Law Made Simple

Living Trusts
Simplified

Living Trusts
Simplified

by Daniel Sitarz
Attorney-at-Law

Nova Publishing Company
Small Business and Consumer Legal Books and Software
Carbondale, Illinois

Editorial assistance by Janet Harris Sitarz, Linda Jorgensen-Buhman, and Melanie Bray. Interior design by Linda Jorgensen-Buhman. Manufactured in the United States.

ISBN 0-935755-53-5   Book only   ($22.95)
ISBN 0-935755-51-9   Book w/CD   ($28.95)

Cataloging-in-Publication Data
    Sitarz, Dan, 1948-
        Living Trusts Simplified / by Daniel Sitarz. -- 1st ed.
        224 p. cm. -- (Law Made Simple series).
        1. Trusts—United States—Popular Works. 2. Trusts—United States—Forms.
        3. Trusts—United States—States—Popular Works. I. Sitarz, Daniel. II. Title. III. Series.
        ISBN 0-935755-53-5, Book only ($22.95); ISBN 0-935755-51-9, Book/CD Set ($28.95).

Nova Publishing Company is dedicated to providing up-to-date and accurate legal information to the public. All Nova publications are periodically revised to contain the latest available legal information.

1st Edition; 1st Printing   June, 2002

This publication is designed to provide accurate and authoritative information in regard to the subject matter covered. It is sold with the understanding that the publisher and author are not engaged in rendering legal, accounting, or other professional services. If legal advice or other expert assistance is required, the services of a competent professional person should be sought.

—From a Declaration of Principles jointly adopted by a Committee of
the American Bar Association and a Committee of Publishers

DISCLAIMER

Because of possible unanticipated changes in governing statutes and case law relating to the application of any information contained in this book, the author, publisher, and any and all persons or entities involved in any way in the preparation, publication, sale, or distribution of this book disclaim all responsibility for the legal effects or consequences of any document prepared or action taken in reliance upon information contained in this book. No representations, either express or implied, are made or given regarding the legal consequences of the use of any information contained in this book. Purchasers and persons intending to use this book for the preparation of any legal documents are advised to check specifically on the current applicable laws in any jurisdiction in which they intend the documents to be effective.

Nova Publishing Company
Small Business and Consumer Legal Books and Software
1103 West College Street
Carbondale, IL 62901
Editorial: (800) 748-1175

Distributed by:
National Book Network
4720 Boston Way
Lanham, MD 20706
Orders: (800) 462-6420

Table of Contents

INTRODUCTION 9

CHAPTER 1: Why Do You Need a Living Trust? 13

    What Is a Living Trust? 14

    Advantages of a Living Trust 15

        Avoiding the Expense and Delay of Probate 15

        Avoiding Having the State Decide Who Will Receive Your Property 15

        Appointing a Trustee to Administer Your Property 18

        Appointing a Trustee to Administer Property for a Minor Child 19

        Other Advantages of a Living Trust 20

    Disadvantages of a Living Trust 20

    Why You Still Need a Will 21

CHAPTER 2: Planning Your Living Trust 22

    Qualifications for Having a Living Trust 22

    Other Estate Planning Tools 23

        Joint Tenancy with Right of Survivorship 23

        Life Insurance 24

        Payable-on-Death Bank Accounts 24

        Living Will 25

        Durable Power of Attorney for Health Care 25

    Steps in Preparing Your Living Trust 25

    Living Trust Preparation Checklist 29

CHAPTER 3: Property Questionnaire 30

    What Property May You Dispose of with Your Living Trust? 30

        Community Property States 31

        Common-Law Property States 33

    Federal Estate Taxes and State Inheritance and Estate Taxes 34

    Property Questionnaire (Instructions) 35

    Property Questionnaire 37

        What Are Your Assets? 37

        What Are Your Liabilities? 45

        What Is the Net Worth of Your Estate? 47

CHAPTER 4: Beneficiary Questionnaire 48

Who May Be a Beneficiary? 48

What Types of Gifts May You Make? 49

Beneficiary Questionnaire 53

    Who Will Receive Which of Your Assets? 53

    Are There Any Other Relatives, Friends, or Organizations to Whom

        You Wish to Leave Gifts? 58

CHAPTER 5: Information for Successor Trustee 60

Overview of Probate Proceedings 60

Choosing a Successor Trustee 62

Affidavit of Assumption of Duties by Successor Trustee 63

Successor Trustee Duties Checklist Instructions 63

Successor Trustee Duties Checklist 65

    Immediate Successor Trustee Duties 65

    Successor Trustee Duties within First Month 65

    Successor Trustee Financial Duties 67

Successor Trustee Information List (Instructions) 68

Successor Trustee Information List 69

    Location of Records 69

    Funeral or Cremation Arrangements 69

    Persons to Contact 70

    Relatives to Contact 71

    Friends to Contact 72

    Newspaper Obituary Information 73

CHAPTER 6: Instructions for Living Trust Forms 74

Completing Your Living Trust Declaration 76

Completing Your Schedule of Assets of Living Trust Form(s) 81

Completing Your Schedule of Beneficiaries of Living Trust Form(s) ... 82

Finishing Your Living Trust Forms 85

CHAPTER 7: Living Trust Forms 86

Living Trust for Single Person or Individual Spouse with

    Children's Trust Included (Instructions) 86

Living Trust for Single Person or Individual Spouse with

    Children's Trust Included (Form) 89

Living Trust for Single Person or Individual Spouse without a

    Children's Trust (Instructions) 93

Living Trust for Single Person or Individual Spouse without a

    Children's Trust (Form) 95

Joint Living Trust of Married Couple with Children's Trust

    Included (Instructions) 98

Joint Living Trust of Married Couple with Children's Trust
    Included (Form) 99
Joint Living Trust of Married Couple without a Children's
    Trust (Instructions) 104
Joint Living Trust of Married Couple without a Children's
    Trust (Form) 105
Assignment to Living Trust by Single Person or Individual
    Spouse (Instructions) 109
Assignment to Living Trust by Single Person or Individual
    Spouse (Form) 111
Joint Assignment to Joint Living Trust by Married Couple (Instructions)...... 112
Joint Assignment to Joint Living Trust by Married Couple (Form) 113
Schedule of Assets of Living Trust for Single Person or
    Individual Spouse (Instructions) 114
Schedule of Assets of Living Trust for Single Person or
    Individual Spouse 115
Schedule of Assets of Joint Living Trust for Husband (Instructions) 116
Schedule of Assets of Joint Living Trust for Husband (Form) 117
Schedule of Assets of Joint Living Trust for Wife (Instructions)................... 119
Schedule of Assets of Joint Living Trust for Wife (Form) 121
Schedule of Beneficiaries of Living Trust for Single Person or
    Individual Spouse (Instructions) 123
Schedule of Beneficiaries of Living Trust for Single Person or
    Individual Spouse (Form) 125
Joint Schedule of Beneficiaries of Joint Living Trust of Married
    Couple (Instructions) 127
Joint Schedule of Beneficiaries of Joint Living Trust of Married
    Couple (Form) 129
New York Notice of Assignment of Property to Living Trust (Instructions) 133
New York Notice of Assignment of Property to Living Trust (Form)............ 135
Registration of Living Trust (Instructions) 136
Registration of Living Trust (Form) 137
Affidavit of Assumption of Duties by Successor Trustee (Instructions) 138
Affidavit of Assumption of Duties by Successor Trustee (Form) 139

CHAPTER 8: Sample Living Trust 140
Living Trust of Mary Ellen Smith 141
Schedule of Assets of Living Trust 145
Schedule of Beneficiaries of Living Trust 146

CHAPTER 9: Completing Your Living Trust 148
Safeguarding Your Living Trust 149
Transferring Property to Your Living Trust 150

CHAPTER 10: Changing Your Living Trust 152
  Amending Your Living Trust 152
  Amendment of Living Trust by Single Person or Individual
      Spouse (Instructions) 154
  Amendment of Living Trust by Single Person or Individual Spouse (Form) .. 155
  Joint Amendment of Joint Living Trust by Married Couple (Instructions) 156
  Joint Amendment of Joint Living Trust by Married Couple (Form) 157
  Revoking Your Living Trust 158
  Revocation of Living Trust by Single Person or Individual
      Spouse (Instructions) 158
  Revocation of Living Trust by Single Person or Individual Spouse (Form) ... 159
  Joint Revocation of Joint Living Trust by Married Couple (Instructions) 160
  Joint Revocation of Joint Living Trust by Married Couple (Form) 161

CHAPTER 11: Supplemental Will 162
  Completing Your Supplemental Will 162
  Supplemental Will (Form) 167

APPENDIX: State Laws Relating to Living Trusts 171

GLOSSARY OF LEGAL TERMS 214

INDEX 221

Introduction

This book is intended to serve as a guide and explanation of the process and legal procedure required in preparing a valid Living Trust without the aid of an attorney. It is part of Nova Publishing Company's Law Made Simple series. The various self-help legal guides in this series are prepared by licensed attorneys who feel that public access to the American legal system is long overdue.

With the proper information, the average person in today's world can easily understand and apply many areas of law. Preparing your own Living Trust is one of these areas. Understandably, there has been strong resistance by many lawyers against making this type of information available to the public. Many lawyer's jobs depend upon doing things that their clients could do just as well if the clients simply had access to the proper information and forms. Lawyers often caution people that antiquated legal language is most important and that of course, only they, the lawyers, can properly prepare and interpret legal documents using such language. Naturally, plain and easily-understood English is not only perfectly proper for use in all legal documents, but in most cases, leads to far less confusion on the part of later readers.

Law in American society today is far more pervasive than ever before. There are legal consequences to virtually every public and most private actions in today's world. Leaving knowledge of the law within the hands of only the lawyers in such a society is not only foolish but dangerous as well. A free society depends in large part, on an informed citizenry. This book and others in Nova's Law Made Simple series are intended to provide the necessary information to those members of the public who wish to use and understand the law for themselves.

This book is designed to assist its readers in understanding the general aspects of the law as it relates to Living Trusts and after-death distribution of property and to assist its readers in the preparation of their own Living Trusts. However, the range of personal finances, property, and desires is infinite and one book cannot hope to cover all potential situations or contingencies. In situations involving complex personal or business property holdings, complicated or substantial financial investments, or unusual or highly-complex post-death distribution plans, readers are advised to seek additional competent legal advice. In addition, estate and inheritance tax laws and regulations are among the most complex laws in existence. Consequently, although a general overview of these laws is provided and the vast majority of people are exempt from federal estate taxes, readers with very large estates, generally, over $1 million (note however, that this exemption amount is scheduled to increase each year to a high of $3.5 million in 2009) or complex financial resources are encouraged to seek the assistance of a tax professional if they wish to limit or lessen the tax consequences of the transfer of any property using a Living Trust.

Regardless of whether or not a lawyer is ultimately retained in certain situations, the legal information in this handbook will enable the reader to understand the framework of law in this country as it relates to Living Trusts. To try and make that task as easy as possible, technical legal jargon has been eliminated whenever possible and plain English used instead. When it is necessary to use a legal term which may be unfamiliar to most people, it will be shown in *italics* and defined when first used. There is a glossary of most legal terms used in trusts at the end of this book for your reference.

Chapter 1 of this guide will explain the usefulness of a valid Living Trust for insuring that your property and money are passed on to the loved ones whom you desire. It will also explain the legal effects of having a Living Trust and the potential consequences of not having one.

In Chapter 2, guidelines are provided for planning the distribution of your estate. Your *estate* consists of all of your assets. Other estate-planning tools, such as wills and powers of attorneys are discussed. In addition, the qualifications necessary for having a Living Trust are explained and a step-by-step outline of the procedures to follow to prepare your own Living Trust using this book are shown.

Chapter 3 provides a discussion of what property may be disposed of using a Living Trust and provides a detailed Property Questionnaire that will allow you to assemble the necessary property and financial information which you will need in preparing your Living Trust. This chapter also includes information on the inheritance and estate tax consequences of the transfer of property at death.

Chapter 4 provides information on who may be a *beneficiary* (one who benefits or receives a gift through a Living Trust). This chapter also explains the various forms your gifts may take and provides a thorough Beneficiary Questionnaire for setting out your decisions regarding who should receive which of your assets.

Chapter 5 includes an overview of information relating to the administration of your estate by your *successor trustee* (the person whom you will choose to administer your trust after your death), information and a checklist for use by your successor trustee, and a final information sheet for your successor trustee's use in locating your assets and administering your *trust estate* (the assets you have transferred to your trust).

In Chapter 6, detailed instructions on how to complete the various trusts forms are provided. The main trust forms and various supplementary forms are provided in Chapter 7. An actual sample Living Trust is shown and its various provisions are explained in Chapter 8. The mechanics of actually preparing your Living Trust and the legal formalities and requirements for signing your Living Trust are set forth in Chapter 9. These requirements, although not at all difficult, must be followed to insure that your Living Trust is acceptable as a valid legal document. Methods and instructions for safeguarding your will are also contained in this chapter.

Chapter 10 contains information regarding when it may be prudent and how to accomplish any changes or alterations to your Living Trust at a later date. Chapter 11 provides instructions to allow you to prepare a standard will in addition to your Living Trust.

The Appendix contains a detailed listing of the individual state legal requirements relating to Living Trusts for each of the 50 states and the District of Columbia. Finally, a Glossary explaining legal terms most often encountered in Living Trusts is included.

As with many routine legal tasks, preparation of a Living Trust is not as difficult as most people fear. With the proper information before them, most people will be able to prepare a legally-valid Living Trust which specifically addresses their individual needs in a matter of a few hours. Read through this manual carefully, follow the step-by-step instructions, and be assured that your wishes will be safely contained in your own Living Trust.

CHAPTER 1:

Why Do You Need a Living Trust?

For most of us, it is very difficult to come to terms with our own mortality. To actually contemplate one's own death is painful. Consequently, very often such thoughts are avoided. However, if you wish to insure that your desires regarding the disposition of your property and possessions after your death are fulfilled, you must confront your mortality and plan accordingly.

Most people's lives are centered on living and, in one way or another, on a close and intimate group of loved ones. These may be relatives, friends, church members, co-workers, or business associates. They are looked to for love, support, and assistance in times of trouble and are asked to share in times of joy. They are often cared about in ways that are difficult to express. But during your life, you at least have the opportunity to show your love and concern in many forms.

It is the purpose of this book to assist you in the difficult task of showing these loved ones your continuing concern for their well-being after you are gone. "You can't take it with you" is a well-worn phrase, but it does strike to the core of the problem of providing for your property and money to be distributed in some fashion on your death. Your entire life has been spent accumulating possessions and wealth for your own comfort and the comfort of your loved ones. Through the proper use of a Living Trust, you have a once-in-a-lifetime opportunity to personally decide what will happen to your accumulated wealth and possessions when you are gone. It is entirely your personal decision. Indeed, it is your legal privilege to make this decision. No one but you has the power to decide, prior to your death, how and to whom your property should be distributed on your demise. But in order to do so, you must take the initiative and overcome the understandable difficulty of these decisions. If you do not take the initiative, upon your death an impersonal court will decide who will receive your wealth.

To actually sit down and decide how your property and possessions should be divided amongst your loved ones in the event of your own death is not an easy task. However, it is you alone who knows your wishes. The property and possessions that you own may be land, your home, personal household furnishings, keepsakes, heirlooms, money, stocks, bonds, or any other type of property. It may be worth thousands of dollars or it may be worth far less. If you are like most people, you want to insure that it is passed on to the persons whom you choose. But then again, if you are like most people, you have put off making these decisions.

What Is a Living Trust?

A trust consists of assets of a *Grantor* (the person who creates the trust) which are managed and distributed by a *Trustee* to benefit one or more *Beneficiaries* (those persons or organizations who will receive property under the trust). A Living Trust provides for all three of these designations to be held by the same person. You are the Grantor, Trustee, and Beneficiary of your Living Trust while you are still alive. Upon your death, your chosen *Successor Trustee* succeeds you in the management of the trust and the distribution of your trust assets to your chosen beneficiaries. A Living Trust is a legal document that allows for the transfer of property to the persons or organizations named in the Living Trust upon the death of the maker of the Living Trust. A Living Trust is only effective for the on-death distribution of property that has been previously transferred to the Living Trust. A Living Trust can be changed, modified, or revoked at any time by the Grantor prior to death. Another name for a Living Trust is a *Revocable* Trust, because during your lifetime you may *revoke*, or cancel the trust at any time. Upon your death, however, your Living Trust becomes irrevocable and can no longer be changed or altered in any way.

An increasingly popular estate planning tool, Living or Revocable Trusts can be effectively used to avoid *probate*. Probate is an official series of court proceedings which begin with either proving a will is valid or determining that no will existed and continues with the distribution of the deceased person's property. To avoid probate, a Living Trust generally provides that all or most of a person's property be transferred to trust ownership. The owner of the property generally retains full control and management of the trust as trustee. In the trust document, beneficiaries are chosen, much the same as in a will. The terms of the trust can actually parallel the terms of a will. The difference is that, upon the death of the creator (Grantor) of the trust, all of the property that has been transferred to trust ownership passes immediately and automatically to the beneficiaries without any court intervention or supervision and without an official probate proceeding.

The owner of the property retains full control over the property until death and the creator of the trust can terminate this type of trust at any time prior to death. After the trust itself is prepared, all of the property that a person wishes placed in the Living Trust (stocks, bonds, bank accounts, real estate deeds, car titles, etc.) is actually transferred to the Living Trust.

It is equally important to understand that for a Living Trust to be valid, it must generally be prepared, signed, and notarized according to certain technical legal procedures. Although a Living Trust is perfectly valid if it is written in plain English and does not use technical legal language, it must be prepared, signed, and notarized in the manner outlined in this book. These procedures are not at all difficult and consist generally of carefully typing your Living Trust in the manner outlined later, and signing it in the manner specified.

In some cases (for example, those involving extremely complicated business or personal financial holdings or the desire to create a complex trust arrangement) it is clearly advisable to consult an attorney for the preparation of your Living Trust. However, in most circumstances and for most people, the terms of a Living Trust that can provide for the necessary protection are relatively routine and may safely be prepared without the added expense of consulting a lawyer.

Advantages of a Living Trust

Avoiding the Expense and Delay of Probate

There are many reasons why it is desirable to have a Living Trust. One of the most important is that through the proper use of a Living Trust most or all of the expense and delay of probate is avoided. During proceedings, an *executor* (a person appointed in a will) or a court-appointed administrator is authorized to collect, appraise, and distribute the assets of the deceased. Normally, the proper use of a Living Trust entirely eliminates or dramatically lessens the expenses of probate, since the disposition of all of your property has been planned in advance by you and takes place automatically upon your death.

Many people desire to avoid having their property be subject to probate proceedings. Although in some situations the probate process has been abused, there are valid reasons for allowing your property to be handled through probate after your death. It provides a process by which the improper distribution of your assets is guarded against by the probate court. Having your property distributed through a probate process also puts a definite limit on the length of time that a creditor can file a claim against your estate.

The drawbacks of probate are that it can substantially delay the distribution of your property while the probate process continues. The probate of an estate can take, generally, from four to 18 months, and sometimes much longer. Additionally, probate costs can be very significant. Court costs, appraisal fees, lawyer's fees, and accounting bills can all cut deeply into the amount of property and funds that will eventually be distributed to your beneficiaries. However, for small estates (generally, under $100,000.00) most states have simplified probate procedures that can be handled without lawyers and can substantially reduce these costs. The probate process itself is complex and will, in almost all cases, require the use of an attorney. The proper use of a Living Trust can allow all or most of your property to pass directly to your chosen beneficiaries immediately upon your death, thus bypassing the probate process entirely. For many, this reason alone justifies the use of a Living Trust.

Avoiding Having the State Decide Who Will Receive Your Property

There are, however, numerous other valuable attributes of a Living Trust. Perhaps the next most important reason to have a Living Trust is to insure that it is you who decides how your estate is distributed on your death and to be assured that those loved ones whom you wish to share in your bounty actually receive your gifts.

What happens to your property and possessions if you do not have a valid and legal method by which to have your property distributed to your chosen *beneficiaries* (those persons or organizations to whom you decide to leave property) upon your death? Law books are filled with many unfortunate cases in which, because of the lack of a valid Living Trust or will, the true desires and wishes of a person as to who should inherit their property have been frustrated. If there is no valid Living Trust or will to use for direction, a probate judge must give a person's property to either the spouse, children, or the closest blood relatives of the deceased person. This result is required, even in situations when it is perfectly clear that the deceased person did not, under any circumstances, want those relatives to inherit the property.

Without such a valid Living Trust or will before him or her, a judge must rely on a legislative scheme which has been devised to make for an orderly distribution of property in all cases where there is no valid Living Trust or will. This scheme is present as law, in one form or another, in all 50 states and is generally referred to as *intestate distribution*.

The terms of state intestate distribution plans are very complex in most states. In general, a person's spouse is first in line to receive the property when there is no Living Trust or will at death. Most states provide that the spouse and children will either share the entire estate or the surviving spouse will take it all in the hopes that the spouse will share it with the children. Generally, the spouse will receive one-half and the children will receive one-half. In many states, if a person dies without a valid Living Trust or will and is survived by a spouse but not by any children, the spouse will inherit the entire estate and the surviving parents, brother, sisters, and any other blood relatives to the deceased will be entitled to nothing.

If there is no surviving spouse or children, the *heirs*, or blood relatives of the deceased will receive the estate. If there is someone or several persons within the next closest relationship level (for example, parents or siblings) who are alive on the death of the person, then these relatives will receive all of the person's property or share it equally with all others alive who are in a similar relationship level. Once a level of blood relationship is found in which there is at least one living person, all persons who are more distantly related inherit nothing.

In addition, these legislative distribution plans are set up on the assumption that family members are the only parties whom a deceased person would wish to have inherit his or her property. Thus, without a Living Trust or will, it is impossible to leave any gifts to close friends, in-laws, blood relatives more distant then any alive, charities, or organizations of any type. If there is no Living Trust or will and if there are no blood relatives alive, the state confiscates all of a person's property under a legal doctrine entitled *escheat*.

As an example of a typical legislative intestate distribution scheme, the following is a general representative outline of the various levels of distribution that are set up in many states. Keep in mind, however, that this example is only an illustration of the method that states may use and is not intended to be used in determining how your own estate would be divided. Check on the listing in the Appendix for your own state's intestate distribution plan for specific details:

- If a spouse and children of the marriage are surviving: $50,000.00 and one-half of the balance of the estate will go to the spouse and one-half of the balance of the estate will go to the children equally. If one of the children has predeceased the parent and leaves surviving children (grandchildren of the deceased parent), then the grandchildren will split the deceased child's share.

- If a spouse and children of the deceased who are not from the present marriage are surviving: One-half of the balance of the estate will go to the spouse and one-half of the balance of the estate will go to the children equally. If one of the children has predeceased the parent and leaves surviving children (grandchildren of the deceased parent), then the grandchildren will split the deceased child's share.

- If a spouse, but no children or parents of the deceased are surviving: All of the estate will go to the spouse.

- If a spouse and one or both parents, but no children are surviving: $50,000.00 and one-half of the balance of the estate will go to the spouse and one-half of the balance of the estate will go to the parents equally. If only one parent is surviving, that parent gets the entire one-half share of the estate.

- If there are children of the deceased, but no spouse surviving: All of the estate goes to the children. If one of the children has predeceased the parent and leaves surviving children (grandchildren of the deceased parent), then the grandchildren will split the deceased child's share.

- If one or both parents, but no spouse or children are surviving: All of the estate will go to the parents equally, or the entire estate will go to the surviving parent.

- If there is no spouse, no children, or no parents surviving: All of the estate will go to brothers and sisters equally. If a brother or sister has predeceased the deceased sibling and has left surviving children, their children will split the deceased brother or sister's share.

- If there is no spouse, no children, no parents, and no brothers and sisters or their children surviving: One-half of the estate will go to the maternal grandparents and one-half will go to the paternal grandparents. If the grandparents on either side have predeceased the decedent, their children will split their share.

- If there is no spouse, no children, no parents, no brothers and sisters or their children, and no grandparents or their children surviving: The estate will pass to the surviving members of the closest level of blood relatives: aunts, uncles, nephews, nieces, great-grandparents, great-uncles, great-aunts, first cousins, great-great-grandparents, second cousins, etc.

- If there are no surviving kin: The estate will be claimed by the state under the doctrine of escheat.

Many disastrous consequences can result from having your property distributed according to a standardized state plan. Take, for example, a situation in which a person and his or her spouse die from injuries sustained in a single accident, but one spouse survives a few hours longer. If there is no Living Trust or will, the result in this scenario is that the property of the first one to die passes to the spouse who survives. A few hours later, on the death of the surviving spouse, the property automatically passes *only* to the relatives of the spouse who survived the longest. The relatives of the first person to die can inherit nothing at all. Obviously, this would not normally be the desired consequence. Under the typical state scheme, luck and chance play a large role in deciding who is to inherit property.

Each state has a complicated and often different method for deciding which particular family members will take property when there is no Living Trust or will. However, the results are often far from the desires of how the person actually wished to have the property distributed. Obviously, under this type of state distribution of your property, the individual circumstances of your family are not taken into consideration at all nor are any intentions that you may have had, regardless of how strongly you may have expressed them during your lifetime. The only way to avoid having the state decide who is to receive your property is to have prepared a legally valid Living Trust or will. If you die without a valid Living Trust or will, the state essentially writes one for you on its own terms.

Appointing a Trustee to Administer Your Property

Another very important reason for having a Living Trust is the ability to appoint a *Successor Trustee* of your own choice. A Successor Trustee is your personal representative for seeing that your wishes, as contained in your Living Trust, are carried out after your death and that your taxes and debts are paid. A Successor Trustee also collects and inventories all of your property and is in charge of seeing that it is distributed according to your wishes as expressed in your Living Trust.

Typically, a spouse, sibling, or other close family member or trusted friend is chosen to act as Successor Trustee. However, it may be any responsible adult whom you would feel confident having this duty. It may even be a local bank or trust company. In that case of course, there will often be a substantial fee charged to your estate for the completion of these generally routine duties by the corporate Successor Trustee. If you choose an individual, he or she should be a resident of your home state. The Living Trusts in this book enable you to appoint your Successor Trustee and an alternate Successor Trustee so that, in the event your first choice cannot perform, it is still your personal choice as to who will administer your Living Trust.

If you do not have a Living Trust or you do not choose an Successor Trustee in your Living Trust, a judge will appoint someone to administer the distribution of your property. Often it will be a local attorney, court official, or bank officer who may not know you or your beneficiaries at all. Your estate will then be distributed by a stranger who will charge your estate a hefty fee for the collection and distribution of your assets.

By appointing your own Successor Trustee, you are also able to waive the posting of a bond by your Successor Trustee. A *bond* is a type of insurance policy that a Trustee would normally have to purchase to insure that he or she carries out his or her duties properly. The cost of the bond would come out of your *Trust Estate* (all of the trust's assets). You also provide that your Successor Trustee will not receive any compensation for serving as Trustee. This will allow more of your assets to reach your beneficiaries, rather than paying for the expenses of administration of your estate.

Appointing a Trustee to Administer Property for a Minor Child

For those with minor children, the appointment of a trustee for any assets to be provided to the children is another very important matter which may be accomplished through the use of a Living Trust. You may set up a Children's Trust within your Living Trust and have your Successor Trustee administer your children's property until a time when you feel that your children will be able to handle their own affairs. Instructions to provide for this alternative are simply stated in a Living Trust, but are more difficult to accomplish without one. If such instruction is not provided for in a Living Trust and a minor child is left money or property by way of the state intestate succession laws, the courts will generally decide who should administer the property. Such court-supervised guardianship of the property or money will automatically end at the child's reaching the legal age of majority in the state (usually 18 years of age). At this age, without a Living Trust to direct otherwise, the child will receive full control over the property and/or money. This may not be the most prudent result, as many 18-year-olds are not capable of managing property or large sums of money. With a Living Trust, it is easy to arrange for the property or money to be held in trust and used to benefit the child until a later age, perhaps 21, 25, or even 30 years of age or older.

Other Advantages of a Living Trust

There are a number of other significant advantages to using a Living Trust to distribute your property upon your death:

- If you own real estate in a state other than that of your legal residence, the use of a Living Trust will allow that real estate to be passed to your beneficiary without an out-of-state probate proceeding.

- If you become incapacitated, a Living Trust allows your chosen Successor Trustee to manage your property. Without a Living Trust, a "conservator" or "guardian" would need to be authorized by a court to handle such matters. The legal proceeding to accomplish this is often long and expensive.

- With a Living Trust, the details of your estate plan remain confidential. Only your chosen Successor Trustee will need to know the actual specifics of your intentions. And even your Successor Trustee need only know the details of your estate plan after your death.

- While you are alive, there are no required trust recordkeeping requirements. You need not have a trust bank account, file a trust federal or state income tax return, or maintain any separate trust records. Of course, it is a good idea to keep careful track of the assets that you will place in the Living Trust.

- You can amend or revoke your Living Trust at any time, without any formal proceedings or actions. Simply use the forms provided later in this book to accomplish these actions.

- Finally, no lawyer is necessary to handle the distribution of your assets upon your death. If you follow the instructions in this book carefully, your chosen Successor Trustee should have no difficulty in distributing your assets to your chosen beneficiaries. This can save not only time, but considerable money as well.

Disadvantages of a Living Trust

There are a few disadvantages to using a Living Trust to distribute your property upon your death:

- First, setting up a Living Trust entails some paperwork. You must carefully prepare a Trust document and the property and beneficiary schedules that will accompany it. You must also make certain that you have the selected property clearly transferred to the trust. If the property has a title or ownership document (such as a car or a piece of real estate), you must change the ownership documents to reflect that the ownership is being transferred to the trust. If the property has no ownership document, then simply listing the chosen property on the Trust Schedule of Assets will effectively transfer the property to the Trust.

- In a very few situations and jurisdictions, there may be some limited transfer taxes, such as real estate transfer taxes or vehicle title transfer fees. In the vast majority of states, transfers of real estate to ownership by a living trust are exempt from any transfer taxes. Even if imposed, such transfer taxes are generally very minimal. Please check specifically with your jurisdiction if this is an issue.

- There may be a few banks or finance companies that will balk at refinancing a property that has the title held by a trust. Most companies should be satisfied if you provide them with your trust document and all of the transfer documents (such as the new deed or title).

- Finally, unlike a probate proceeding, there is no cutoff date for the filing of creditor's claims against the estate of a person who dies with a Living Trust. For the vast majority of people, this is not a problem as most estates do not have large unpaid liabilities. However, if you feel that your estate may be subject to large claims, you may wish to use a will, rather than a Living Trust, to distribute your property upon death.

Why You Still Need a Will

Even if you have used a Living Trust and the various estate planning tools outlined in the next chapter to attempt to have your estate avoid probate, a will is still highly recommended. There may be assets that you have neglected, forgotten about, or that will not be uncovered until your death. If you have used a trust, joint property agreements, and other estate planning tools, these unknown or forgotten assets may wind up passing to your heirs as intestate property and causing probate proceedings to be instituted. Through the use of a simple will, you can avoid this possibility. Chapter 11 provides a simple basic will for you to create to supplement your Living Trust.

Although it can be short and simple, a Living Trust is an important document which can accomplish many tasks. The proper use of a Living Trust can eliminate much confusion for those left behind. Since it provides a clear and legal record of your wishes, it can avoid feuding and squabbles among your family members. Perhaps most importantly, it can make your last wishes come true.

CHAPTER 2:
Planning Your Living Trust

A Living Trust is the cornerstone of any comprehensive arrangement to plan for the distribution of your property upon your death. In this chapter, the basic qualifications for having a Living Trust are outlined. Various other estate planning tools which may be useful in certain situations are also detailed. Finally, an overview of the steps you will take in preparing your own Living Trust is presented.

Qualifications for Having a Living Trust

Are you legally qualified to have a Living Trust? In general, if you are over 18 years of age and of "sound mind," you will qualify.

The requirement to have a "sound mind" refers to the ability to understand the following:

- That you are signing a Living Trust
- That you know who your beneficiaries are
- That you understand the nature and extent of your assets

Having a "sound mind" refers only to the moment when you actually *execute* (sign) the Living Trust. A person who is suffering from a mental illness, a person who uses drugs or alcohol, or even a person who is senile may legally sign a Living Trust. This is acceptable as long as the Living Trust is signed and understood during a period when the person is lucid and has sufficient mental ability to understand the extent of his or her property, who is to receive that property, and that it is a Living Trust that is being signed.

The fact that a person has a physical incapacity makes no difference in his or her right to sign a Living Trust. Regardless if a person is blind, deaf, cannot speak, is physically very weak, or is illiterate; as long as they understand what it is they are doing and what they are signing, the "sound mind" requirement is met.

Related to the requirement that the Grantor have a "sound mind" at the time of signing the Living Trust is the requirement that the Living Trust be signed without any undue influence, fraud, or domination by others. In other words, the Living Trust must be freely signed and reflect the wishes of the person signing it for it to be legally valid. You do not ever have to sign a Living Trust that is not exactly what you desire. Do not let anyone coerce or force you to sign a Living Trust that does not accurately reflect your own personal wishes. If you are in a situation of this nature, it is highly recommended that you immediately seek the assistance of a competent lawyer.

Other Estate Planning Tools

The use of a Living Trust is one of the most popular and widespread legal tools for planning for the distribution of your *estate*. Your estate consists of everything that you own, whether it is real estate or personal property. As explained in Chapter 1, through the use of a Living Trust you can accomplish the planned distribution of your estate property and many other goals. However, there may be other objectives in your planning that cannot be accomplished solely through the use of a Living Trust. Other estate planning documents may be necessary to achieve all of your goals.

There are three basic reasons that other estate planning tools may be useful in certain situations: avoidance of probate, reducing taxes, and health care considerations.

First, many people desire to avoid having their property be subject to probate proceedings. The drawbacks of probate are that it can delay the distribution of your property while the probate process continues. The probate of an estate can take, generally, from four to 18 months, and sometimes much longer. Additionally, probate costs can be substantial. Court costs, appraisal fees, lawyer's fees, and accounting bills can all cut deeply into the amount of property and funds that will eventually be distributed to your beneficiaries. However, for small estates (generally, under $100,000.00), most states have simplified probate procedures which can be handled without lawyers and can substantially reduce these costs.

There are various methods for avoiding having property pass to others through the probate process. The three most important are as follows:

Joint Tenancy with Right of Survivorship

Upon one owner's death, any property held as joint tenants with right of survivorship passes automatically to the surviving owner without probate or court intervention of any kind. Under the laws of most states, the description of ownership on the deed or other title document must specifically state that the property is being held by the people as "joint tenants with right of survivorship." If not, the property is usually presumed to be held as "tenants-in-common," which means that each owner owns a certain specific share of the property which they may leave by way of a Living Trust or other estate planning device, such as a will. Some states have another class of property known as "tenancy-by-the-entirety" which is, essentially, a joint tenancy specifically for spouses. More information on property ownership is provided in Chapter 3.

Life Insurance

Another common method of passing funds to a person on death while avoiding probate is through the use of life insurance. By making the premium payments throughout your life, you are accumulating assets for distribution on your death. The life insurance benefits are paid directly to your chosen beneficiaries without probate court intervention. However, life insurance benefits are still considered part of your taxable estate. For more information on insurance, you are advised to consult an insurance professional.

Payable-on-Death Bank Accounts

This type of property ownership consists of a bank account held in trust for a named beneficiary. It may also be referred to as a "Totten" trust or "Bank" trust account. It is a very simple method for providing that the assets in a bank account are paid immediately to a beneficiary on your death without the beneficiary having any control over the account during your life, as is the case with a joint bank account. This trust-type bank account allows for the property to be transferred without probate and is very simple to set up. Any type of bank account, whether checking, savings, money market, or even certificates of deposit, may be designated as a payable-on-death account by filling out simple forms at your financial institution.

The second major use for estate planning tools is to attempt to lessen or completely avoid the payment of any taxes on the transfer of property upon death. Upon death, the transfer of property may be subject to federal estate taxes, state estate taxes, and state inheritance taxes. However, much of the taxation of estates (most importantly, federal taxation) does not become a factor unless your estate is valued at over $1 million. Thus, for most people, the need to pursue complicated tax avoidance estate plans is unnecessary. For reference however, some details regarding taxation of estates are provided in Chapter 3. The complexity of tax laws and the methods to avoid taxes through estate planning is beyond the scope of this book. If your estate is over $1 million, it may be wise to seek the assistance of a tax professional.

The third main purpose of estate planning is a relatively new concern. Recent advances in medical technology have allowed modern medicine in many cases, to significantly extend the lives of many people. In addition, many people have become aware of the possibility of their lives being continued indefinitely through technological life-support procedures. Two legal documents have been developed to deal with these concerns: the Living Will and Durable Power of Attorney for Health Care.

Living Will

A *living will* is a document that can be used to state your desire that extraordinary life-support means not be used to artificially prolong your life in the event that you are stricken with a terminal disease or injury. Its use has been recognized in the vast majority of states in recent years. You may wish to consult Nova Publishing Company's book *Living Wills Simplified* which provides information regarding the necessary forms and instructions for preparation of a living will in each state.

Durable Power of Attorney for Health Care

This relatively new legal document has been developed to allow a person to appoint another person to handle all their health care affairs in the event that he or she becomes incapacitated or incompetent. Generally, this document will only take effect upon a person becoming unable to manage his or her own affairs. This type of document may be used to delegate the legal authority to make health care decisions to another person. This document may be carefully tailored to fit your needs and concerns and may be used in conjunction with a living will. It can be a valuable tool for dealing with difficult health care situations. Instructions and forms for preparing a basic durable power of attorney are also provided in Nova Publishing Company's book, *Living Wills Simplified*.

This book provides the information necessary to prepare the two basic legal documents in estate planning: a Living Trust and a will. Regardless of what other types of estate planning tools you eventually decide are appropriate in your situation, these two basic documents are necessary complements to any successful estate plan. If you believe that your situation warrants additional estate planning, please consult an experienced financial planner, tax professional, or attorney. You may, of course, also wish to research and prepare any of the above documents yourself without the aid of an attorney or accountant.

Steps in Preparing Your Living Trust

There are several steps that must be followed to properly prepare your Living Trust using this book. None of them are very difficult or overly complicated. However, they must be done carefully in order to effectively accomplish what you set out to do: be assured that your property is left to those loved ones whom you choose and that your loved ones are properly cared for after your death.

What follows is a brief outline of the necessary steps which must be followed to prepare a valid Living Trust with this book. You will probably refer back to this chapter several times in the course of preparing your own Living Trust to be certain that you are on the right track and have not left out any steps.

① Read through this entire book. You are advised to read carefully through this entire book before you actually begin preparing your own Living Trust. By doing this you will gain an overview of the entire process and will have a much better idea of where you are heading before you actually begin the preparation of your Living Trust.

② Fill in the Property Questionnaire contained in Chapter 3 and the Beneficiary Questionnaire in Chapter 4. These questionnaires are designed to compile all of the necessary personal information for your Living Trust preparation. Information regarding your personal and business assets, percentages of ownership of these assets, marital relationship, names and addresses of relatives, and many other items will be gathered together in these questionnaires for your use. As you fill in these questionnaires, you will begin making the actual decisions regarding distribution of your assets. In addition, in Chapter 5, you will fill out a Successor Trustee Information List which will provide important data for use by your chosen Successor Trustee.

③ Review your own state's legal requirements as contained in the Appendix. The Appendix contains a concise listing of the laws relating to Living Trusts in every state. Although the standard Living Trust clauses used in this book will alleviate most of the concerns raised by these legal requirements, there may be certain of your own state's requirements that will affect how you decide to prepare your own Living Trust.

④ Read through all of the pre-assembled Living Trusts and decide which trust most clearly fits your needs. This is one of the most important steps in the process and one which must be done very carefully. The Living Trusts are, for the most part, self-explanatory and you should be able to easily decide which one applies to your situation. However, you are advised to read through each one before you decide on the final choice for your own Living Trust.

⑤ Make a photocopy of your own chosen Living Trust form. These photocopies will be your Living Trust preparation worksheets. After you have done this, fill in the appropriate information on the photocopies using your Property and Beneficiary Questionnaires.

⑥ Type a clean original of your Living Trust as explained in Chapter 9. With your filled-in photocopy worksheet before you, this should be a relatively easy task of simply copying the provisions that you have selected.

⑦ Proofread your entire Living Trust very carefully to be certain that it is exactly what you want. If there are any typographical errors or if you want to change some provision, no matter how slight, you must retype that page of your Living Trust. Do not make any corrections on the Living Trust itself.

⑧ Take your completed Living Trust before a notary public and formally sign your Living Trust in front of him or her. This is known as the *execution* of your Living Trust.

⑨ Make a photocopy of your original, signed Living Trust and give it to the Successor Trustee whom you have named in your Living Trust. You may also wish to give the Successor Trustee a copy of the Successor Trustee Information List from Chapter 5. Store the original of your Living Trust in a safe place as outlined in Chapter 9.

⑩ Review your Living Trust periodically and amend or revoke your Living Trust if necessary, as detailed in Chapter 10.

⑪ Prepare and execute a will to supplement the use of your Living Trust, as explained in Chapter 11.

That's all there is to it. Actually, that may sound like a lot of work and bother, but realize that you would have to follow many of the same steps even if a lawyer were to prepare your Living Trust. However, in that case, you would give the lawyer all of the information and he or she would simply prepare a Living Trust in much the same fashion that you will use in this book. The difference, of course, is that you must pay an often exorbitant price to have this done by a lawyer. Additionally, by preparing your Living Trust yourself and doing so at your own pace, you are certain to take more care and give more thought to the entire process than if you have someone else prepare it for you.

Living Trust Preparation Checklist

☐ Read this entire book first

☐ Fill in the Property and Beneficiary Questionnaires

☐ Review your state's legal requirements

☐ Choose the appropriate Living Trust

☐ Make a photocopy rough-draft version of your Living Trust and fill it in

☐ Type an original of your Living Trust

☐ Carefully proofread your Living Trust

☐ Go before a notary public and sign your Living Trust

☐ Give a copy of your Living Trust to your Successor Trustee and safeguard the original

☐ Review your Living Trust periodically and make any changes in a formal manner

☐ Prepare and execute a will to supplement your Living Trust

CHAPTER 3:
Property Questionnaire

The methods and manners of distribution of your property upon your death using a Living Trust are discussed in this chapter. Your *assets* consist of different types of property. It may be personal property, real estate, "community" property, stocks, bonds, cash, heirlooms, or keepsakes. Regardless of the type of property you own, there are certain general rules which must be kept in mind as you prepare your Living Trust.

In addition, in this chapter you will prepare an inventory of all of your assets and liabilities. This will allow you to have before you a complete listing of all of the property that you own as you begin to consider which beneficiaries should receive which property.

It is also important to understand that laws of different states may apply to a single Living Trust. The laws of the state in which you have your principal residence will be used to decide the validity of the Living Trust as to any personal property and real estate located in that state. However, if any real estate outside of your home state is mentioned in the Living Trust, then the laws of the state in which that real estate is found will govern the disposition of that particular real estate. Thus, if you own property outside of the state where you live, when you check the Appendix for information concerning specific state laws, be certain to check both your own state's laws and those of the state in which your other property is located.

What Property May You Dispose of with Your Living Trust?

In general, you may dispose of any property that you own which has effectively been transferred to the Living Trust at the time of your death. This simple fact, however, contains certain factors which require further explanation. There are forms of property which you may "own," but which may not be transferred by way of a Living Trust. In addition, you may own only a percentage or share of certain other property. In such situations, only that share or percentage which you actually own may be transferred by your Living Trust. Finally, there are types of property ownership which are automatically transferred to another party at your death, regardless of the presence of a Living Trust.

In the first category of property which cannot be transferred by Living Trust are properties which have a designated beneficiary outside of the provisions of your Living Trust. These types of properties include:

- Life insurance policies
- Retirement plans
- IRAs and KEOGHs
- Pension plans
- Trust bank accounts
- Payable-on-death bank accounts
- U.S. Savings Bonds, with payable-on-death beneficiaries

In general, if there is already a valid determination of who will receive the property upon your death (as there is, for example, in the choice of a life insurance beneficiary), you may not alter this choice of beneficiary through the use of your Living Trust. If you wish to alter your choice of beneficiary in any of these cases, please alter the choice directly with the holder of the particular property (for instance, the life insurance company or bank).

The next category of property which may have certain restrictions regarding its transfer by Living Trust is property in which you may own only a certain share or percentage. Examples of this may be a partnership interest in a company or jointly-held property. Using a Living Trust, you may leave only that percentage or fraction of the ownership of the property that is actually yours. For business interests, it is generally advisable to pass the interest which you own to a beneficiary intact. The forced sale of the share of a business for estate distribution purposes often results in a lower value being placed on the share. Of course, certain partnership and other business ownership agreements require the sale of a partner's or owner's interest upon death. These buy-out provisions will be contained in any ownership or partnership documents that you may have. Review such documentation carefully to determine both the exact share of your ownership and any post-death arrangements.

The ownership rights and shares of property owned jointly must be considered. This is discussed below under common law property states, although most joint ownership laws also apply in community property states as well. Another example of property in which only a certain share is actually able to be transferred by Living Trust is a spouse's share of marital property in states which follow community property designation of certain jointly-owned property. The following is a discussion of the basic property law rules in both community property and common law property states. The rules regarding community property only apply to married persons in those states that follow this type of property designation. If you are single, please disregard this section and use the common-law property states rules below to determine your ownership rights.

Community Property States

Several states, mostly in the western United States, follow the community property type of marital property system. Please refer to the Appendix to see if your state has this type of system. The system itself is derived from ancient Spanish law. It is a relatively simple concept. All property owned by either spouse during a marriage is divided into two types: *separate property* and *community property*.

Separate property consists of all property considered owned entirely by one spouse. Separate property, essentially, is all property owned by the spouse prior to the marriage and kept separate during the marriage; and all property received individually by the spouse by gift or inheritance during the marriage. All other property is considered community property. In other words, all property acquired during the marriage by either spouse, unless by gift or inheritance, is community property. Community property is considered to be owned in equal shares by each spouse, regardless of whose efforts actually went into acquiring the property. (Major exceptions to this general rule are Social Security and Railroad retirement benefits, which are considered to be separate property by Federal law).

Specifically, separate property generally consists of:

- All property owned by a spouse prior to a marriage (if kept separate)
- All property a spouse receives by gift or inheritance during a marriage (if kept separate)
- All income derived from separate property (if kept separate), except in Texas and Idaho, where income from separate property is considered community property

Community property generally consists of:

- All property acquired by either spouse during the course of a marriage, unless it is separate property (thus it is community property unless acquired by gift or inheritance or is income from separate property)
- All pensions and retirement benefits earned during a marriage (except Social Security and Railroad retirement benefits)
- All employment income of either spouse acquired during the marriage
- All separate property which is mixed or co-mingled with community property during the marriage

Thus, if you are a married resident of a community property state, the property which you may dispose of by Living Trust consists of all of your separate property and one-half of your jointly-owned marital community property. The other half of the community property automatically becomes your spouse's sole property on your death.

Residents of community property states may also own property jointly as tenant-in-common or as joint tenants. These forms of property ownership are discussed on the following pages.

Common-Law Property States

Residents of all other states are governed by a common-law property system, which was derived from English law. Under this system, there is no rule which gives 50 percent ownership of the property acquired during marriage to each spouse.

In common-law states, the property which you may dispose of with your Living Trust consists of all the property held by title in your name, any property that you have earned or purchased with your own money, and any property that you may have been given as a gift or inherited, either before or during your marriage.

If your name alone is on a title document in these states (for instance, a deed or automobile title), then you own it solely. If your name and your spouse's name are on the document, you generally own it as *tenants-in-common*, unless it specifically states that your ownership is to be as joint tenants or if your state allows for a *tenancy-by-the-entireties* (a form of joint tenancy between married persons). There is an important difference between these types of joint ownership: namely, survivorship.

With property owned as tenants-in-common, the percentage or fraction that each tenant-in-common owns is property which may be disposed of under a Living Trust. If the property is held as joint tenants or as tenants-by-the-entireties, the survivor automatically receives the deceased party's share. Thus, in your Living Trust, you may not dispose of any property held in joint tenancy or tenancy-by-the-entirety since it already has an automatic legal disposition upon your death. For example: if two persons own a parcel of real estate as equal tenants-in-common, each person may leave a half-interest in the property to the beneficiary of their choice by their Living Trust. By contrast, if the property is owned as joint tenants with right of survivorship, the half-interest that a person owns will automatically become the surviving owner's property upon death.

In common-law states, you may dispose of any property that has your name on the title in whatever share that the title gives you, unless the title is held specifically as joint tenants or tenants-by-the-entireties. You may also dispose of any property that you earned or purchased with your own money, and any property that you have been given as a gift or inherited. If you are married, however, there is a further restriction on your right to dispose of property by Living Trust.

All common-law states protect spouses from total disinheritance by providing a statutory scheme under which a spouse may choose to take a minimum share of the deceased spouse's estate, regardless of what a Living Trust or a will states. This effectively prevents any spouse from being entirely disinherited through the use of the common-law rules of property (name on the title equals ownership of property).

In most states, the spouse has a right to a one-third share of the deceased spouse's estate, regardless of what the deceased spouse's Living Trust or will states. However, all states are slightly different in how they apply this type of law and some allow a spouse to take up to one-half of the estate. Please check your particular state's laws on this aspect in the Appendix. The effect of these statutory provisions is to make it impossible to disinherit a spouse entirely. If you choose to leave nothing to your spouse under your Living Trust or by other means (such as will, life insurance or joint tenancies), he or she may take it anyway, generally from any property which you tried to leave to others. The details of each state's spousal statutory share are outlined in the Appendix.

Some states also allow a certain family allowance or homestead allowance to the spouse or children to insure that they are not abruptly cut off from their support by any terms of a Living Trust. These allowances are generally of short duration and for relatively minor amounts of money and differ greatly from state to state.

Thus, the property which you may dispose of by Living Trust is as follows:

- **In community property states**: All separate property (property which was brought into a marriage, or obtained by gift or inheritance during the marriage) and one-half of the community property (all other property acquired during the marriage by either spouse). If you are single, follow the common law rules below. Note that you may not use your Living Trust to dispose of property for which a beneficiary has been chosen by the terms of the ownership of the property itself (for example: life insurance).
- **In common-law states**: Your share of all property in which your name is on the title document, unless it is held as joint tenants or tenants-by-the-entireties and your share of all other property which you own, earned, or purchased in your own name. Please check the Appendix for information relating to the spouse's minimum statutory share of an estate. Note that you may not use your Living Trust to dispose of property for which a beneficiary has been chosen by the terms of the ownership of the property itself (for example: life insurance)

Federal Estate Taxes and State Inheritance and Estate Taxes

Various taxes may apply to property transfers upon death. In general, there are two main type of taxes: estate taxes and inheritance taxes. An estate tax is a government tax on the privilege of being allowed to transfer property onto others upon your death. This tax is assessed against the estate itself and is paid out of the estate before the assets are distributed to the beneficiaries. An inheritance tax is a tax on property received and is paid by the person who has actually inherited the property. The federal government assesses an estate tax. Various states impose additional estate taxes and inheritance taxes. Additionally, the federal government and a few states apply a gift tax on property transfers during a person's life. Nevada is the only state which does not impose any estate, inheritance, or gift taxes. Basic information regarding each state's tax situation is provided in the Appendix.

With regard to estate taxes, recent changes in the federal Income Tax Code, as it relates to estate taxes, have released an estimated 95 percent of the American public from any federal estate tax liability on their death. The current IRS rules provide for the equivalent of an exemption from all estate tax for the first $1 million of a person's assets. This exemption amount is scheduled to rise to $3.5 million by 2009. In addition, all of the value of a person's estate that is left to a spouse is exempt from any federal estate tax. Even if your particular assets are over this minimum exemption, there are still methods to lessen or eliminate your tax liability. These methods, however, are beyond the scope of this book. Therefore, if your assets (or your joint assets, if married) total over approximately $1 million, it is recommended that you consult a tax professional prior to preparing your Living Trust.

State estate taxes are, as a rule, also very minimal or even nonexistent until the value of your estate is over $1 million. Most state's estate tax laws are tied directly to the federal estate tax regulations and thus allow for the same level of exemption equivalent from state estate taxes on death if the estate property totals under $1 million. A few states may impose an additional level of estate tax. The details of each state's estate tax situation are outlined in the Appendix.

Less than half of the states impose an inheritance tax on the receipt of property resulting from the death of another. There are generally relatively high exemptions allowed and the inheritance taxes are usually scaled in such a way that spouses, children, and close relatives pay much lower rates than more distant relatives or unrelated persons.

From a planning standpoint, the changes in the federal estate tax have virtually eliminated any consideration of tax consequences from the preparation of a Living Trust for most Americans. Other factors, however, will affect the planning of your Living Trust.

Property Questionnaire

Before you begin to actually prepare your own Living Trust, you must understand what your assets are, who your beneficiaries are to be, and what your personal desires are as to how those assets should be distributed among your beneficiaries.

Since you may only give away property which you actually own, before you prepare your Living Trust it is helpful to gather all of the information regarding your personal financial situation together in one place. The following Property Questionnaire will assist you in that task.

Determining who your dependents are, what their financial circumstances are, what gifts you wish to leave them, and whether you wish to make other persons or organizations beneficiaries under your Living Trust are questions that will be answered as you complete the Beneficiary Questionnaire in Chapter 4.

Together, these two Questionnaires should provide you with all of the necessary information to make the actual preparation of your Living Trust a relatively easy task. In addition, the actual process of filling out these questions will gently force you to think about and make the important decisions which must be made in the planning and preparation of your Living Trust.

Mark down each piece of property that you wish to place in the Living Trust. When you have finished completing this Questionnaire, have it before you as you select and fill in your personal Living Trust in Chapter 7.

It may also be prudent to leave a photocopy of these Questionnaires with the original of your Living Trust and provide a copy to your Successor Trustee, in order to provide a readily-accessible inventory of your assets and list of your beneficiaries for use by your Successor Trustee in managing your estate.

Property Questionnaire

What Are Your Assets?

Cash And Bank Accounts

(Individual accounts can be left by living trust, provided the account ownership has been effectively transferred to the trust; joint tenancy and payable-on-death accounts cannot.)

Checking Account $ _____
Bank   _____
Account #   _____
Name(s) on account   _____

Checking Account $ _____
Bank   _____
Account #   _____
Name(s) on account   _____

Savings Account $ _____
Bank   _____
Account #   _____
Name(s) on account   _____

Savings Account $ _____
Bank   _____
Account #   _____
Name(s) on account   _____

Certificate of Deposit $
Held by   _____
Expiration date   _____
Name(s) on account   _____

Other Account $ _____
Bank   _____
Account #   _____
Name(s) on account   _____

Total Cash $ _____

Life Insurance and Annuity Contracts

(Life insurance benefits cannot be left by living trust.)

Ordinary Life $ _____
Company _____
Policy # _____
Beneficiary _____
Address _____

Ordinary Life $ _____
Company _____
Policy # _____
Beneficiary _____
Address _____

Endowment $ _____
Company _____
Policy # _____
Beneficiary _____
Address _____

Term $ _____
Company _____
Policy # _____
Beneficiary _____
Address _____

Annuity Contract $ _____
Company _____
Policy # _____
Beneficiary _____
Address _____

Total Insurance $ _____

Accounts and Notes Receivable

(Debts payable to you may be left by living trust.)

Accounts $ _____
Due from _____
Address _____

Accounts $ _____
Due from   _____
Address   _____

Accounts $ _____
Due from   _____
Address   _____

Notes $ _____
Due from   _____
Address   _____

Notes $ _____
Due from   _____
Address   _____

Notes $ _____
Due from   _____
Address   _____

Other Debts $ _____
Due from   _____
Address   _____

Other Debts $ _____
Due from   _____
Address   _____

Other Debts $ _____
Due from   _____
Address   _____

Total Accounts & Notes $ _____

Stocks

(Ownership of individually-held stocks and mutual funds may be left by living trust, provided the assets have been effectively transferred to the trust.)

Company   _____
CUSIP or Certificate #   _____
and type of shares   _____
Value $ _____

Company _____
CUSIP or Certificate # _____
and type of shares _____
Value $ _____

Company _____
CUSIP or Certificate # _____
and type of shares _____
Value $ _____

Company _____
CUSIP or Certificate # _____
and type of shares _____
Value $ _____

Company _____
CUSIP or Certificate # _____
and type of shares _____
Value $ _____

Company _____
CUSIP or Certificate # _____
and type of shares _____
Value $ _____

Company _____
CUSIP or Certificate # _____
and type of shares _____
Value $ _____

Total Stocks $ _____

Bonds

(Ownership of individually-held bonds may be left by living trust, provided the assets have been effectively transferred to the trust.)

Company _____
CUSIP or Certificate # _____
and type of shares _____
Value $ _____

Company _____

CUSIP or Certificate # _____

and type of shares _____

Value $ _____

Company _____

CUSIP or Certificate # _____

and type of shares _____

Value $ _____

Company _____

CUSIP or Certificate # _____

and type of shares _____

Value $ _____

Company _____

CUSIP or Certificate # _____

and type of shares _____

Value $ _____

Company _____

CUSIP or Certificate # _____

and type of shares _____

Value $ _____

Company _____

CUSIP or Certificate # _____

and type of shares _____

Value $ _____

Total Bonds $ _____

Business Interests

(Ownership of business interests may generally be left by living trust, provided the assets have been effectively transferred to the trust.)

Individual Proprietorship

Name _____

Location _____

Type of business _____

Your net value $ _____

Sole Proprietorship
Name   _____
Location   _____
Type of business   _____
Your net value $ _____

Interest in Partnership
Name   _____
Location   _____
Type of business   _____
Gross value $ _____
Percentage interest   _____
Your net value $ _____

Interest in Partnership
Name   _____
Location   _____
Type of business   _____
Gross value $ _____
Percentage interest   _____
Your net value $ _____

Close Corporation Interest
Name   _____
Location   _____
Type of business   _____
Gross value $ _____
Percentage shares held   _____
Your net value $ _____

Total Business Value $ _____

Real Estate

(Property owned individually or as tenants-in-common may be left by living trust, provided the assets have been effectively transferred to the trust. Property held in joint tenancy or tenancy-by-entirety may not be left by living trust, unless it has first been transferred to ownership as tenants-in-common and then transformed to ownership by the trust.)

Personal Residence
Location   _____
Value $ _____
How held and percent held? (Joint Tenants, Tenancy in Common, etc?)
                     _____ / _____ %
Value of your share $ _____

Vacation Home

Location   _____

Value $ _____

How held and percent held? (Joint Tenants, Tenancy in Common, etc?)

     _____ / _____ %

Value of your share $ _____

Vacant Land

Location   _____

Value $ _____

How held and percent held? (Joint Tenants, Tenancy in Common, etc?)

     _____ / _____ %

Value of your share $ _____

Income property

Location   _____

Value $ _____

How held and percent held? (Joint Tenants, Tenancy in Common, etc?)

     _____ / _____ %

Value of your share $ _____

Total Real Estate $ _____

Personal Property

(Personal property owned individually or as a tenant-in-common may be left by living trust, provided the assets have been effectively transferred to the trust. Patents, copyrights, and trademarks require special transfer forms.)

Car $ _____

Description   _____

Car $ _____

Description   _____

Boat/other vehicles $ _____

Description   _____

Household furnishings $ _____

Description   _____

     _____

     _____

     _____

     _____

     _____

Jewelry and furs $ _____
Description _____

Artwork $ _____
Description _____

Total Personal Property $ _____

Miscellaneous Assets

Royalties, Patents, Copyrights $ _____
Description _____

Heirlooms $ _____
Description _____
           _____
           _____
           _____
           _____
           _____

Other $ _____
Description _____

Other $ _____
Description _____

Total Miscellaneous $ _____

Employee Benefit and Pension/Profit-Sharing Plans

(Retirement benefits cannot be left by living trust)

Company   _____
Plan type   _____
Net value $ _____

Company   _____
Plan type   _____
Net value $ _____

Company   _____
Plan type   _____
Net value $ _____

Total Benefit Value $ _____

Total Assets

(Insert totals from previous pages)

Cash Total	$	_____
Life Insurance Total	$	_____
Accounts & Notes Total	$	_____
Stocks Total	$	_____
Bonds Total	$	_____
Business Total	$	_____
Real Estate Total	$	_____
Personal Property Total	$	_____
Miscellaneous Total	$	_____
Pension Total	$	_____
TOTAL ASSETS	$	_____

What Are Your Liabilities?

Notes and Loans Payable

Payable to _____
Address _____
Term _____   Interest rate _____
Amount due $ _____

Payable to _____
Address _____
Term _____   Interest rate _____
Amount due $ _____

Total Notes and Loans Payable $ _____

Accounts Payable

Payable to _____
Address _____
Term _____   Interest rate _____
Amount due $ _____

Payable to _____
Address _____
Term _____   Interest rate _____
Amount due $ _____

Total Accounts Payable $ _____

Mortgages Payable

Property location _____

_____

Payable to _____

Address _____

Term _____ Interest rate _____

Amount due $ _____

Property location _____

_____

Payable to _____

Address _____

Term _____ Interest rate _____

Amount due $ _____

Total Mortgages Payable $ _____

Taxes Due

Federal Income $ _____

State Income $ _____

Personal Property $ _____

Real Estate $ _____

Payroll $ _____

Other $ _____

Total Taxes Due $ _____

Credit Card Accounts

Credit Card Account # _____

Credit Card Company _____

Address _____

Amount due $ _____

Credit Card Account # _____

Credit Card Company _____

Address _____

Amount due $ _____

Total Credit Card Accounts Payable $ _____

Miscellaneous Liabilities

To whom due _____

Address _____

Term _____ Interest rate _____

Amount due $ _____

To whom due _____

Address _____

Term _____ Interest rate _____

Amount due $ _____

To whom due _____

Address _____

Term _____ Interest rate _____

Amount due $ _____

Total Miscellaneous Liabilities $ _____

Total Liabilities

(Insert totals from previous pages)

Total Notes and Loans Payable $ _____
Total Accounts Payable $ _____
Total Mortgages Payable $ _____
Total Taxes Due $ _____
Total Credit Card Accounts $ _____
Total Miscellaneous Liabilities $ _____

TOTAL LIABILITIES $ _____

What Is the Net Worth of Your Estate?

TOTAL ASSETS $ _____

minus (-)

TOTAL LIABILITIES $ _____

equals (=)

YOUR TOTAL NET WORTH $ _____

CHAPTER 4:
Beneficiary Questionnaire

In this chapter you will determine both who you would like your beneficiaries to be and what specific property you will leave to each beneficiary through your Living Trust. There is an explanation of the various methods that you may use to leave gifts to your beneficiaries. Finally, there is a Beneficiary Questionnaire which you will use to actually make the decisions regarding which beneficiaries will receive which property.

Who May Be a Beneficiary?

Any person or organization who receives property under a Living Trust is termed a *beneficiary* of that Living Trust. Any person or organization you choose may receive property under your Living Trust. This includes any family members, the named Successor Trustee, any illegitimate children (if named specifically), corporations, charities, creditors, debtors, any friends, acquaintances, or even strangers.

A few states also have restrictions on the right to leave property to charitable organizations and churches. These restrictions are usually in two forms: a time limit prior to death when changes to a Living Trust which leave large amounts of money or property to a charitable organization are disallowed and also a percentage limit on the amount of a person's estate which may be left to a charitable organization (often a limit of 50 percent). The reasoning behind this rule is to prevent abuse of a dying person's desire to be forgiven. There have been, in the past, unscrupulous individuals or organizations who have obtained last minute changes in a Living Trust in an attempt to have the bulk of a person's estate left to them or their group. If you intend to leave large sums of money or property to a charitable organization or church, please check with an attorney in your area to see if there are any restrictions of this type in force in your state.

Under this same category as to who may be a beneficiary under your Living Trust are issues related to marriage, divorce, and children. First and foremost, you are advised to review your Living Trust periodically and make any necessary changes as your marital or family situation may dictate. If you are divorced, married, remarried, or widowed, adopt, or have a child, there may be unforeseen consequences based on the way you have written your Living Trust. Your Living Trust should be prepared with regard to how your life is presently arranged. It should, however, always be reviewed and updated each time there is a substantial change in your life.

What Types of Gifts May You Make?

There are various standard terms and phrases that may be employed when making gifts under your Living Trust. The Living Trust clauses which are employed in this book incorporate these standard terms. Using these standard phrases, you may make a gift of any property that is owned by the Living Trust at your death to any beneficiary whom you choose.

A few type of gifts are possible but are not addressed in the Living Trusts that may be prepared using this book. Simple shared gifts (for example: "All my property to my children, Alice, Bill, and Carl, in equal shares") are possible using this book. However, any complex shared gift arrangements will require the assistance of an attorney. In addition, you may impose simple conditions on any gifts in Living Trusts prepared using this book. However, complex conditional gifts that impose detailed requirements that the beneficiary must comply with in order to receive the gift are also beyond the scope of this book. Finally, although it is possible to leave any gifts under your Living Trust in many types of additional complicated trusts, a simple trust for leaving gifts to children is the only trust available for Living Trusts prepared using this book. If you desire to leave property in trust to an adult or in a complex trust arrangement, you are advised to seek professional advice.

The terms that you use to make any gifts can be any that you desire, as long as the gift is made in a clear and understandable manner. Someone reading the Living Trust at a later date, perhaps even a stranger appointed by a court, must be able to determine exactly what property you intended to be a gift and exactly who it is you intended to receive it. If you follow the few rules which follow regarding how to identify your gifts and beneficiaries, your intentions will be clear to whomever may need to interpret your Living Trust in the future:

(1) Always describe the property in as detailed and clear a manner as possible. For example: do not simply state "my car;" instead state "a 1994 Buick Skylark, serial #123456789." Describe exactly what it is you wish for each beneficiary to receive. You may make any type of gift that you wish, either a cash gift, a gift of a specific piece of personal property or real estate, or a specific share of your total *trust estate* (all of the property that has been effectively transferred to the trust). If you wish to give some of your trust estate in the form of portions of the total, it is recommended to use fractional portions. For example, if you wish to leave your trust estate in equal shares to two persons, use "One-half of my total trust estate to . . ." for each party.

(2) In your description of the property, you should be as specific and precise as possible. For land, it is suggested that you use the description exactly as shown on the

deed to the property. For personal property, be certain that your description clearly differentiates your gift from any other property.

Always describe the beneficiaries is as precise and clear a manner as is possible. For example: do not simply state "my son;" instead state "my son, Robert Edward Smith, of Houston Texas." This is particularly important if the beneficiary is an adopted child.

③ Never provide a gift to a group or class of people without specifically stating their individual names. For example: do not simply state "my sisters;" instead state "my sister Katherine Mary Jones, my sister Elizabeth Anne Jones, and my sister Annette Josephine Jones."

④ You may put simple conditions on the gift if they are reasonable and not immoral or illegal. For example: you may say "This gift is to be used to purchase daycare equipment for the church nursery;" but you may not say "I give this gift to my sister only if she divorces her deadbeat husband Ralph Edwards."

⑤ You should always provide for an alternate beneficiary for the purpose of allowing you to designate someone to receive the gift if your first choice to receive the gift dies before you do (or, in the case of a organization chosen as primary beneficiary, is no longer in business). Your choice for alternate beneficiary may be one or more persons or an organization. In addition, you may delete the alternate beneficiary choice and substitute the words "the residue" instead. The result of this change will be that if your primary beneficiary dies before you do, your gift will pass under your residuary clause, which is discussed next.

⑥ Although not a technical legal requirement, a residuary clause is included in every Living Trust in this book. With it, you will choose the person, persons, or organization to receive anything not covered by other clauses of your Living Trust. Even if you feel that you have given away everything that you own under other clauses of your Living Trust, this can be a very important clause.

If, for any reason, any other gifts under your Living Trust are not able to be completed, this clause goes into effect. For example, if a beneficiary refuses to accept your gift or the chosen beneficiary has died and no alternate was selected, or both the beneficiary and alternate have died, the gift is put back into your trust estate and would pass under the residuary clause. If there is no residuary clause included in your Living Trust, any property not disposed of under your Living Trust could potentially be forfeited to the state.

In addition, you may use this clause to give all of your trust estate (except your specific gifts) to one or more persons. For example: you make specific gifts of

$1,000.00 to a sister and a car to a friend. By then naming your spouse as the residuary clause beneficiary, you will have gifted everything in your trust estate to your spouse—except the $1,000.00 and the car. You could then name your children, in equal shares, as the alternate residuary beneficiaries. In this manner, if your spouse were to die first, your children would then equally share your entire estate—except the $1,000.00 and the car.

Be sure to clearly identify the beneficiary by full name. The space provided for an identification of the relationship of the beneficiary can be simply a descriptive phrase like "my wife," "my brother-in-law," or "my best friend." It does not mean that the beneficiary must be related to you personally.

⑦ A survivorship clause should be included in every Living Trust. This provides for a period of survival for any beneficiary. For Living Trusts prepared using this book, the period is set at 30 days. The practical effect of this is to be certain that your property passes under your Living Trust and not that of a beneficiary who dies shortly after receiving your gift.

Without this clause in your Living Trust it would be possible that property would momentarily pass to a beneficiary under your Living Trust. When that person dies (possibly immediately if a result of a common accident or disaster) your property could wind up being left to the person whom your beneficiary designated, rather than to your alternate beneficiary.

⑧ Be sure to review your Living Trust each time there is a change in your family circumstances. Please see Chapter 10 for a discussion regarding changing your Living Trust.

⑨ Finally, property may be left to your children in trust using the Children's Trust Clause that is included in Living Trusts for persons with children. Please refer to the discussion of the Children's Trust in Chapter 6.

If you state your gifts simply, clearly, and accurately, you can be assured that they will be able to be carried out after your death regardless of who may be required to interpret the language in your Living Trust.

Beneficiary Questionnaire

Who Will Receive Which of Your Assets?

Spouse

Spouse _____

    Maiden name _____

    Date of marriage _____

    Date of birth _____

    Address _____

    Current income $ _____

    Amount, specific items, or share of trust estate that you desire to leave _____

    _____

    _____

    Alternate beneficiary _____

Children

Child _____

    Date of birth _____

    Address _____

    _____

    Spouse's name (if any) _____

    Current income $ _____

    Amount, specific items, or share of trust estate that you desire to leave _____

    _____

    _____

    Alternate beneficiary _____

Child _____

    Date of birth _____

    Address _____

    _____

    Spouse's name (if any) _____

    Current income $ _____

    Amount, specific items, or share of trust estate that you desire to leave _____

    _____

    _____

    Alternate beneficiary _____

Child _____
    Date of birth _____
    Address _____
    _____

    Spouse's name (if any) _____
    Current income $ _____
    Amount, specific items, or share of trust estate that you desire to leave _____
    _____
    _____

    Alternate beneficiary _____

Child _____
    Date of birth _____
    Address _____
    _____

    Spouse's name (if any) _____
    Current income $ _____
    Amount, specific items, or share of trust estate that you desire to leave _____
    _____
    _____

    Alternate beneficiary _____

Child _____
    Date of birth _____
    Address _____
    _____

    Spouse's name (if any) _____
    Current income $ _____
    Amount, specific items, or share of trust estate that you desire to leave _____
    _____
    _____

    Alternate beneficiary _____

Grandchildren

Grandchild _____
    Date of birth _____
    Address _____
    _____

    Spouse's name (if any) _____
    Current income $ _____
    Amount, specific items, or share of trust estate that you desire to leave _____
    _____
    _____

    Alternate beneficiary _____

Grandchild _____
    Date of birth _____
    Address _____
    _____
    Spouse's name (if any) _____
    Current income $ _____
    Amount, specific items, or share of trust estate that you desire to leave _____
    _____
    _____
    Alternate beneficiary _____

Grandchild _____
    Date of birth _____
    Address _____
    _____
    Spouse's name (if any) _____
    Current income $ _____
    Amount, specific items, or share of trust estate that you desire to leave _____
    _____
    _____
    Alternate beneficiary _____

Grandchild _____
    Date of birth _____
    Address _____
    _____
    Spouse's name (if any) _____
    Current income $ _____
    Amount, specific items, or share of trust estate that you desire to leave _____
    _____
    _____
    Alternate beneficiary _____

Grandchild _____
    Date of birth _____
    Address _____
    _____
    Spouse's name (if any) _____
    Current income $ _____
    Amount, specific items, or share of trust estate that you desire to leave _____
    _____
    _____
    Alternate beneficiary _____

Grandchild _____
   Date of birth _____
   Address _____
   _____
   Spouse's name (if any) _____
   Current income $ _____
   Amount, specific items, or share of trust estate that you desire to leave _____
   _____
   _____
   Alternate beneficiary _____

Parents

Parent _____
   Date of birth _____
   Address _____
   _____
   Spouse's name (if any) _____
   Current income $ _____
   Amount, specific items, or share of trust estate that you desire to leave _____
   _____
   _____
   Alternate beneficiary _____

Parent _____
   Date of birth _____
   Address _____
   _____
   Spouse's name (if any) _____
   Current income $ _____
   Amount, specific items, or share of trust estate that you desire to leave _____
   _____
   _____
   Alternate beneficiary _____

Siblings

Sibling _____
   Date of birth _____
   Address _____
   _____
   Spouse's name (if any) _____
   Current income $ _____
   Amount, specific items, or share of trust estate that you desire to leave _____
   _____
   _____
   Alternate beneficiary _____

Sibling _____

    Date of birth _____

    Address _____

    _____

    Spouse's name (if any) _____

    Current income $ _____

    Amount, specific items, or share of trust estate that you desire to leave _____

    _____

    _____

    Alternate beneficiary _____

Sibling _____

    Date of birth _____

    Address _____

    _____

    Spouse's name (if any) _____

    Current income $ _____

    Amount, specific items, or share of trust estate that you desire to leave _____

    _____

    _____

    Alternate beneficiary _____

Sibling _____

    Date of birth _____

    Address _____

    _____

    Spouse's name (if any) _____

    Current income $ _____

    Amount, specific items, or share of trust estate that you desire to leave _____

    _____

    _____

    Alternate beneficiary _____

Other Dependents

Other Dependent _____

    Date of birth _____

    Address _____

    _____

    Spouse's name (if any) _____

    Current income $ _____

    Amount, specific items, or share of trust estate that you desire to leave _____

    _____

    _____

    Alternate beneficiary _____

Other Dependent _____
    Date of birth _____
    Address _____

    _____
    Spouse's name (if any) _____
    Current income $ _____
    Amount, specific items, or share of trust estate that you desire to leave _____

    _____

    _____
    Alternate beneficiary _____

Other Dependent _____
    Date of birth _____
    Address _____

    _____
    Spouse's name (if any) _____
    Current income $ _____
    Amount, specific items, or share of trust estate that you desire to leave _____

    _____

    _____
    Alternate beneficiary _____

Are There Any Other Relatives, Friends, or Organizations to Whom You Wish to Leave Gifts?

Name _____
    Relationship _____
    Address _____

    _____
    Spouse's name (if any) _____
    Current income $ _____
    Amount, specific items, or share of trust estate that you desire to leave _____

    _____
    Alternate beneficiary _____

Name _____
    Relationship _____
    Address _____

    _____
    Spouse's name (if any) _____
    Current income $ _____
    Amount, specific items, or share of trust estate that you desire to leave _____

    _____
    Alternate beneficiary _____

Name _____

    Relationship _____

    Address _____

    _____

    Spouse's name (if any) _____

    Current income $ _____

    Amount, specific items, or share of trust estate that you desire to leave _____

    _____

    Alternate beneficiary _____

Name _____

    Relationship _____

    Address _____

    _____

    Spouse's name (if any) _____

    Current income $ _____

    Amount, specific items, or share of trust estate that you desire to leave _____

    _____

    Alternate beneficiary _____

Name _____

    Relationship _____

    Address _____

    _____

    Spouse's name (if any) _____

    Current income $ _____

    Amount, specific items, or share of trust estate that you desire to leave _____

    _____

    Alternate beneficiary _____

Name _____

    Relationship _____

    Address _____

    _____

    Spouse's name (if any) _____

    Current income $ _____

    Amount, specific items, or share of trust estate that you desire to leave _____

    _____

    Alternate beneficiary _____

CHAPTER 5:
Information for Successor Trustee

In this chapter, various information relating to the Successor Trustee of your Living Trust and the probate process is provided. In many respects, your Successor Trustee will perform duties similar to those that a chosen executor would perform if property was left by a will. Later in this chapter are various lists of duties that need to be performed by either your Successor Trustee or an executor of your will. You may designate either or both to perform most of these duties. However, the actual collection and distribution of your assets under the terms of your Living Trust must be handled by your Successor Trustee alone (or with the assistance of any attorney or other professional, if necessary). The official duties of the Successor Trustee under the terms of the Living Trust cannot be delegated to someone else. Many of the other duties that are listed at the end of this chapter can, however, be handled by other parties.

Overview of Probate Proceedings

Before actually planning your Living Trust, an overview of how the legal system operates after a person's death may be useful to keep in mind. The system of court administration of the estates of deceased parties is generally entitled probate. How to avoid the probate court was the subject of one of the first self-help law books to challenge the legal establishment's monopoly on law. Probate however, despite what many lawyers would have you believe, is not all that mysterious a matter.

Upon the death of a person who has left a will or a person who has not left a will, in most states there is a general sequence of events which takes place. First, the executor appointed in the will (who, hopefully, has been notified of his or her duties in advance) locates the will and files it with the proper authority. If necessary, the executor arranges for the funeral and burial. A lawyer is most often hired to handle the probate proceeding. Upon presenting the will to the probate court, the will is *proved*, which means that it is determined whether or not the document presented is actually the deceased's will. This may be done in most states with a "Self-Proving Affidavit" which is prepared and notarized at the time your will is signed or it is done with the actual testimony of those people who witnessed the signing of the will.

Upon proof that it is a valid will, the executor is officially given legal authority to gather together all of the estate's property. This authority for the executor to administer the estate is generally referred to as *letters testamentary*. The probate court also officially appoints the parties who are designated as guardians of any minor children and any trustees. If no executor was chosen in the will, or if the one chosen cannot serve, the probate court will appoint one. The order of preference for appointment is commonly as follows: surviving spouse, next of kin, a person having an interest in the estate or claims against the estate.

If the will is shown to be invalid, or if there is no will, the same sequence of events generally is followed. However, in this case, the party appointed to administer the estate is usually titled an *administrator* of the estate rather than an executor. The court orders granting authority to an administrator are generally referred to as *letters of administration*.

After the executor or administrator is given authority, he or she handles the collection of assets, the management of the estate, the arrangement of any necessary appraisals, and the payment of any debts and taxes until such time as all creditor's claims have been satisfied and other business of the estate completed. An inventory of all of the assets is typically the first official act of an executor. Creditors, by the way, only have a certain time period in which to make a claim against an estate. The same holds true for any *contests* of the will (challenges to the validity of a will). Contesting a will is a fairly rare occurrence and is most difficult if the will was properly prepared and signed by a competent, sane adult.

The executor will generally also be empowered under state law to provide an allowance for the surviving spouse and children until such time as all affairs of the deceased person are completed and the estate is closed.

Upon completion of all business and payment of all outstanding charges against the estate, an accounting and inventory of the estate's assets are then presented to the probate court by the executor. At this time, if everything appears to be in order, the executor is generally empowered to distribute all of the remaining property to the persons or organizations named in the will and probate is officially closed. The entire probate process generally takes from six to 18 months to complete. The distribution of your property and money is usually handled solely by the executor (with a lawyer's help to be certain that all legal requirements are fulfilled).

Upon the death of a person who has signed a valid Living Trust, there is a slightly different sequence of events which takes place. First, the Successor Trustee appointed in the Living Trust (who, hopefully, has been notified of his or her duties in advance) locates the Living Trust. The Successor Trustee has the immediate legal authority to gather together all of the estate's property. This authority for the Successor Trustee to administer the estate is provided for in the terms of the Trust itself and does not have to be granted by a probate court.

The Successor Trustee handles the collection of assets, management of the estate, and payment of any debts and taxes until such time as all creditor's claims have been satisfied and other business of the estate completed. An inventory of all of the assets is typically the first official act of an Successor Trustee. The Successor Trustee is then generally empowered to distribute all of the remaining property to the persons or organizations named in the Living Trust, without any court proceeding of any kind.

If your assets are distributed under a probate proceeding, the entire probate process generally takes from six to 18 months to complete, and may take much longer. If your property is distributed under a probate proceeding, court approval of all aspects of the disbursement must normally be obtained, which is a cumbersome and very time-consuming requirement for your executor that will almost always require the help of an attorney. Under a Living Trust, the distribution of your property and money is usually handled solely by the Successor Trustee. This is done without court approval of the disbursement and will most likely not require the assistance of an attorney.

Choosing a Successor Trustee

Your choice of who should be your Successor Trustee is a personal decision. A spouse, sibling, or other trusted party is usually chosen to act as Successor Trustee, although a bank officer, accountant, or attorney may also be chosen. The person chosen should be someone you trust and someone whom you feel can handle or at least efficiently delegate the complicated tasks of making an inventory of all of your property and distributing it to your chosen beneficiaries. The person chosen should be a resident of the state in which you currently reside. In addition, all states require that Successor Trustees be competent, of legal age (generally, over 18) and a citizen of the U.S. It is generally not wise to appoint two or more persons as co-Successor Trustees. It is preferable to appoint your first choice as primary Successor Trustee and the other person as alternate Successor Trustee.

In your Living Trust, you will grant the Successor Trustee broad powers to manage your estate and also provide that he or she not be required to post a bond in order to be appointed to serve as Successor Trustee. This provision can save your estate considerable money, depending upon its size. The fees for Successor Trustee bonds are based upon the size of the estate and can amount to hundreds of dollars every year that your estate is being managed. By waiving this bond requirement, these potential bond fees can be eliminated and the money saved passed on to your beneficiaries.

You should discuss your choice with the person chosen to be certain that they will be willing to act as Successor Trustee. In addition, it is wise to provide your Successor Trustee, in advance, with a copy of the Living Trust, a copy of your Property and Beneficiary Questionnaires, and a copy of the information contained in this chapter.

Affidavit of Assumption of Duties by Successor Trustee

Upon your death, under the terms of the Living Trust, your Successor Trustee is automatically authorized to take over the administration and distribution of the trust assets. No court proceedings are necessary to officially authorize the Successor Trustee to begin to manage the Trust. However, some banks, real estate companies, or other financial institutions may require an Affidavit signed by the Successor Trustee that states that he or she has officially assumed the duties and responsibilities of acting as the Successor Trustee. A form for this purpose is provided in Chapter 7 of this book. You may wish to leave a completed, but unsigned copy of this form with the copy of the Living Trust that you provide to your Successor Trustee so that he or she may complete the form quickly and easily upon your demise.

Successor Trustee Duties Checklist Instructions

Provided on the following pages is a checklist of items that your Successor Trustee may have to deal with after your death. Although this list is extensive, there may be other personal tasks that are not included. Scanning this list can give you an idea of the scope and range of the Successor Trustee's duties. You can provide invaluable assistance to your Successor Trustee by being aware of their duties and providing them with information to help them. This listing is divided into two time periods, immediate and first month. These time periods are approximations and many of the duties may be required to be performed either before or after the exact time specified. All of the immediate and first month duties can be delegated to others. The duties in the Financial listing cannot be delegated to others, although your Successor Trustee may use the assistance of professionals, such as accountants, appraisers, or lawyers, if necessary.

Successor Trustee Duties Checklist

Immediate Successor Trustee Duties

- ☐ Contact mortuary or funeral home regarding services

- ☐ Contact cemetery regarding burial or cremation

- ☐ Contact local newspaper with obituary information

- ☐ Contact relatives and close friends

- ☐ Contact employer and business associates

- ☐ Contact lawyer and accountant

- ☐ Arrange for pallbearers

- ☐ Arrange for immediate care of decedent's children

- ☐ Arrange for living expenses for decedent's spouse

- ☐ Contact veterans' organizations

Successor Trustee Duties within First Month

- ☐ Contact life insurance agent and report death

- ☐ Contact general insurance agent

- ☐ Contact medical and health insurance companies

- ☐ Contact Medicare

- ☐ Contact union regarding pensions and death benefits

- ☐ Contact employer regarding pensions and death benefits

- ☐ Contact military regarding pensions and death benefits

- ☐ Contact Social Security Administration

- ☐ Obtain death certificates from attending physician

- ☐ Contact IRA or KEOGH account trustees

- ☐ Contact county recorder

- ☐ Contact post office

- ☐ Contact Department of Motor Vehicles

- ☐ Arrange for management of business or real estate holdings

- ☐ Review all of decedent's records and legal documents

- ☐ Contact gas, telephone, electric, trash, and water companies

- ☐ Contact newspaper and magazine subscription departments

- ☐ Contact credit card companies

Successor Trustee Financial Duties

(These cannot be delegated.)

- ☐ Begin inventory of assets

- ☐ Arrange for appraisal of assets

- ☐ Begin collection of assets

- ☐ Contact banks, savings and loans, and credit unions

- ☐ Contact mortgage companies

- ☐ Contact stockbroker and investment counselor

- ☐ Open bank accounts for trust

- ☐ Open decedent's safe deposit box

- ☐ Inventory all trust assets

- ☐ Collect all monies and property due to decedent

- ☐ Pay all taxes due and file all necessary tax returns

- ☐ Provide notice to all creditors

- ☐ Pay all debts and expenses of decedent, including funeral expenses

- ☐ Arrange for sale of trust assets, if necessary

- ☐ Distribute all remaining assets according to Living Trust

- ☐ Close trust books and affairs

Successor Trustee Information List

The following listing will provide your Successor Trustee with valuable information that will make performance of his or her difficult task much easier. Included in this questionnaire is information relating to the location of your records, any funeral or burial arrangements that you have made, lists of important persons that the Successor Trustee will need to contact after your death, and information that will assist your Successor Trustee in preparing any obituary listing. It may be very difficult to confront the need for this information. Please take the time to provide this valuable record of information for your Successor Trustee. After your death, they may be under tremendous emotional stress and this information will help them perform their necessary duties with the least difficulty. You will probably wish to give this information list and a copy of your Living Trust to the person whom you have chosen as your Successor Trustee.

Successor Trustee Information List

Location of Records

Original of will _____

Original of codicil _____

Trust documents _____

Safe deposit box and key _____

Bankbook and savings passbook _____

Treasury bills and certificates of deposit _____

Social Security records _____

Real estate deeds and mortgage documents _____

Veteran's information _____

Stock certificates and bonds _____

Promissory notes and loan documents _____

Business records _____

Partnership records _____

Corporation records _____

Automobile titles _____

Income tax records _____

Credit card records _____

Birth certificate _____

Warranties _____

Other important papers _____

_____

Funeral or Cremation Arrangements

Name of mortuary, funeral service, or crematorium _____

Name of person contacted _____

Phone _____

Address _____

_____

Arrangements made _____

_____

_____

_____

Name of cemetery _____

Name of person contacted _____

Phone _____

Address _____

_____

Arrangements made _____

_____

_____

_____

Location of memorial or church service _____

Name of person contacted _____

Phone _____

Address _____

_____

Arrangements made _____

_____

_____

Persons to Contact

Clergy _____

Address _____

City, State, Zip _____

Phone _____

Lawyer _____

Address _____

City, State, Zip _____

Phone _____

Accountant _____

Address _____

City, State, Zip _____

Phone _____

Life insurance agent _____

Address _____

City, State, Zip _____

Phone _____

General insurance agent _____

Address _____

City, State, Zip _____

Phone _____

Employer _____

Address _____

City, State, Zip _____

Phone _____

Military unit _____

Address _____

City, State, Zip _____

Phone _____

Relatives to Contact

Relative name _____

Address _____

City, State, Zip _____

Phone _____

Relative name _____

Address _____

City, State, Zip _____

Phone _____

Relative name _____

Address _____

City, State, Zip _____

Phone _____

Relative name _____

Address _____

City, State, Zip _____

Phone _____

Relative name _____

Address _____

City, State, Zip _____

Phone _____

Relative name _____

Address _____

City, State, Zip _____

Phone _____

Relative name _____

Address _____

City, State, Zip _____

Phone _____

Friends to Contact

Friend name _____
Address _____
City, State, Zip _____
Phone _____

Friend name _____
Address _____
City, State, Zip _____
Phone _____

Friend name _____
Address _____
City, State, Zip _____
Phone _____

Friend name _____
Address _____
City, State, Zip _____
Phone _____

Friend name _____
Address _____
City, State, Zip _____
Phone _____

Friend name _____
Address _____
City, State, Zip _____
Phone _____

Friend name _____
Address _____
City, State, Zip _____
Phone _____

Friend name _____
Address _____
City, State, Zip _____
Phone _____

Newspaper Obituary Information

Name _____

Date of birth _____

Place of birth _____

Current residence _____

Former residence _____

Occupation _____

_____

Education _____

_____

Military service _____

_____

Club, union, civic, or fraternal organizations _____

_____

_____

Special achievements _____

_____

_____

_____

_____

Survivors _____

_____

_____

_____

_____

_____

Date of death _____

Place of service _____

_____

Date of service _____

Time of service _____

Memorial contribution preference _____

_____

_____

CHAPTER 6:
Instructions for Living Trust Forms

In this chapter are the instructions for four separate Living Trusts that have been prepared for certain general situations, and for the various other forms that may need to accompany the one that you choose. The forms themselves are contained in the following chapter. For your reference, the four Trust forms are as follows:

- **Living Trust for Single Person or Individual Spouse with Children's Trust Included**

   This Living Trust is appropriate for use by a married or single person with one or more minor children, who desires to place the property and assets that may be left to the child(ren) in an ongoing trust fund. In most cases, a married person may desire to choose the other spouse as both Successor Trustee and Trustee for any children's trust, although this is not a legal requirement.

- **Living Trust for Single Person or Individual Spouse without a Children's Trust**

   This Living Trust is appropriate for use by a single person or individual spouse with or without children. If the person has children, this form is to be used only if the person desires that any assets to be transferred to the children at the grantor's death be held not in a children's trust, but be transferred directly to the children upon the death of the grantor. This will normally be used only when any children are already above the legal age of minority.

- **Joint Living Trust of Married Couple with Children's Trust Included**

   This Living Trust is appropriate for use by a married couple with one or more minor children, who desire to jointly enter into a Living Trust and to place the property and assets which may be left to their child(ren) in an ongoing trust fund. It is designed so that the surviving spouse will manage the Living Trust after the death of the other spouse. If both spouses die or become incapacitated, the chosen Successor Trustee will take over the management of the Living Trust.

- **Joint Living Trust of Married Couple without a Children's Trust**

   This Living Trust is appropriate for joint use by a married couple with or without children. With this trust, the couple enters jointly into a trust agreement. If the couple has children, this form is to be used only if the couple desires that any assets to be transferred to the child(ren) at each spouse's death not be held in a children's trust. This will normally be used only when any children are already above the legal age of minority.

The additional forms that you may need and that are contained in the next chapter are as follows:

- **Assignment to Living Trust by Single Person or Individual Spouse**
  This form may be used if an assignment of ownership of personal property to an individual Living Trust is necessary.

- **Joint Assignment to Joint Living Trust by Married Couple**
  This form may be used if an assignment of ownership of personal property to a Joint Living Trust is necessary.

- **Schedule of Assets of Living Trust for Single Person or Individual Spouse**
  This form should be used to list the assets of a single person or an individual spouse who is setting up an individual Living Trust. Please remember that any assets that have ownership documents must be transferred to the ownership of the trust using the appropriate method of documentary transfer (such as a deed or title).

- **Schedule of Assets of Joint Living Trust for Husband**
  This form should be used by a husband who is setting up a Joint Living Trust with his wife. This form allows for any of the husband's separate property and shared property to be assigned to the trust. Please remember that any assets that have ownership documents must be transferred to the ownership of the trust using the appropriate method of documentary transfer (such as a deed or title).

- **Schedule of Assets of Joint Living Trust for Wife**
  This form should be used by a wife who is setting up a Joint Living Trust with her husband. This form allows for any of the wife's separate property and shared property to be assigned to the trust. Please remember that any assets that have ownership documents must be transferred to the ownership of the trust using the appropriate method of documentary transfer (such as a deed or title).

- **Schedule of Beneficiaries of Living Trust for Single Person or Individual Spouse**
  This form should be used to list the beneficiaries of a single individual or an individual spouse who is setting up an individual Living Trust.

- **Joint Schedule of Beneficiaries of Joint Living Trust of Married Couple**
  This form should be used to list the joint beneficiaries of a husband and wife who are setting up a Joint Living Trust.

- **New York Notice of Assignment of Property to Living Trust**
  The State of New York has an additional requirement that a Notice of Assignment must be prepared for any personal property that has been assigned to a Living

Trust. This form simply uses a copy of any Schedule of Assets of Living Trust form to serve as the listing of property that has been assigned to the Living Trust.

- **Registration of Living Trust**
  A handful of states require that the Living Trust be registered in the local court by the trustee of the Living Trust. The purpose is to give the court jurisdiction over the Living Trust should any disputes arise. However, since there are no penalties or consequences from failing to register the Living Trust in these states, the requirement is not mandatory. You may use this simple form to comply with the registration requirements if your state is one that requires this. Please check the Appendix listing for your home state requirements.

- **Affidavit of Assumption of Duties by Successor Trustee**
  Upon your death, under the terms of the Living Trust, your Successor Trustee is automatically authorized to take over the administration and distribution of the Living Trust assets. No court proceedings are necessary to officially authorize the Successor Trustee to begin to manage the Living Trust. However, some banks, real estate companies, or other financial institutions may require an Affidavit signed by the Successor Trustee that states that he or she has officially assumed the duties and responsibillities of acting as the Successor Trustee. You may wish to leave a completed, but unsigned copy of this form with the copy of the Living Trust that you provide to your Successor Trustee so that he or she may complete the form quickly and easily upon your demise.

These Living Trust forms are intended to be used as simplified worksheets in preparing your own personal Living Trust. They should be filled-in by hand and then retyped according to the following instructions and the instructions contained in Chapter 9. (*Note*: if you have a version of this book with an enclosed CD, please follow the instructions on the "ReadMe" file which accompanied the CD). These Living Trusts are not intended to be filled-in and used "as is" as an original Living Trust. Such use would most likely result in an invalid Living Trust. They must be retyped. Be certain to carefully follow all of the instructions for use of these forms. They are not difficult to fill out, but must be prepared properly in order to be legally valid. In order to prepare any of the Living Trusts in this chapter, you should follow the simple steps listed on the following pages.

Completing Your Living Trust Declaration

Carefully read through all of the clauses in the blank Living Trusts to determine which trust is suitable in your situation. Choose the Living Trust that is most appropriate. Make a photocopy of the Living Trust that you choose to use as a worksheet. If you wish, you may use this book itself as a worksheet (unless it is a library book!)

As you fill in the information for each clause, keep in mind the following instructions:

Title Section

Title Clause: The title is mandatory for all Living Trusts. Fill in the name blank with your full legal name (such as the "Andrea Ann Doria Living Trust"). If you have been known under more than one name, use only your principal name. If you are completing a joint Living Trust as a husband and wife, you should name the trust under your joint names (such as the "Andrea Ann Doria and Peter William Doria Living Trust").

Declaration of Trust Section

Identification and Date Clause: The identification clause is mandatory and must be included in all Living Trusts. In the first blank, include any other names which you are known by. Do this by adding the phrase: "also known as" after your principal full name. For example: "John James Smith, also known as Jimmy John Smith." In the spaces provided for your residence, use the location of your principal residence; that is, where you currently live permanently. If you are completing a joint Living Trust as a husband and wife, fill in both of your full names in the spaces provided. Fill in the date when you wish the Living Trust to take effect.

Name of Trust Clause: Fill in your own name prior to the title of the trust (for example: "The John Smith Living Trust"). If you are completing a joint Living Trust as a husband and wife, fill in both of your full names in the spaces provided.

Marital and Parental Status Clause: Depending upon your current marital and parental status you will choose one of the following clauses. If you have children, list the appropriate information for each child. This clause should be included in your Living Trust after the phrase "My marital status is that...:

- I am single and have no children."
- I am currently married to [name of spouse] and we have no children."
- I was previously married to [name of spouse] and that marriage ended on [date] by [death, divorce, or annulment] and we had no children."
- I am single and have [number] child[ren] currently living. Their names and dates of birth are:"
- I am currently married to [name of spouse] and we have [number] child[ren] currently living. Their names and dates of birth are:"
- I was previously married to [name of spouse] and that marriage ended on [date] by [death, divorce, or annulment] and we have [number] child[ren] currently living. Their names and dates of birth are:"

Trusteeship Clause: Under this clause, you declare that you will act as the Trustee of the Trust and any subtrusts which may be created by the Trust (such as a Children's Trust). In addition, if you are completing a joint Living Trust as a husband and wife, there is an additional clause under this section which states that each of you will have the right to act as Trustee of the trust and any subtrusts (for example: a Children's Trust) while you are both alive. Upon the death of either spouse, the surviving spouse will act as Trustee.

Property Transfer Section

No additional information need be filled-in in this section. This section of your trust provides that you are transferring ownership of all of the property listed on your Schedule of Assets of Living Trust to the trust itself. You are also reserving the right to make any changes to your Schedule of Assets at any time, as long as they are in writing, notarized, and attached to the trust. You are also agreeing to prepare any additional paperwork that may be necessary to complete any such transfers of ownership, such as completing a deed or title transfer if necessary.

If you are completing a joint Living Trust as a husband and wife, you are agreeing to transfer the property listed on your own individual Schedule of Assets of Joint Living Trust. It is also noted that the property that each of you transfer as "separate" property will retain its character as "separate" property even after transfer to the trust.

Grantor's Rights Section

No additional information need be filled-in for this section. Under this section, you retain full lifetime control of all of the trust's assets that you have transferred in the above section (and by other transfer documents, if necessary). Regarding your home, you specifically state that you retain the right of possession for your entire life and that any transfer to the trust does not interfere with any rights to homestead exemptions that you may have under state law. If you are completing a joint Living Trust as a husband and wife, each of you will have such rights as long as each of you is alive.

Successor Trustee Section

This section is included in every Living Trust in this book. With this clause, you will make your choice of Successor Trustee and alternative Successor Trustee, the persons who will administer and distribute your trust assets upon your death or who will take over the management of your trust upon your incapacitation. You also provide that any such incapacitation be certified by a physician before the Successor Trustee may assume management of your trust. The chosen alternate Successor Trustee will assume the powers of the Trustee only if the Successor Trustee that you have chosen is not surviving or is otherwise unable to serve. A spouse, sibling, or other trusted party is usually chosen to act as Successor Trustee. The person chosen should be a resident of the state in which you currently reside. You also provide that he or she not be required to post a bond in order to be appointed to serve as Successor Trustee and that he or she will not be compensated for their service as Trustee. Finally, you note that any reference to "trustee" in your document also refers to the Successor or alternative Successor Trustee. Be sure to clearly identify the Successor Trustee and alternate Successor Trustee by full name and address.

Trustee's Powers Section

In this section, no additional information needs to be filled-in and you grant any Trustee broad powers to manage your trust assets. The powers are granted without court supervision and without oversight by anyone else. The powers granted are the same power and authority as an individual person has over their own property.

Additional Trustee Powers Section

No additional information need be filled-in in this section. This section provides a detailed enumeration of the powers that are granted to the Trustee. Although in the previous section you granted any powers granted by law, many businesses and financial institutions require that a trustee's actual power to perform a specific act be spelled-out in a trust document. As you can see, the powers granted to the trustee are very extensive and approximate the power that an individual would have over his or her property.

Incapacitation Section

No additional information needs to be filled-in for this section. This section goes into effect in the event that a grantor becomes incapacitated during his or her lifetime. This incapacitation must be certified by a physician, as noted in the Successor Trustee section above. In this event, the Successor Trustee is bound to manage the Trust solely for the benefit of the grantor and in accordance with the grantor's accustomed manner of living. Thus, any beneficiaries of the trust cannot demand that the Successor Trustee stop spending trust assets to care for an incapacitated grantor and save the trust assets for them.

Children's Trust Fund Section

This clause will only be present in the Living Trusts which relate to children. It is with this clause that you may set up a Trust Fund for any gifts you have made to your minor children. You also may delay the time when they will actually have unrestricted control over your gift. It is not recommended, however, to attempt to delay receipt of control beyond the age of 35.

In this section, you will fill in two ages. First, you will select an age that a child must be under for the Children's Trust section to take effect. You may desire the gifts under the main Trust to be held in the Children's Trust for any child under the age of, say, 30 years of age. Then you will also select an age when the Children's Trust will terminate and the then-adult will receive the property with no restrictions, for example, 35 years of age. The ages that you select may be any reasonable age.

The terms of the trust provide that the trustee may distribute any or all of the income or principal to the children as he or she deems necessary to provide for their health, support, and education. The trust will terminate when either the specific age is reached, all of the money is spent prior to that age, or the child dies prematurely. Upon termination, any remaining trust funds will be distributed to the child (beneficiary), if surviving. If the child is not surviving at the age when the trust is to terminate, the trust funds will be distributed to the heirs of the beneficiary (if there are any). If there are none, then the trust funds remaining will revert back to the residue of your trust (as noted on your Schedule of Beneficiaries of Living Trust) and be distributed accordingly. Additionally, since the Trustee of the Children's Trust is the same person who is Successor Trustee, you have already granted the Trustee broad powers to manage the trust and also provided that he or she not be required to post a bond nor allowed compensation for services rendered.

Termination of Trust Section

This section provides that the Trust shall become irrevocable upon the death of the grantor. Upon that event, the Successor Trustee will then be empowered to pay all of the valid debts, last expenses, and taxes of the grantor and then distribute the trust assets as specified on the Schedule of Beneficiaries of Living Trust. It is also noted in any of the Trusts which contain a Children's Trust that any such distributions to beneficiaries are subject to the terms of the Children's Trust. This section also provides that the Schedule of Beneficiaries may be amended at any time (before it becomes irrevocable) by a written, notarized amendment which is attached to the Trust.

If you are completing a Joint Living Trust as a husband and wife, this section provides that upon the death of the first spouse to die, the Trustee (who will generally be the surviving spouse) shall pay all of the valid debts, last expenses, and taxes of the deceased spouse and then distribute the trust assets as specified on the deceased spouse's Schedule of Beneficiaries of Joint Living Trust. The Trust will become irrevocable upon the death of the surviving spouse, and in that event, the Successor Trustee will then be empowered to pay all of the valid debts, last expenses, and taxes of the grantor and then distribute the trust assets as specified on the Schedule of Beneficiaries of Joint Living Trust of the final spouse to die.

Survivorship Section

This clause is included in every Living Trust. This clause provides for two possibilities. First, it provides for a required period of survival for any beneficiary to receive a gift under your Living Trust. The practical effect of this is to be certain that your property passes under your Living Trust and not that of a beneficiary who dies shortly after receiving your gift. The second portion of this clause provides for a determination of how your property should pass in the eventuality that both you and a beneficiary (most likely your spouse) should die in a manner that makes it impossible to determine who died first.

Without this clause in your Living Trust it would be possible that property would momentarily pass to a beneficiary under your Living Trust. When that person dies (possibly immediately if a result of a common accident or disaster) your property could wind up being left to the person whom your beneficiary designated, rather than to your alternate beneficiary. If you and your spouse are both preparing individual Living Trusts, it is a good idea to be certain that each of your Living Trusts contains identical survivorship clauses. If you are each other's primary beneficiary, it is also wise to attempt to coordinate who your alternate beneficiaries may be in the event of a simultaneous death.

Amendments and Revocations Section

This form of trust reserves the right to allow you to cancel (revoke) or amend this trust or any of the schedules at any time. However, any changes (amendments) must be in writing, notarized, and attached to the original trust document to be valid. If you are completing a Joint Living Trust as a husband and wife, you agree that while both of you are still alive, you will only have the right to jointly amend the Trust. However, a surviving spouse will have the right to individually amend the trust. In addition, you will agree that either spouse will have the right to unilaterally revoke the Living Trust. You will also have the right to jointly revoke the Trust at any time.

Governing Law Section

You will fill in the number of pages, including all schedules, and the state of your legal residence where indicated after you have properly typed or had your Living Trust typed. The laws of the state of your principal residence will govern any questions regarding the operation of the trust or the actions of any trustee.

Signature Section

The signature lines of your Living Trust will be completed in front of a notary public as indicated in the instructions in Chapter 9.

Notary Acknowledgment Section

This section will be completed by a notary public as indicated in the instructions in Chapter 9.

Completing Your Schedule of Assets of Living Trust Form(s)

On this form, you will include a listing of all of the property that you wish to transfer into the trust. This document should be attached to the Living Trust when completed. It is relatively simple to complete. Simply fill in the title information (name and date of trust) and then carefully list the property that you have chosen to include in the trust.

Please refer to the Property Questionnaire in Chapter 3 that you completed to be certain that you include all of the property that you desire to be held in trust.

Always describe the property in as detailed and clear a manner as possible. For example: do not simply state "my car," instead state "a 1994 Buick Skylark, serial #123456789." In your description of the property, you should be as specific and precise as possible. For land, it is suggested that you use the description exactly as shown on the deed to the property. For personal property, be certain that your description clearly differentiates your gift from any other property.

(Note for married couples completing Joint Living Trust: You will each complete a separate Schedule of Assets of Living Trust form. On each of these forms, you will note which shared property you wish to add to the trust and which separately-owned property you wish to transfer to the trust. Please refer back to the discussion regarding common-law and community property in Chapter 3 and your completed Property Questionnaire to complete this form.)

Very Important Note: If the particular asset that you list on this Schedule has any type of ownership document, such as a title, deed, stock certificate, or similar document, you must also transfer the ownership of the asset to the trust by completing a new deed, title, or other transfer paperwork. Simply listing the asset on this form does not transfer it to the trust if an ownership document is required. For those items of personal property for which no such ownership document exists (such as a stereo system, appliances, antiques, etc.), the listing on the Schedule of Assets of Living Trust will effectively transfer the ownership to the Trust.

This Schedule of Assets will become a part of the Living Trust. It should be stapled to the original of the trust document. Any time that any changes are made to the assets that are to be included in the Living Trust, this schedule must be changed and an Amendment to Living Trust form should be filled out as explained in Chapter 10.

Completing Your Schedule of Beneficiaries of Living Trust Form(s)

Using this form, you will direct how your property will be distributed by your Successor Trustee upon your death. You will select your beneficiaries, alternate beneficiaries, and the property that each of them will receive. Please refer back to your Beneficiary Questionnaire that you completed in Chapter 4 to prepare this form. The information that you compiled for that Questionnaire will be your guide for preparing your Living Trust, both in terms of being certain that you have disposed of all of your Trust assets, and in terms of being certain that you have left gifts to all those persons or organizations that you wished to. Using the clauses in this section, you will be able to prepare a Living Trust in which you may:

- Make specific gifts of cash, real estate, or personal property to anyone
- Make specific gifts of certain shares of your trust assets
- Make a gift of the rest (residue) of your assets to anyone

Specific Gifts Clause: Use this type of clause to provide specific gifts to your beneficiaries. If chosen, add this clause or clauses after the phrase "Upon the death of the grantor of the trust and the payment of all debts, taxes, and liabilities of the grantee, the Successor Trustee shall then distribute the remaining assets of the trust as follows:

To my [relationship], [name of beneficiary], or if not surviving, to my [relationship], [name of alternate beneficiary], the following trust assets shall be distributed:"

For making specific gifts, use as many of the "To my…" paragraphs as is necessary to complete your chosen gifts. In these paragraphs, you may make any type of gift that you wish, either a cash gift, a gift of a specific piece of personal property or real estate, or a specific share of your total trust estate. If you wish to give some of your trust estate in the form of portions of the total, it is recommended to use fractional portions. For example, if you wish to leave your trust estate in equal shares to two persons, name both parties after "To my…" and state "one-half of my total trust estate to each party."

Although none of the Living Trusts in this book contain a specific clause which states that you give one person your entire trust estate, you may make such a gift using this clause by simply stating after "The following trust assets shall be distributed:…"

"My entire trust estate"

Be sure that you do not attempt to give any other gifts. However, you should still include the residuary clause in your Living Trust, which is explained on the following pages.

You may only give away property that the trust itself owns. Be certain that any property included in any of the gift clauses is also included on your Schedule of Assets and has been effectively transferred to the Trust. In your description of the property, you should be as specific and precise as possible. For land, it is suggested that you use the description exactly as shown on the deed to the property. For personal property, be certain that your description clearly differentiates your gift from any other property. For example: "The blue velvet coat which was a gift from my brother John." Use serial numbers, colors, or any other descriptive words to clearly indicate the exact nature of the gift. For cash gifts, specifically indicate the amount of the gift. For gifts of securities, state the amount of shares and the name of the company. You may add simple conditions to the gifts that you make, if you desire. For example: You may state "$1,000.00 to the Centerville Church for use in purchasing a new roof for the church." Complex conditions, however, are not possible in this clause, and immoral or illegal conditions are not acceptable.

Be sure to clearly identify the beneficiary and alternate beneficiary by full name. You can also name joint beneficiaries, such as several children, if you choose. The space provided for an identification of the relationship of the beneficiary can be simply a descriptive phrase like "my wife," "my brother-in-law," or "my best friend." It does not mean that the beneficiary must be related to you personally.

The choice of alternate beneficiary is for the purpose of allowing you to designate someone to receive the gift if your first choice to receive the gift dies before you do (or, in the case of a organization chosen as primary beneficiary, is no longer in business). In this or any of the other gift clauses, your choice for alternate beneficiary may be one or more persons or an organization. It is recommended to always specifically name your beneficiary(s), rather than using a description only, such as "my children." In addition, you may delete the alternate beneficiary choice and substitute the words "the residue" instead. The result of this change will be that if your primary beneficiary dies before you do, your gift will pass under your residuary clause, which is discussed below. If additional gifts are desired, simply photocopy an additional page.

Residuary Clause: Although not a technical legal requirement, a residuary clause is included in every Living Trust in this book. With it, you will choose the person, persons, or organization to receive anything not covered by other clauses of your Living Trust. Even if you feel that you have given away everything that your trust owns under other clauses of your Living Trust, this can be a very important clause.

If, for any reason, any other gifts under your Living Trust are not able to completed, this clause goes into effect. For example, if a beneficiary refuses to accept your gift or the chosen beneficiary has died and no alternate was selected or both the beneficiary and alternate has died, the gift is put back into your trust estate and will pass under the residuary clause. If there is no residuary clause included, any property not disposed of could potentially be forfeited to the state.

In addition, you may use this clause to give all of your estate (except your specific gifts) to one or more persons. For example: you make specific gifts of $1,000.00 to a sister and a car to a friend. By then naming your spouse as the residuary clause beneficiary, you will have gifted everything in your trust estate to your spouse—except the $1,000.00 and the car. You could then name your children, in equal shares, as the alternate residuary beneficiaries. In this manner, if your spouse were to die first, your children would then equally share your entire trust estate—except the $1,000.00 and the car.

Be sure to clearly identify the beneficiary by full name. The space provided for an identification of the relationship of the beneficiary can be simply a descriptive phrase like "my wife," or "my brother-in-law," or "my best friend." It does not mean that the beneficiary must be related to you personally.

Finishing Your Living Trust Forms

After you have filled in all of the appropriate information, carefully re-read your entire Living Trust and your Schedules of Assets and Beneficiaries. Be certain that they contain all of the correct information that you desire. Then starting at the beginning of the Living Trust forms, cross out all of the words and phrases in the Living Trust forms that do not apply in your situation. After all of the extraneous information has been crossed out, look over the sample Living Trust in Chapter 8 to see how a completed Living Trust should look. Then turn to Chapter 9 for instructions on typing and final preparation of your Living Trust.

CHAPTER 7:
Living Trust Forms

Living Trust for Single Person or Individual Spouse with Children's Trust Included

This Living Trust is appropriate for use by an individual married person or a single person with one or more minor children, who desires to place the property and assets which may be left to the children in a trust fund. In most cases, a married person may desire to choose the other spouse as both successor trustee and trustee for any of their children's trusts, although this is not a legal requirement.

Fill in each of the appropriate blanks in this Living Trust, a Schedule of Assets of Living Trust, and a Schedule of Beneficiaries of Living Trust using the information which you included in your Property and Beneficiary Questionnaires. Cross out any information that is not appropriate to your situation. You will then complete the preparation of all your forms following the instructions in Chapter 9.

To complete this form, you will need the following information:

①   The name of the Living Trust (generally, your full name is the name of the trust, such as the "Gwendolyn Smith Living Trust").

②   Your complete name,
The date on which you wish the Living Trust to take effect,
The name of the Living Trust,
Your complete name, and
Your marital status and the names of any children (see page 77 for the correct phrase).

③   No information needed.

④   No information needed.

⑤   The names and addresses of your chosen Successor Trustee and Alternative Successor Trustee.

⑥   No information needed.

⑦   No information needed.

⑧   No information needed.

⑨Ⓐ   The age of your child(ren) under which you wish the Children's Trust to take effect, and
The age of each child when the Children's Trust will terminate.

⑨Ⓑ   No information needed.

⑩   No information needed.
⑪   No information needed.
⑫   No information needed.
⑬   The number of pages of the Living Trust, including schedules, and
      The state of your legal residence.
⑭   Your signature and printed name (do not sign unless in front of a notary public).
⑮   The Notary Acknowledgment section (to be completed by notary public).

Living Trust for Single Person or Individual Spouse with Children's Trust Included

① Title

LIVING TRUST OF _____

② Declaration of Trust

I, _____ , the grantor of this trust, declare and make this Living Trust on _____ (date).

This trust will be known as the _____ Living Trust.

I, _____ , will be trustee of this trust and any subtrusts created under this trust.

My marital status is that _____ .

③ Property Transfer

I transfer ownership to this trust of all of the assets which are listed on the attached Schedule of Assets of Living Trust, which is specifically made a part of this trust. I reserve the right to add or delete any of these assets at any time. In addition, I will prepare a separate Deed, Assignment, or any other documents necessary to carry out such transfers. Any additions or deletions to the Schedule of Assets of Living Trust must be written, notarized, and attached to this document to be valid.

④ Grantor's Rights

Until I die, I retain all rights to all income, profits, and control of the trust property. If my principal residence is transferred to this trust, I retain the right to possess and occupy it for my life, rent-free and without charge. I will remain liable for all taxes, insurance, maintenance, related costs, and expenses. The rights that I retain are intended to give me a beneficial interest in my principal residence such that I do not lose any eligibility that I may have for a state homestead exemption for which I am otherwise qualified.

⑤ Successor Trustee

Upon my death or if it is certified by a licensed physician that I am physically or mentally unable to manage this trust and my financial affairs, then I appoint _____

_____ (name), of _____
_____ (address), as Successor Trustee, to serve without bond and without compensation. If this successor trustee is not surviving or otherwise unable to serve, I appoint _____ (name), of _____
_____ (address), as Alternate Successor Trustee, also to serve without bond and without compensation. The successor trustee or alternative successor trustee shall not be liable for any actions taken in good faith. References to "trustee" in this document shall include any successor or alternative successor trustees.

⑥ Trustee's Powers

In addition to any powers, authority, and discretion granted by law, I grant the trustee any and all powers to perform any acts, in his or her sole discretion and without court approval, for the management and distribution of this trust and any subtrusts created by this trust. I intend the trustee to have the same power and authority to manage and distribute the trust assets as an individual owner has over his or her own wholly-owned property.

⑦ Additional Trustee Powers

The trustee's powers include, but are not limited to: the power to sell trust property, borrow money, and encumber that property, specifically including trust real estate, by mortgage, deed of trust, or other method; the power to manage trust real estate as if the trustee were the absolute owner of it, including the power to lease or grant options to lease the property, make repairs or alterations, and insure against loss; the power to sell or grant options for the sale or exchange of any trust property, including stocks, bonds, and any other form of security; the power to invest trust property in property of any kind, including but not limited to bonds, notes, mortgages, and stocks; the power to receive additional property from any source and add to any trust created by this trust; the power to employ and pay reasonable fees to accountants, lawyers, or investment consultants for information or advice relating to the trust; the power to deposit and hold trust funds in both interest-bearing and non-interest-bearing accounts; the power to deposit funds in bank or other accounts uninsured by FDIC coverage; the power to enter into electronic fund transfer or safe deposit arrangements with financial institutions; the power to continue any business of the grantor; the power to institute or defend legal actions concerning the trust or grantor's affairs; and the power to execute any document necessary to administer any children's trust created in this trust.

⑧ Incapacitation

Should the successor trustee or alternative successor trustee assume management of this trust during the lifetime of the grantor, the successor trustee or alternative successor trustee shall manage the trust solely for the proper health care, support, maintenance, comfort, and/or welfare of the grantor, in accordance with the grantor's accustomed manner of living.

⑨ Children's Trust Fund

Ⓐ If any of my children who are named as beneficiaries on the attached Schedule of Beneficiaries of Living Trust are under _____ years old on my death, I direct that any property that I give them under this trust be held in an individual children's trust for each child under the following terms, until each shall reach the age of _____ years old.

Ⓑ In the trustee's sole discretion, the trustee may distribute any or all of the principal, income, or both as deemed necessary for the beneficiary's health, support, welfare, and education. Any income not distributed shall be added to the trust principal. Any such trust shall terminate when the beneficiary reaches the required age, dies prior to reaching the required age, or all trust funds have been distributed. Upon termination, any remaining undistributed principal and income shall pass to the beneficiary; or if not surviving, to the beneficiary's heirs; or if none, to the residue of the main trust created by this document.

⑩ Termination of Trust

Upon my death, this trust shall become irrevocable. The successor trustee shall then pay my valid debts, last expenses, and estate taxes from the assets of this trust. The successor trustee shall then distribute the remaining trust assets in the manner shown on the attached Schedule of Beneficiaries of Living Trust which is specifically made a part of this trust, subject to the provisions of any children's trust which is created by this document. I reserve the right to add and/or delete any beneficiaries at any time. Any additions or deletions to the Schedule of Beneficiaries of Living Trust must be written, notarized, and attached to this document to be valid.

⑪ Survivorship

All beneficiaries named in the Schedule of Beneficiaries of Living Trust must survive me by thirty (30) days to receive any gift under this living trust. If any beneficiary and I should die simultaneously, I shall be conclusively presumed to have survived that beneficiary for purposes of this living trust.

⑫ Amendments and Revocations

I reserve the right to amend any or all of this trust at any time. The amendments must be written, notarized, and attached to this document to be valid. I also reserve the right to revoke this trust at any time. A revocation of this trust must be written, notarized, and attached to this document to be valid.

⑬ Governing Law

This trust, containing _____ pages, was created on the date noted above and will be governed under the laws of the State of _____ .

⑭ Signature

_____

Signature of Grantor

_____

Printed Name of Grantor

⑮ Notary Acknowledgment

State of _____
County of _____

On _____ , _____ came before me personally and, under oath, stated that he or she is the person described in the above document and he or she signed the above document in my presence. I declare under penalty of perjury that the person whose name is subscribed to this instrument appears to be of sound mind and under no duress, fraud, or undue influence.

_____

Notary Public
My commission expires _____

Living Trust for Single Person or Individual Spouse without a Children's Trust

This Living Trust is appropriate for use by an single person or an individual married person with or without children. If the person has children, this form is to be used only if the person desires that any assets to be transferred to the children at the grantor's death not be held in a children's trust, but rather be transferred directly to the children upon the death of the grantor. This will normally be used only when any children are already above the legal age of minority.

Fill in each of the appropriate blanks in this Living Trust, a Schedule of Assets of Living Trust, and a Schedule of Beneficiaries of Living Trust using the information which you included in your Property and Beneficiary Questionnaires. Cross out any information that is not appropriate to your situation. You will then complete the preparation of all your forms following the instructions in Chapter 9.

To complete this form, you will need the following information:

①   The name of the Living Trust (generally, your full name is the name of the trust, such as the "Gwendolyn Smith Living Trust").

②   Your complete name,
The date on which you wish the Living Trust to take effect,
The name of the Living Trust,
Your complete name, and
Your marital status and the names of any children (see page 77 for the correct phrase).

③   No information needed.

④   No information needed.

⑤   The names and addresses of your chosen Successor Trustee and Alternative Successor Trustee.

⑥   No information needed.

⑦   No information needed.

⑧   No information needed.

⑨   No information needed.

⑩   No information needed.

⑪   No information needed.

⑫   The number of pages of the Living Trust, including schedules, and
The state of your legal residence.

⑬   Your signature and printed name (do not sign unless in front of a notary public).

⑭   The Notary Acknowledgment section (to be completed by notary public).

Living Trust for Single Person or Individual Spouse without a Children's Trust

① Title

LIVING TRUST OF _____

② Declaration of Trust

I, _____ , the grantor of this trust, declare and make this
Living Trust on _____ (date).

This trust will be known as the _____ Living Trust.

I, _____ , will be trustee of this trust.

My marital status is that _____ .

③ Property Transfer

I transfer ownership to this trust of all of the assets which are listed on the attached
Schedule of Assets of Living Trust, which is specifically made a part of this trust. I reserve
the right to add or delete any of these assets at any time. In addition, I will prepare a
separate Deed, Assignment, or any other documents necessary to carry out such transfers.
Any additions or deletions to the Schedule of Assets of Living Trust must be written,
notarized, and attached to this document to be valid.

④ Grantor's Rights

Until I die, I retain all rights to all income, profits, and control of the trust property. If my
principal residence is transferred to this trust, I retain the right to possess and occupy it for
my life, rent-free and without charge. I will remain liable for all taxes, insurance, maintenance, related costs, and expenses. The rights that I retain are intended to give me a
beneficial interest in my principal residence such that I do not lose any eligibility that I may
have for a state homestead exemption for which I am otherwise qualified.

⑤ Successor Trustee

Upon my death or if it is certified by a licensed physician that I am physically or mentally
unable to manage this trust and my financial affairs, then I appoint _____
_____ (name), of _____
_____ (address), as Successor Trustee, to serve without bond and without
compensation. If this successor trustee is not surviving or otherwise unable to serve, I

appoint _____ (name), of _____
_____ (address), as Alternate Successor
Trustee, also to serve without bond and without compensation. The successor trustee or
alternative successor trustee shall not be liable for any actions taken in good faith. References
to "trustee" in this document shall include any successor or alternative successor trustees.

⑥ Trustee's Powers

In addition to any powers, authority, and discretion granted by law, I grant the trustee any
and all powers to perform any acts, in his or her sole discretion and without court approval, for the management and distribution of this trust. I intend the trustee to have the
same power and authority to manage and distribute the trust assets as an individual owner
has over his or her own wholly-owned property.

⑦ Additional Trustee Powers

The trustee's powers include, but are not limited to: the power to sell trust property,
borrow money, and encumber that property, specifically including trust real estate, by mortgage, deed of trust, or other method; the power to manage trust real estate as if the trustee
were the absolute owner of it, including the power to lease or grant options to lease the
property, make repairs or alterations, and insure against loss; the power to sell or grant
options for the sale or exchange of any trust property, including stocks, bonds, and any
other form of security; the power to invest trust property in property of any kind, including but
not limited to bonds, notes, mortgages, and stocks; the power to receive additional property
from any source and add to any trust created by this trust; the power to employ and pay
reasonable fees to accountants, lawyers, or investment consultants for information or advice relating to the trust; the power to deposit and hold trust funds in both interest-bearing
and non-interest-bearing accounts; the power to deposit funds in bank or other accounts
uninsured by FDIC coverage; the power to enter into electronic fund transfer or safe deposit arrangements with financial institutions; the power to continue any business of the grantor;
and the power to institute or defend legal actions concerning the trust or grantor's affairs.

⑧ Incapacitation

Should the successor trustee or alternative successor trustee assume management of this trust
during the lifetime of the grantor, the successor trustee or alternative successor trustee shall
manage the trust solely for the proper health care, support, maintenance, comfort, and/or
welfare of the grantor, in accordance with the grantor's accustomed manner of living.

⑨ Termination of Trust

Upon my death, this trust shall become irrevocable. The successor trustee shall then pay
my valid debts, last expenses, and estate taxes from the assets of this trust. The successor
trustee shall then distribute the remaining trust assets in the manner shown on the attached
Schedule of Beneficiaries of Living Trust which is specifically made a part of this trust.

Any additions or deletions to the Schedule of Beneficiaries of Living Trust must be written, notarized, and attached to this document to be valid.

⑩ Survivorship

All beneficiaries named in the Schedule of Beneficiaries of Living Trust must survive me by thirty (30) days to receive any gift under this living trust. If any beneficiary and I should die simultaneously, I shall be conclusively presumed to have survived that beneficiary for purposes of this living trust.

⑪ Amendments and Revocations

I reserve the right to amend any or all of this trust at any time. The amendments must be written, notarized, and attached to this document to be valid. I also reserve the right to revoke this trust at any time. A revocation of this trust must be written, notarized, and attached to this document to be valid.

⑫ Governing Law

This trust, containing _____ pages, was created on the date noted above and will be governed under the laws of the State of _____ .

⑬ Signature

_____

Signature of Grantor

_____

Printed Name of Grantor

⑭ Notary Acknowledgment

State of _____
County of _____

On _____ , _____ came before me personally and, under oath, stated that he or she is the person described in the above document and he or she signed the above document in my presence. I declare under penalty of perjury that the person whose name is subscribed to this instrument appears to be of sound mind and under no duress, fraud, or undue influence.

_____

Notary Public
My commission expires _____

Joint Living Trust of Married Couple with Children's Trust included

This Living Trust is appropriate for use by a married couple with one or more minor children, and the married couple desire to jointly enter into a Living Trust and place the property and assets which may be left to their child(ren) in a trust fund.

Fill in each of the appropriate blanks in this particular Living Trust, a Schedule of Assets of Joint Living Trust for Husband, a Schedule of Assets of Joint Living Trust for Wife, and a Joint Schedule of Beneficiaries of Joint Living Trust using the information which you included in your Property and Beneficiary Questionnaires. Please note that each spouse must complete a separate Schedule of Assets. Cross out any information that is not appropriate to your situation. You will then complete the preparation of all your forms following the instructions in Chapter 9.

To complete this form, you will need the following information:

①   The name of the Living Trust (generally, both of your full names will be the name of the trust, such as the "Gwendolyn Smith and Robert Smith Living Trust").

②   Both of your complete names,
The date on which you wish the Living Trust to take effect,
The name of the Living Trust,
Both of your complete names, and
Your marital status and the names of any children (see page 77 for the correct phrase).

③   No information needed.

④   No information needed.

⑤   No information needed.

⑥   The names and addresses of your chosen Successor Trustee and Alternative Successor Trustee.

⑦   No information needed.

⑧   No information needed.

⑨Ⓐ   The age of your child(ren) under which you wish the Children's Trust to take effect, and
The age of each child when the Children's Trust will terminate.

⑨Ⓑ   No information needed.

⑩   No information needed.

⑪   No information needed.

⑫   No information needed.

⑬   The number of pages of the Living Trust, including schedules, and
The state of your legal residence.

⑭   Your signatures and printed names (do not sign unless in front of a notary public).

⑮   The Notary Acknowledgment section (to be completed by notary public).

Joint Living Trust of Married Couple with Children's Trust Included

① Title

LIVING TRUST OF _____ and

_____

② Declaration of Trust

We, _____ and _____ , the grantors of this trust, declare and make this Living Trust on _____ (date).

This trust will be known as the _____ and _____ Living Trust.

We, _____ and _____ , will be trustees of this trust and any subtrusts created under this trust. Either trustee may act for and represent the trust in any transaction. Upon the death of either trustee, the surviving grantor shall serve as sole trustee of this trust.

Our marital status is that _____ .

③ Property Transfer

The husband transfers his ownership to this trust of all of the assets which are listed on the attached Schedule of Assets of Joint Living Trust for Husband, which is specifically made a part of this trust. The property listed on the Schedule of Assets of Joint Living Trust for Husband shall retain its character as the shared or separate property of the Husband. The wife also transfers her ownership to this trust of all of the assets which are listed on the attached Schedule of Assets of Joint Living Trust for Wife, which is specifically made a part of this trust. The property listed on the Schedule of Assets of Joint Living Trust for Wife shall retain its character as the shared or separate property of the Wife. We reserve the right to add or delete any of these assets at any time. In addition, we will prepare a separate Deed, Assignment, or any other documents necessary to carry out such transfers. Any additions or deletions to any of the Schedules of Assets of Living Trust must be written, notarized, and attached to this document to be valid.

④ Grantor's Rights

As long as we are both alive, we retain all rights to all income, profits, and control of the shared property listed on the attached Schedule of Assets of Joint Living Trust for Husband and Schedule of Assets of Joint Living Trust for Wife. As long as the Husband is alive, he shall retain all rights to all income, profits, and control of the separate property listed on Schedule of Assets of Joint Living Trust for Husband. As long as the Wife is alive, she shall retain all rights to all income, profits, and control of the separate property listed on Schedule of Assets of Joint Living Trust for Wife. If our principal residence is transferred to this trust, we retain the right to possess and occupy it for our lives, rent-free, and without charge. We will remain liable for all taxes, insurance, maintenance, related costs, and expenses. The rights that we retain are intended to give us a beneficial interest in our principal residence such that we do not lose any eligibility that we may have for a state homestead exemption for which we are otherwise qualified.

⑤ Successor Trustee

Upon the death of the surviving grantor or if it is certified by a licensed physician that either the sole surviving grantor or both grantors are physically or mentally unable to manage this trust and his or her financial affairs, then we appoint _____ _____ (name), of _____ _____ (address), as Successor Trustee of this trust and any subtrusts created by this trust, to serve without bond and without compensation. If this successor trustee is not surviving or otherwise unable to serve, we appoint _____ _____ (name), of _____ _____ (address), as Alternate Successor Trustee, also to serve without bond and without compensation. The successor trustee or alternative successor trustee shall not be liable for any actions taken in good faith. References to "trustee" in this document shall include any successor or alternative successor trustees.

⑥ Trustee's Powers

In addition to any powers, authority, and discretion granted by law, we grant the trustee any and all powers to perform any acts, in his or her sole discretion and without court approval, for the management and distribution of this trust and any subtrusts created by this trust. We intend the trustee to have the same power and authority to manage and distribute the trust assets as an individual owner has over his or her own wholly-owned property.

⑦ Additional Trustee Powers

The trustee's powers include, but are not limited to: the power to sell trust property, borrow money, and encumber that property, specifically including trust real estate, by mortgage, deed of trust, or other method; the power to manage trust real estate as if the trustee were the absolute owner of it, including the power to lease or grant options to lease the property, make repairs or alterations, and insure against loss; the power to sell or grant options for the sale or exchange of any trust property, including stocks, bonds, and any other form of security; the power to invest trust property in property of any kind, including but not limited to bonds, notes, mortgages, and stocks; the power to receive additional property from any source and add to any trust created by this trust; the power to employ and pay reasonable fees to accountants, lawyers, or investment consultants for information or advice relating to the trust; the power to deposit and hold trust funds in both interest-bearing and non-interest-bearing accounts; the power to deposit funds in bank or other accounts uninsured by FDIC coverage; the power to enter into electronic fund transfer or safe deposit arrangements with financial institutions; the power to continue any business of the grantor; the power to institute or defend legal actions concerning the trust or grantor's affairs; and the power to execute any document necessary to administer any children's trust created in this trust.

⑧ Incapacitation

Should the successor trustee or alternative successor trustee assume management of this trust during the lifetime of the grantor(s), the successor trustee or alternative successor trustee shall manage the trust solely for the proper health care, support, maintenance, comfort, and/or welfare of the grantor(s), in accordance with the grantor's accustomed manner of living.

⑨ Children's Trust Fund

Ⓐ If any of our children who are named as beneficiaries on the attached Joint Schedule of Beneficiaries of Joint Living Trust are under _____ years old on the death of the surviving grantor, we direct that any property that we give them under this trust be held in an individual children's trust for each child under the following terms, until each shall reach the age of _____ years old.

Ⓑ In the trustee's sole discretion, the trustee may distribute any or all of the principal, income, or both as deemed necessary for the beneficiary's health, support, welfare, and education. Any income not distributed shall be added to the trust principal. Any such trust shall terminate when the beneficiary reaches the required age, dies prior to reaching the required age, or all trust funds have been distributed. Upon termination, any remaining undistributed principal and income shall pass to the beneficiary; or if not surviving, to the beneficiary's heirs; or if none, to the residue of the main trust created by this document.

⑩ Termination of Trust

Upon the death of the first grantor to die, the trustee shall pay from the assets of the trust all valid debts, last expenses, and estate taxes due upon the death of the first grantor to die. The trustee shall then distribute the trust assets of the deceased spouse as specified on the attached Joint Schedule of Beneficiaries of Joint Living Trust, subject to the provisions of any children's trust which is created by this document. Upon the death of the surviving grantor, this trust shall become irrevocable. The successor trustee shall then pay all valid debts, last expenses, and estate taxes from the assets of this trust. The successor trustee shall then distribute the remaining trust assets in the manner shown on the attached Joint

Schedule of Beneficiaries of Joint Living Trust which is specifically made a part of this trust, subject to the provisions of any children's trust which is created by this document. Any additions or deletions to the Joint Schedule of Beneficiaries of Joint Living Trust must be written, notarized, and attached to this document to be valid.

⑪ Survivorship

All beneficiaries named in the Joint Schedule of Beneficiaries of Joint Living Trust must survive the last surviving grantor by thirty (30) days to receive any gift under this living trust. If any beneficiary and the last surviving grantor should die simultaneously, then the last surviving grantor shall be conclusively presumed to have survived that beneficiary for purposes of this living trust.

⑫ Amendments and Revocations

We reserve the right to jointly amend any or all of this trust at any time. Upon the death of either grantor, the surviving grantor may amend this trust. The amendments must be written, notarized, and attached to this document to be valid. We also reserve the right to individually or jointly revoke this trust at any time. Upon the death of either grantor, the surviving grantor may revoke this trust. A revocation of this trust must be written, notarized, and attached to this document to be valid. If the trust is revoked, the property shall revert to the grantors based on the ownership rights in the property before the property was transferred to the trust.

⑬ Governing Law

This trust, containing _____ pages, was created on the date noted above and will be governed under the laws of the State of _____ .

⑭ Signature

_____   _____
Signature of Grantor   Signature of Grantor

_____   _____
Printed Name of Grantor   Printed Name of Grantor

⑮ Notary Acknowledgment

State of _____
County of _____

On _____ , _____ and _____ _____ came before me personally and, under oath, stated that they are the persons described in the above document and they signed the above document in my presence. I declare under penalty of perjury that the persons whose names are subscribed to this instrument appear to be of sound mind and under no duress, fraud, or undue influence.

_____

Notary Public
My commission expires _____

Joint Living Trust of Married Couple without a Children's Trust

This Living Trust is appropriate for joint use by a married couple with or without children. With this trust, the couple will jointly enter into a trust agreement. If the couple has children, this form is to be used only if the couple desires that any assets to be transferred to the child(ren) at either spouse's death not be held in a children's trust. This will normally be used only when any children are already above the legal age of minority.

Fill in each of the appropriate blanks in this Living Trust, a Schedule of Assets of Joint Living Trust for Husband, a Schedule of Assets of Joint Living Trust for Wife, and a Joint Schedule of Beneficiaries of Joint Living Trust using the information which you included in your Property and Beneficiary Questionnaires. Please note that each spouse must complete a separate Schedule of Assets. Cross out any information that is not appropriate to your situation. You will then complete the preparation of all your forms following the instructions in Chapter 9.

To complete this form, you will need the following information:

① The name of the Living Trust (generally, both of your full names will be the name of the trust, such as the "Gwendolyn Smith and Robert Smith Living Trust").

② Both of your complete names,
The date on which you wish the Living Trust to take effect,
The name of the Living Trust,
Both of your complete names, and
Your marital status and the names of any children (see page 77 for the correct phrase).

③ No information needed.

④ No information needed.

⑤ The names and addresses of your chosen Successor Trustee and Alternative Successor Trustee.

⑥ No information needed.

⑦ No information needed.

⑧ No information needed.

⑨ No information needed.

⑩ No information needed.

⑪ No information needed.

⑫ The number of pages of the Living Trust, including schedules, and
The state of your legal residence.

⑬ Your signatures and printed names (do not sign unless in front of a notary public).

⑭ The Notary Acknowledgment section (to be completed by notary public).

Joint Living Trust of Married Couple without a Children's Trust

① Title

LIVING TRUST OF _____ and

_____

② Declaration of Trust

We, _____ and _____ , the grantors of this trust, declare and make this Living Trust on _____ (date).

This trust will be known as the _____ and _____ Living Trust.

We, _____ and _____ , will be trustees of this trust created under this trust. Either trustee may act for and represent the trust in any transaction. Upon the death of either trustee, the surviving grantor shall serve as sole trustee of this trust.

Our marital status is that _____ .

③ Property Transfer

The husband transfers his ownership to this trust of all of the assets which are listed on the attached Schedule of Assets of Joint Living Trust for Husband, which is specifically made a part of this trust. The property listed on the Schedule of Assets of Joint Living Trust for Husband shall retain its character as the shared or separate property of the Husband. The wife also transfers her ownership to this trust of all of the assets which are listed on the attached Schedule of Assets of Joint Living Trust for Wife, which is specifically made a part of this trust. The property listed on the Schedule of Assets of Joint Living Trust for Wife shall retain its character as the shared or separate property of the Wife. We reserve the right to add or delete any of these assets at any time. In addition, we will prepare a separate Deed, Assignment, or any other documents necessary to carry out such transfers. Any additions or deletions to any of the Schedules of Assets of Joint Living Trust must be written, notarized, and attached to this document to be valid.

④ Grantor's Rights

As long as we are both alive, we retain all rights to all income, profits, and control of the shared property listed on the attached Schedule of Assets of Joint Living Trust for Husband and Schedule of Assets of Joint Living Trust for Wife. As long as the Husband is alive, he shall retain all rights to all income, profits, and control of the separate property listed on Schedule of Assets of Joint Living Trust for Husband. As long as the Wife is alive, she shall retain all rights to all income, profits, and control of the separate property listed on Schedule of Assets of Joint Living Trust for Wife. If our principal residence is transferred to this trust, we retain the right to possess and occupy it for our lives, rent-free, and without charge. We will remain liable for all taxes, insurance, maintenance, related costs, and expenses. The rights that we retain are intended to give us a beneficial interest in our principal residence such that we do not lose any eligibility that we may have for a state homestead exemption for which we are otherwise qualified.

⑤ Successor Trustee

Upon the death of the surviving grantor or if it is certified by a licensed physician that either the sole surviving grantor or both grantors are physically or mentally unable to manage this trust and his or her financial affairs, then we appoint _____ (name), of _____ (address), as Successor Trustee of this trust and any subtrusts created by this trust, to serve without bond and without compensation. If this successor trustee is not surviving or otherwise unable to serve, we appoint _____ (name), of _____ _____ (address), as Alternate Successor Trustee, also to serve without bond and without compensation. The successor trustee or alternative successor trustee shall not be liable for any actions taken in good faith. References to "trustee" in this document shall include any successor or alternative successor trustees.

⑥ Trustee's Powers

In addition to any powers, authority, and discretion granted by law, we grant the trustee any and all powers to perform any acts, in his or her sole discretion and without court approval, for the management and distribution of this trust and any subtrusts created by this trust. We intend the trustee to have the same power and authority to manage and distribute the trust assets as an individual owner has over his or her own wholly-owned property.

⑦ Additional Trustee Powers

The trustee's powers include, but are not limited to: the power to sell trust property, borrow money, and encumber that property, specifically including trust real estate, by mortgage, deed of trust, or other method; the power to manage trust real estate as if the trustee were the absolute owner of it, including the power to lease or grant options to lease the property, make repairs or alterations, and insure against loss; the power to sell or grant options for the sale or exchange of any trust property, including stocks, bonds, and any other form of security; the power to invest trust property in property of any kind, including but not limited to bonds, notes, mortgages, and stocks; the power to receive additional property from any source and add to any trust created by this trust; the power to employ and pay reasonable fees to accountants, lawyers, or investment consultants for information or advice relating to the trust; the power to deposit and hold trust funds in both interest-bearing and non-interest-bearing accounts; the power to deposit funds in bank or other accounts uninsured by FDIC coverage; the power to enter into electronic fund transfer or safe deposit arrangements with financial institutions; the power to continue any business of the grantor; and the power to institute or defend legal actions concerning the trust or grantor's affairs.

⑧ Incapacitation

Should the successor trustee or alternative successor trustee assume management of this trust during the lifetime of the grantor(s), the successor trustee or alternative successor trustee shall manage the trust solely for the proper health care, support, maintenance, comfort, and/or welfare of the grantor(s), in accordance with the grantor's accustomed manner of living.

⑨ Termination of Trust

Upon the death of the first grantor to die, the trustee shall pay from the assets of the trust all valid debts, last expenses, and estate taxes due upon the death of the first grantor to die. The trustee shall then distribute the trust assets of the decased spouse as specified on the attached Joint Schedule of Beneficiaries of Joint Living Trust. Upon the death of the surviving grantor, this trust shall become irrevocable. The successor trustee shall then pay all valid debts, last expenses, and estate taxes from the assets of this trust. The successor trustee shall then distribute the remaining trust assets in the manner shown on the attached Joint Schedule of Beneficiaries of Joint Living Trust which is specifically made a part of this trust. Any additions or deletions to the Joint Schedule of Beneficiaries of Joint Living Trust must be written, notarized, and attached to this document to be valid.

⑩ Survivorship

All beneficiaries named in the Joint Schedule of Beneficiaries of Joint Living Trust must survive the last surviving grantor by thirty (30) days to receive any gift under this living trust. If any beneficiary and the last surviving grantor should die simultaneously, then the last surviving grantor shall be conclusively presumed to have survived that beneficiary for purposes of this living trust.

⑪ Amendments and Revocations

We reserve the right to jointly amend any or all of this trust at any time. Upon the death of either grantor, the surviving grantor may amend this trust. The amendments must be written, notarized, and attached to this document to be valid. We also reserve the right to individually or jointly revoke this trust at any time. Upon the death of either grantor, the surviving grantor may revoke this trust. A revocation of this trust must be written, notarized, and attached to this document to be valid. If the trust is revoked, the property shall revert to the grantors based on the ownership rights in the property before the property was transferred to the trust.

⑫ Governing Law

This trust, containing _____ pages, was created on the date noted above and will be governed under the laws of the State of _____ .

⑬ Signature

_____   _____
Signature of Grantor   Signature of Grantor

_____   _____
Printed Name of Grantor   Printed Name of Grantor

⑭ Notary Acknowledgment

State of _____
County of _____

On _____ , _____ and _____ _____ came before me personally and, under oath, stated that they are the persons described in the above document and they signed the above document in my presence. I declare under penalty of perjury that the persons whose names are subscribed to this instrument appear to be of sound mind and under no duress, fraud, or undue influence.

_____
Notary Public
My commission expires _____

Assignment to Living Trust by Single Person or Individual Spouse

This form may be used if an assignment of ownership of personal property to an individual or joint Living Trust is necessary.

An assignment of property is used for the transfer of personal property to the trust. Recall that you must complete transfer paperwork if the property in question is real estate, patents, copyrights, trademarks, motor vehicles, boats, stocks, bonds, or some other form of property that has ownership documents (such as a deed or title). For property with no ownership documentation, generally, the listing of property to be held by the trust on the Schedule of Trust Assets, effectively transfers ownership of property to the trust. Thus, an assignment of property is not normally a legal necessity. However, some businesses or financial institutions may require this particular document to verify that the property has been technically "assigned" to the trust. In addition, this form is also necessary for assigning patents, copyrights, or trademarks to the trust. If such occasions arise, you may use this document.

To complete this form, you will need the following information:

①   Date of assignment,
     Full name of grantor,
     Name of Living Trust, and
     Date original Living Trust was created.
②   Full description of property to be assigned to the trust.
③   No information needed.
④   No information needed.
⑤   Your signature and printed name (do not sign unless in front of a notary public).
⑥   The Notary Acknowledgment section (to be completed by notary public).

Assignment to Living Trust by Single Person or Individual Spouse

ASSIGNMENT TO LIVING TRUST

① This Assignment to Living Trust is made on _____ (date) , between _____ , the grantor, and the _____ _____ Living Trust dated _____ .

② The grantor transfers and conveys possession, ownership, and all right, title, and intent in the following property to the Living Trust:

③ The grantor warrants that he or she owns this property and that he or she has the full authority to transfer and convey the property to the Living Trust. Grantor also warrants that the property is transferred free and clear of all liens, indebtedness, or liabilities.

④ Signed and delivered to the Living Trust on the above date.

⑤
_____

Signature of Grantor

_____

Printed Name of Grantor

⑥ **Notary Acknowledgment**

State of _____
County of _____

On _____ , _____ came before me per-sonally and, under oath, stated that he or she is the person described in the above document and he or she signed the above document in my presence. I declare under penalty of perjury that the person whose name is subscribed to this instrument appears to be of sound mind and under no duress, fraud, or undue influence.

_____

Notary Public
My commission expires _____

Joint Assignment to Joint Living Trust by Married Couple

This form may be used if an assignment of shared ownership of personal property to a Joint Living Trust is necessary.

An assignment of property is used for the transfer of personal property to the trust. Recall that you must complete transfer paperwork if the property in question is real estate, patents, copyrights, trademarks, motor vehicles, boats, stocks, bonds, or some other form of property that has ownership documents (such as a deed or title). For property with no ownership documentation, generally, the listing of property to be held by the trust on the Schedule of Trust Assets effectively transfers ownership of property to the trust. Thus, an assignment of property is not normally a legal necessity. However, some businesses or financial institutions may require this particular document to verify that the property has been technically "assigned" to the trust. In addition, this form is also necessary to assign patents, copyrights, or trademarks to the trust. If such occasions arise, you may use this document.

To complete this form, you will need the following information:

1. Date of assignment,
   Full name of grantors,
   Name of Joint Living Trust, and
   Date original Joint Living Trust was created.
2. Full description of property to be assigned to the trust.
3. No information needed.
4. No information needed.
5. Your signatures and printed names (do not sign unless in front of a notary public).
6. The Notary Acknowledgment section (to be completed by notary public).

Joint Assignment to Joint Living Trust by Married Couple

JOINT ASSIGNMENT TO LIVING TRUST

① This Joint Assignment to Living Trust is made on _____ (date), between _____ and _____ , the grantors, and the _____ and _____ Joint Living Trust dated _____ .

② The grantors transfer and convey possession, ownership, and all right, title, and intent in the following property to the Joint Living Trust:

③ The grantors warrant that they own this property and that they have the full authority to transfer and convey the property to the Joint Living Trust. Grantors also warrant that the property is transferred free and clear of all liens, indebtedness, or liabilities.

④ Signed and delivered to the Joint Living Trust on the above date.

⑤

_____   _____
Signature of Grantor   Signature of Grantor

_____   _____
Printed Name of Grantor   Printed Name of Grantor

⑥ **Notary Acknowledgment**

State of _____
County of _____

On _____ , _____ and _____
_____ came before me personally and, under oath, stated that they are the persons described in the above document and they signed the above document in my presence. I declare under penalty of perjury that the persons whose names are subscribed to this instrument appear to be of sound mind and under no duress, fraud, or undue influence.

_____
Notary Public
My commission expires _____

Schedule of Assets of Living Trust for Single Person or Individual Spouse

This form should be used to list the assets of a single person or an individual spouse who is setting up an individual Living Trust. Please remember that any assets that have ownership documents must be transferred to the ownership of the trust using the appropriate method of documentary transfer (such as a deed or title).

Please refer to your Property Questionnaire to determine which property you desire to transfer to your Living Trust. The listing of property on this Schedule will effectively transfer the ownership of the property to the trust, unless an additional transfer of ownership document is necessary. Even if such additional paperwork is necessary, you should list the property on this Schedule of Assets. Please refer to the property instructions in Chapters 3 and 6 for details of how to list the property.

To complete this form, you will need the following information:

1. Date of assignment,
   Full name of grantor,
   Name of Living Trust, and
   Date original Living Trust was created.
2. Full description of property to be transferred to the trust.
3. Your signature and printed name (do not sign unless in front of a notary public).
4. The Notary Acknowledgment section (to be completed by notary public).

Schedule of Assets of Living Trust for Single Person or Individual Spouse

SCHEDULE OF ASSETS OF LIVING TRUST

(1) This Schedule of Assets of Living Trust is made on _____ (date), by _____ , the grantor, to the _____ _____ Living Trust dated _____ .

(2) All grantor's right, title, and interest in the following property shall be the property of the trust:

(3)

_____
Signature of Grantor

_____
Printed Name of Grantor

(4) **Notary Acknowledgment**

State of _____
County of _____

On _____ , _____ came before me personally and, under oath, stated that he or she is the person described in the above document and he or she signed the above document in my presence. I declare under penalty of perjury that the person whose name is subscribed to this instrument appears to be of sound mind and under no duress, fraud, or undue influence.

_____
Notary Public
My commission expires _____

Schedule of Assets of Joint Living Trust for Husband

This form should be used by a husband who is setting up a Joint Living Trust with his wife. This form allows for any of the husband's separate property and shared property to be assigned to the trust. Please remember that any assets that have ownership documents must be transferred to the ownership of the trust using the appropriate method of documentary transfer (such as a deed or title).

Please refer to your Property Questionnaire to determine which property you desire to transfer to your Living Trust. The listing of property on this Schedule will effectively transfer the ownership of the property to the trust, unless an additional transfer of ownership document is necessary. Even if such additional paperwork is necessary, you should list the property on this Schedule of Assets. Please refer to the property instructions in Chapters 3 and 6 for details of how to list the property and for information on how to determine which of your property is separate and which is shared or jointly-owned. The shared property that you list on this Schedule should match the shared property that is listed by your spouse on her Schedule of Assets.

To complete this form, you will need the following information:

①   Date of assignment,
       Full name of grantor,
       Name of Joint Living Trust, and
       Date original Joint Living Trust was created.
②   Full description of husband's separate property to be transferred to the trust.
③   Full description of husband's shared property to be transferred to the trust.
④   Your signature and printed name (do not sign unless in front of a notary public).
⑤   The Notary Acknowledgment section (to be completed by notary public).

Schedule of Assets of
Joint Living Trust for Husband

SCHEDULE OF ASSETS OF JOINT LIVING TRUST FOR HUSBAND

① This Schedule of Assets of Joint Living Trust for Husband is made on _____ (date), by _____ , the co-grantor, to the _____ _____ and _____ Living Trust dated _____ .

② All husband's right, title, and interest in the following separate property shall be the property of the trust:

③ All husband's right, title, and interest in the following shared property shall be the property of the trust:

④
_____

Signature of Grantor

_____

Printed Name of Grantor

⑤ Notary Acknowledgment

State of _____

County of _____

On _____ , _____ came before me per-
sonally and, under oath, stated that he is the person described in the above document and he
signed the above document in my presence. I declare under penalty of perjury that the person
whose name is subscribed to this instrument appears to be of sound mind and under no duress,
fraud, or undue influence.

_____

Notary Public
My commission expires _____

Schedule of Assets of Joint Living Trust for Wife

This form should be used by a wife who is setting up a Joint Living Trust with her husband. This form allows for any of the wife's separate property and shared property to be assigned to the trust. Please remember that any assets that have ownership documents must be transferred to the ownership of the trust using the appropriate method of documentary transfer (such as a deed or title).

Please refer to your Property Questionnaire to determine which property you desire to transfer to your Joint Living Trust. The listing of property on this Schedule will effectively transfer the ownership of the property to the trust, unless an additional transfer of ownership document is necessary. Even if such additional paperwork is necessary, you should list the property on this Schedule of Assets. Please refer to the property instructions in Chapters 3 and 6 for details of how to list the property and for information on how to determine which of your property is separate and which is shared . The shared property that you list on this Schedule should match the shared property that is listed by your spouse on his Schedule of Assets.

To complete this form, you will need the following information:

① Date of assignment,
  Full name of grantor,
  Name of Joint Living Trust, and
  Date original Joint Living Trust was created.
② Full description of wife's separate property to be transferred to the trust.
③ Full description of wife's shared property to be transferred to the trust.
④ Your signature and printed name (do not sign unless in front of a notary public).
⑤ The Notary Acknowledgment section (to be completed by notary public).

Schedule of Assets of
Joint Living Trust for Wife

SCHEDULE OF ASSETS OF JOINT LIVING TRUST FOR WIFE

1. This Schedule of Assets of Joint Living Trust for Wife is made on _____ (date), by _____ , the co-grantor, to the _____ _____ and _____ Living Trust dated _____ .

2. All wife's right, title, and interest in the following separate property shall be the property of the trust:

3. All wife's right, title, and interest in the following shared property shall be the property of the trust:

④ _____

Signature of Grantor

_____

Printed Name of Grantor

⑤ **Notary Acknowledgment**

State of _____
County of _____

On _____ , _____ came before me per-
sonally and, under oath, stated that she is the person described in the above document and she
signed the above document in my presence. I declare under penalty of perjury that the person
whose name is subscribed to this instrument appears to be of sound mind and under no duress,
fraud, or undue influence.

_____

Notary Public
My commission expires _____

Schedule of Beneficiaries of Living Trust for Single Person or Individual Spouse

This form should be used to list the beneficiaries of a single person or an individual spouse who is setting up an individual Living Trust.

Please refer to your Beneficiary Questionnaire to determine which property you desire to leave to which beneficiaries of your Living Trust. Please refer to the property and beneficiary instructions in Chapters 3, 4, and 6 for details of how to list the property and beneficiaries.

To complete this form, you will need the following information:

① Date of assignment,
Full name of grantor,
Name of Living Trust, and
Date original Living Trust was created.

② For each item of property, complete the following:
Name of beneficiary,
Relationship of beneficiary,
Name of alternative beneficiary (if main beneficiary has died first),
Relationship of alternative beneficiary, and
Full description of property to be transferred.

③ For your residuary clause, complete the following:
Name of residuary beneficiary,
Relationship of residuary beneficiary,
Name of alternative residuary beneficiary (if main beneficiary has died first), and
Relationship of alternative residuary beneficiary.

④ No information needed.

⑤ Your signature and printed name (do not sign unless in front of a notary public).

⑥ The Notary Acknowledgment section (to be completed by notary public).

Schedule of Beneficiaries of Living Trust for Single Person or Individual Spouse

SCHEDULE OF BENEFICIARIES OF LIVING TRUST

(1) This Schedule of Beneficiaries is made on _____ (date), by _____ , the grantor, to the _____ _____ Living Trust dated _____ .

(2) Upon the death of the grantor of the trust and the payment of all debts, taxes, and liabilities of the grantor, the Successor Trustee shall distribute the remaining assets of the Trust as follows:

To _____ (name), my _____ (relationship), or if not surviving, to _____ (name), my _____ (relationship), the following trust assets shall be distributed:

To _____ (name), my _____ (relationship), or if not surviving, to _____ (name), my _____ (relationship), the following trust assets shall be distributed:

To _____ (name), my _____ (relationship), or if not surviving, to _____ (name), my _____ (relationship), the following trust assets shall be distributed:

To _____ (name), my _____ (relationship), or if not surviving, to _____ (name), my _____ (relationship), the following trust assets shall be distributed:

To _____ (name), my _____ (relationship), or if not surviving, to _____ (name), my _____ (relationship), the following trust assets shall be distributed:

③ All the rest and residue of the trust assets shall be distributed to _____ _____ (name), my _____ (relationship), or if not surviving, to _____ (name), my _____ (relationship).

④ If any of the Beneficiaries named on this Schedule of Beneficiaries is subject to the terms of any children's trust in the main trust document to which this Schedule pertains, then any property distributed to such Beneficiary shall be subject to the terms of any such children's trust.

④

_____
Signature of Grantor

_____
Printed Name of Grantor

⑤ **Notary Acknowledgment**

State of _____
County of _____

On _____ , _____ came before me personally and, under oath, stated that he or she is the person described in the above document and he or she signed the above document in my presence. I declare under penalty of perjury that the person whose name is subscribed to this instrument appears to be of sound mind and under no duress, fraud, or undue influence.

_____
Notary Public
My commission expires _____

Joint Schedule of Beneficiaries of Joint Living Trust of Married Couple

This form should be used to list the beneficiaries of a husband and wife who are setting up a Joint Living Trust.

Using this form, the husband will complete a section under which he will leave his share of the shared property and any of his separately-owned property which is listed on his Schedule of Assets of Joint Living Trust for Husband. Additionally, the wife will complete a section under which she will leave her share of the shared property and any of her separately-owned property which is listed on her Schedule of Assets of Joint Living Trust for Wife.

Please refer to your Beneficiary Questionnaire to determine which property you desire to leave to which beneficiaries of your Joint Living Trust. Please refer to the property and beneficiary instructions in Chapters 3, 4, and 6 for details of how to list the property and beneficiaries.

To complete this form, you will need the following information:

①   Date of assignment,
Full name of grantor,
Name of Joint Living Trust, and
Date original Joint Living Trust was created.

②   For each item of property to be left by husband, complete the following:
Name of beneficiary,
Relationship of beneficiary,
Name of alternative beneficiary (if main beneficiary has died first),
Relationship of alternative beneficiary, and
Full description of property to be transferred.

③   For the husband's residuary clause, complete the following:
Name of residuary beneficiary,
Relationship of residuary beneficiary,
Name of alternative residuary beneficiary (if main beneficiary has died first), and
Relationship of alternative residuary beneficiary.

④   For each item of property to be left by wife, complete the following:
Name of beneficiary,
Relationship of beneficiary,
Name of alternative beneficiary (if main beneficiary has died first),
Relationship of alternative beneficiary, and
Full description of property to be transferred.

⑤ For the wife's residuary clause, complete the following:
   Name of residuary beneficiary,
   Relationship of residuary beneficiary,
   Name of alternative residuary beneficiary (if main beneficiary has died first), and
   Relationship of alternative residuary beneficiary.
⑥ No information needed.
⑦ Your signatures and printed names (do not sign unless in front of a notary public).
⑧ The Notary Acknowledgment section (to be completed by notary public).

Joint Schedule of Beneficiaries of Joint Living Trust of Married Couple

JOINT SCHEDULE OF BENEFICIARIES OF JOINT LIVING TRUST

① This Joint Schedule of Beneficiaries is made on _____ (date), by _____ and _____ , the co-grantors, to the _____ and _____ _____ Joint Living Trust dated _____ .

② Upon the death of the husband and the payment of all debts, taxes, and liabilities of the husband, the Trustee shall distribute the assets of the Trust listed on the Schedule of Assets of Joint Living Trust for Husband as follows:

To _____ (name), my _____ (relationship), or if not surviving, to _____ (name), my _____ (relationship), the following trust assets shall be distributed:

To _____ (name), my _____ (relationship), or if not surviving, to _____ (name), my _____ (relationship), the following trust assets shall be distributed:

To _____ (name), my _____ (relationship), or if not surviving, to _____ (name), my _____ (relationship), the following trust assets shall be distributed:

To _____ (name), my _____
(relationship), or if not surviving, to _____ (name), my
_____ (relationship), the following trust assets shall be distributed:

To _____ (name), my _____
(relationship), or if not surviving, to _____ (name), my
_____ (relationship), the following trust assets shall be distributed:

③ All the rest and residue of the husband's trust assets shall be distributed to _____
_____ (name), my _____ (relationship), or if not
surviving, to _____ (name), my _____
(relationship).

④ Upon the death of the wife and the payment of all debts, taxes, and liabilities of the wife,
the Trustee shall distribute the assets of the Trust listed on the Schedule of Assets of Joint
Living Trust for Wife as follows:

To _____ (name), my _____
(relationship), or if not surviving, to _____ (name), my
_____ (relationship), the following trust assets shall be distributed:

To _____ (name), my _____
(relationship), or if not surviving, to _____ (name), my
_____ (relationship), the following trust assets shall be distributed:

To _____ (name), my _____
(relationship), or if not surviving, to _____ (name), my
_____ (relationship), the following trust assets shall be distributed:

To _____ (name), my _____
(relationship), or if not surviving, to _____ (name), my
_____ (relationship), the following trust assets shall be distributed:

To _____ (name), my _____
(relationship), or if not surviving, to _____ (name), my
_____ (relationship), the following trust assets shall be distributed:

To _____ (name), my _____
(relationship), or if not surviving, to _____ (name), my
_____ (relationship), the following trust assets shall be distributed:

⑤ All the rest and residue of the wife's trust assets shall be distributed to _____
_____ (name), my _____ (relationship), or if not
surviving, to _____ (name), my _____
(relationship).

⑥ If any of the Beneficiaries named on this Joint Schedule of Beneficiaries are subject to the terms of any children's trust in the main trust document to which this Schedule pertains, then any property distributed to such Beneficiary shall be subject to the terms of any such children's trust.

⑦

_____   _____
Signature of Grantor   Signature of Grantor

_____   _____
Printed Name of Grantor   Printed Name of Grantor

⑧ **Notary Acknowledgment**

State of _____
County of _____

On _____ , _____ and _____
_____ came before me personally and, under oath, stated that they are the persons described in the above document and they signed the above document in my presence. I declare under penalty of perjury that the persons whose names are subscribed to this instrument appear to be of sound mind and under no duress, fraud, or undue influence.

_____
Notary Public
My commission expires _____

New York Notice of Assignment of Property to Living Trust

This form may be used by residents of New York to provide notice that real or personal property has been assigned to the trust. You should attach a copy of your completed and notarized Schedule of Assets of Living Trust to this form.

To complete this form, you will need the following information:

① Full name of grantor,
Name of Living Trust, and
Date original Living Trust was created.
② Your signature and printed name (do not sign unless in front of a notary public).
③ The Notary Acknowledgment section (to be completed by notary public).

New York Notice of Assignment of Property to Living Trust

NOTICE OF ASSIGNMENT OF PROPERTY TO LIVING TRUST

① I, _____ , as grantor, hereby provide Notice that all of the property listed on the attached Schedule of Assets of Living Trust has been transferred to the _____ Living Trust on the date of _____ .

②

_____
Signature of Grantor

_____
Printed Name of Grantor

③ **Notary Acknowledgment**

State of _____
County of _____

On _____ , _____ came before me personally and, under oath, stated that he or she is the person described in the above document and he or she signed the above document in my presence. I declare under penalty of perjury that the person whose name is subscribed to this instrument appears to be of sound mind and under no duress, fraud, or undue influence.

_____
Notary Public
My commission expires _____

Registration of Living Trust

Residents of a number of states are required to register the main details regarding the existence of a Living Trust with their local courts. Please check the Appendix listing for your state to determine if such registration is required in your state. Note also that even though such registration may technically be required for your state, there are no penalties or consequences for failing to do so.

(1) Full name of trustee,
   Name of Living Trust, and
   Date original Living Trust was created.
(2) No information needed.
(3) Your signature and printed name (do not sign unless in front of a notary public).
(4) The Notary Acknowledgment section (to be completed by notary public).

Registration of Living Trust

REGISTRATION OF LIVING TRUST

① I, _____ , am Trustee of the _____
_____ Living Trust, which was created on the date of
_____ , by the grantor, _____ .

② I hereby acknowledge that I accept the office of Trustee of the Trust, and am now acting
as Trustee of the Trust.

③

_____

Signature of Trustee

_____

Printed Name of Trustee

④ **Notary Acknowledgment**

State of _____

County of _____

On _____ , _____ came before me personally and, under oath, stated that he or she is the person described in the above document and he or she signed the above document in my presence. I declare under penalty of perjury that the person whose name is subscribed to this instrument appears to be of sound mind and under no duress, fraud, or undue influence.

_____

Notary Public
My commission expires _____

Affidavit of Assumption of Duties by Successor Trustee

This document may be used if your Successor Trustee is having any difficulty with a business or financial institution accepting his or her authority to act on behalf of the Trust. Some may insist on written verification that states that the Successor Trustee actually has the power to act on behalf of the Trust. If this is the case, this form should satisfy those institutions or businesses. The Successor Trustee will need to attach a certified copy of the grantor's death certificate to this form.

①   Date of Affidavit, and
    Full name of Successor Trustee.
②   Date of creation of Living Trust,
    Full name of grantor,
    Name of Living Trust, and
    Full name of Successor Trustee.
③   Date of death of grantor, and
    Name of grantor.
④   No information needed.
⑤   Your signature and printed name (do not sign unless in front of a notary public).
⑥   The Notary Acknowledgment section (to be completed by notary public).

Affidavit of Assumption of Duties by Successor Trustee

AFFIDAVIT OF ASSUMPTION OF DUTIES BY SUCCESSOR TRUSTEE

① On this date, _____ , I, _____ , being of legal age and being duly sworn, declare the following:

② On the date of _____ , the grantor, _____ _____ , created the _____ Living Trust. The Living Trust provides that upon the death of the grantor, I, _____ _____ , become Trustee of the Trust.

③ On the date of _____ , the grantor, _____ _____ , died, as established in the certified copy of the Certificate of Death, which is attached to this Affidavit.

④ I hereby accept the office of Trustee of the Trust, and am now acting as Trustee of the Trust.

⑤
_____
Signature of Trustee

_____
Printed Name of Trustee

⑥ **Notary Acknowledgment**

State of _____
County of _____

On _____ , _____ came before me per-sonally and, under oath, stated that he or she is the person described in the above document and he or she signed the above document in my presence. I declare under penalty of perjury that the person whose name is subscribed to this instrument appears to be of sound mind and under no duress, fraud, or undue influence.

_____
Notary Public
My commission expires _____

CHAPTER 8:
Sample Living Trust

In this chapter, a complete sample Living Trust is presented. By reviewing this sample, you will be able to see what a completed Living Trust should look like and how the various parts are put together. Examine the clauses to see how your typewritten final Living Trust should look upon completion. In this sample Living Trust, a Mrs. Mary Smith is the fictional grantor. Mrs. Smith is married to Mr. John Smith, and they have two minor children who live with them. In her Living Trust, Mrs. Smith wishes to accomplish the following:

- Leave her oval diamond necklace to a friend
- Leave her brown mink coat to her mother
- Leave $10,000.00 to each of her children, to be held in trust if they are under the age of 21 upon her death until they are 30
- Leave all the rest of her trust estate to her husband
- Appoint her husband to act as Successor Trustee of the Living Trust and Trustee of the children's trust

By filling in the appropriate blanks in these Living Trust clauses, the fictional Mrs. Mary Smith is able to easily and quickly prepare a Living Trust which accomplishes all of her desires. She has transferred the desired personal property to her trust using a Schedule of Assets of Living Trust and she has designated what each beneficiary shall receive upon her death using the Schedule of Beneficiaries of Living Trust. Mrs. Smith has chosen not to place any real estate into her Trust since she holds title to her and her husband's home as a joint tenant with her husband. Thus, her husband will automatically own the entire piece of real estate upon her death and the property will not be required to be probated. Although it appears that Mrs. Smith has managed to provide that all of her desires for the distribution of her property upon her death will be accomplished without the expense or delay of probate, she would still be wise to complete a basic will for use as a backup in the event of unforeseen acquisitions of property. Also note that should she acquire additional personal property, Mrs. Smith will need to amend her Schedule of Assets to provide for a transfer of such property into the Trust.

She may rest assured that by having properly prepared and signed a Living Trust, her wishes will be carried out upon her death. Since Mrs. Smith chose to prepare an individual Living Trust rather than a Joint Living Trust, it would be advisable that Mrs. Smith's husband also prepare a Living Trust for himself which includes similar provisions for survivorship and reciprocal provisions for a children's trust fund.

LIVING TRUST OF MARY ELLEN SMITH

Declaration of Trust

I, Mary Ellen Smith, the grantor of this trust, declare and make this Living Trust on June 4, 2003.

This trust will be known as the Mary Ellen Smith Living Trust. I, Mary Ellen Smith, will be trustee of this trust and any subtrusts created under this trust. My marital status is that I am married to John Henry Smith and we have two (2) children whose names and dates of birth are: Alice Mary Smith (June 4, 1995), and Bradley John Smith (April 16, 2000).

Property Transfer

I transfer ownership to this trust of all of the assets which are listed on the attached Schedule of Assets of Living Trust, which is specifically made a part of this trust. I reserve the right to add or delete any of these assets at any time. In addition, I will prepare a separate Deed, Assignment, or any other documents necessary to carry out such transfers. Any additions or deletions to the Schedule of Assets of Living Trust must be written, notarized, and attached to this document to be valid.

Grantor's Rights

Until I die, I retain all rights to all income, profits, and control of the trust property. If my principal residence is transferred to this trust, I retain the right to possess and occupy it for my life, rent-free and without charge. I will remain liable for all taxes, insurance, maintenance, related costs, and expenses. The rights that I retain are intended to give me a beneficial interest in my principal residence such that I do not lose any eligibility that I may have for a state homestead exemption for which I am otherwise qualified.

Successor Trustee

Upon my death or if it is certified by a licensed physician that I am physically or mentally unable to manage this trust and my financial affairs, then I appoint John Henry Smith, of 123 Main Street, Centerville, IL, as Successor Trustee, to serve without bond and without compensation. If this successor trustee is not surviving or otherwise unable to serve, I appoint Elizabeth Joan Allen, of 234 Broadway, Centerville, IL, as Alternate Successor Trustee, also to serve without bond and without compensation. The successor trustee or alternative successor trustee shall not be liable for any actions taken in good faith. References to "trustee" in this document shall include any successor or alternative successor trustees.

Trustee's Powers

In addition to any powers, authority, and discretion granted by law, I grant the trustee any and all powers to perform any acts, in his or her sole discretion and without court approval, for the management and distribution of this trust and any subtrusts created by this trust. I intend the trustee to have the same power and authority to manage and distribute the trust assets as an individual owner has over his or her own wholly-owned property.

Additional Trustee Powers

The trustee's powers include, but are not limited to: the power to sell trust property, borrow money, and encumber that property, specifically including trust real estate, by mortgage, deed of trust, or other method; the power to manage trust real estate as if the trustee were the absolute owner of it, including the power to lease or grant options to lease the property, make repairs or alterations, and insure against loss; the power to sell or grant options for the sale or exchange of any trust property, including stocks, bonds, and any other form of security; the power to invest trust property in property of any kind, including but not limited to bonds, notes, mortgages, and stocks; the power to receive additional property from any source and add to any trust created by this trust; the power to employ and pay reasonable fees to accountants, lawyers, or investment consultants for information or advice relating to the trust; the power to deposit and hold trust funds in both interest-bearing and non-interest-bearing accounts; the power to deposit funds in bank or other accounts uninsured by FDIC coverage; the power to enter into electronic fund transfer or safe deposit arrangements with financial institutions; the power to continue any business of the grantor; the power to institute or defend legal actions concerning the trust or grantor's affairs; and the power to execute any document necessary to administer any children's trust created in this trust.

Incapacitation

Should the successor trustee or alternative successor trustee assume management of this trust during the lifetime of the grantor, the successor trustee or alternative successor trustee shall manage the trust solely for the proper health care, support, maintenance, comfort, and/or welfare of the grantor, in accordance with the grantor's accustomed manner of living.

Children's Trust Fund

If any of my children who are named as beneficiaries on the attached Schedule of Beneficiaries of Living Trust are under twenty-one (21) years old on my death, I direct that any property that I give them under this trust be held in an individual children's trust for each child under the following terms, until each shall reach the age of thirty (30) years old.

In the trustee's sole discretion, the trustee may distribute any or all of the principal, income, or both as deemed necessary for the beneficiary's health, support, welfare, and education. Any income not distributed shall be added to the trust principal. Any such trust shall terminate when the beneficiary reaches the required age, dies prior to reaching the required age, or all trust funds have been distributed. Upon termination, any remaining undistributed principal and income shall pass to the beneficiary; or if not surviving, to the beneficiary's heirs; or if none, to the residue of the main trust created by this document.

Termination of Trust

Upon my death, this trust shall become irrevocable. The successor trustee shall then pay my valid debts, last expenses, and estate taxes from the assets of this trust. The successor trustee shall then distribute the remaining trust assets in the manner shown on the attached Schedule of Beneficiaries of Living Trust which is specifically made a part of this trust, subject to the provisions of any children's trust which is created by this document. I reserve the right to add and/or delete any beneficiaries at any time. Any additions or deletions to the Schedule of Beneficiaries of Living Trust must be written, notarized, and attached to this document to be valid.

Survivorship

All beneficiaries named in the Schedule of Beneficiaries of Living Trust must survive me by thirty (30) days to receive any gift under this living trust. If any beneficiary and I should die simultaneously, I shall be conclusively presumed to have survived that beneficiary for purposes of this living trust.

Amendments and Revocations

I reserve the right to amend any or all of this trust at any time. The amendments must be written, notarized, and attached to this document to be valid. I also reserve the right to revoke this trust at any time. A revocation of this trust must be written, notarized, and attached to this document to be valid.

Governing Law

This trust, containing seven (8) pages, was created on the date noted above and will be governed under the laws of the State of Illinois.

Signature

Mary Ellen Smith
_____
Signature of Grantor

Mary Ellen Smith
_____
Printed Name of Grantor

Notary Acknowledgments

State of Illinois
County of Johnson

On June 4, 2003, Mary Ellen Smith came before me personally and, under oath, stated that she is the person described in the above document and she signed the above document in my presence. I declare under penalty of perjury that the person whose name is subscribed to this instrument appears to be of sound mind and under no duress, fraud, or undue influence.

Sally Lincoln
_____
Notary Public
My commission expires 12/31/2005

SCHEDULE OF ASSETS OF LIVING TRUST

This Schedule of Assets of Living Trust is made on June 4, 2003, by Mary Ellen Smith, the grantor, to the Mary Ellen Smith Living Trust dated June 4, 2003.

All grantor's right, title, and interest in the following property shall be the property of the trust:

An oval diamond necklace purchased from Tiffany and Co., and described as an oval-cut diamond of .75 carats set in a white-gold setting on an 18-inch white-gold braided necklace

A brown mink coat purchased from Henderson Furriers, size small, and described as a thigh-length light-brown mink coat with two (2) slash-side pockets, manufactured by Hanson and Company of Chicago, IL

$20,000.00 in funds held in a trust account for the Mary Ellen Smith Trust in the Bank of Centerville, Centerville, IL, account #123456789

Mary Ellen Smith
_____
Signature of Grantor

Mary Ellen Smith
_____
Printed Name of Grantor

State of Illinois
County of Johnson

On June 4, 2003, Mary Ellen Smith came before me personally and, under oath, stated that she is the person described in the above document and she signed the above document in my presence. I declare under penalty of perjury that the person whose name is subscribed to this instrument appears to be of sound mind and under no duress, fraud, or undue influence.

Sally Lincoln
_____
Notary Public
My commission expires 12/31/2005

SCHEDULE OF BENEFICIARIES OF LIVING TRUST

This Schedule of Beneficiaries is made on June 4, 2003, by Mary Ellen Smith, the grantor, to the Mary Ellen Smith Living Trust dated June 4, 2003.

Upon the death of the grantor of the trust and the payment of all debts, taxes, and liabilities of the grantor, the Successor Trustee shall distribute the remaining assets of the Trust as follows:

To Annie Janet Jones, my friend, or if not surviving, to Helen Mary Barrett, my mother, the following trust assets shall be distributed:

An oval diamond necklace purchased from Tiffany and Co., and described as an oval-cut diamond of .75 carats set in a white-gold setting on an 18-inch white-gold braided necklace

To Helen Mary Barrett, my mother, or if not surviving, to Annie Janet Jones, my friend, the following trust assets shall be distributed:

A brown mink coat purchased from Henderson Furriers, size small, and described as a thigh-length light-brown mink coat with two (2) slash-side pockets, manufactured by Hanson and Company of Chicago, IL

To Alice Mary Smith and Bradley John Smith, my children, in equal shares, or if not surviving, to John Henry Smith, my husband, the following trust assets shall be distributed:

$20,000.00 in funds held in a trust account for the Mary Ellen Smith Trust in the Bank of Centerville, Centerville, IL, account #123456789

All the rest and residue of the trust assets shall be distributed to John Henry Smith, my husband, or if not surviving, to Alice Mary Smith and Bradley John Smith, my children, in equal shares.

If any of the Beneficiaries named on this Schedule of Beneficiaries is subject to the terms of any children's trust in the main trust document to which this Schedule pertains, then any property distributed to such Beneficiary shall be subject to the terms of any such children's trust.

Mary Ellen Smith
_____
Signature of Grantor

Mary Ellen Smith _____
Printed Name of Grantor

State of Illinois
County of Johnson

On June 4, 2003, Mary Ellen Smith came before me personally and, under oath, stated that she is the person described in the above document and she signed the above document in my presence. I declare under penalty of perjury that the person whose name is subscribed to this instrument appears to be of sound mind and under no duress, fraud, or undue influence.

Sally Lincoln _____
Notary Public
My commission expires 12/31/2005

CHAPTER 9:
Completing Your Living Trust

As you have noted in the sample Living Trust in the previous chapter, there is nothing very complicated about the arrangement of your Living Trust. This chapter will explain how to put your own Living Trust together and properly type it yourself or have it typed and readied for your signatures. Using your Property and Beneficiary Questionnaires as a guide, you should already have selected and filled in the appropriate information on one of the Living Trusts from Chapter 7 and on the appropriate Schedules of Assets and Beneficiaries.

Below are instructions for preparing the final version of your Living Trust. As you go about preparing your Living Trust, take your time and be very careful to proofread the original before you sign it to be certain that it exactly states your desires.

①　On the photocopy worksheet version of your Living Trust and Schedules, cross out all of the instructions, circled numbers, and any other extraneous material which is not to become a part of your Living Trust. Carefully re-read the entire worksheet version of your Living Trust to be certain that it is exactly as you wish.

②　After making any necessary changes, type or have typed the entire Living Trust and the appropriate Schedules on good quality letter-sized (8½" x 11") paper. (*Note*: If you are using the CD version of the forms, please complete them using the instructions contained on your "ReadMe" file which is on the CD.)

③　After you have completed typing your Living Trust and Schedules, fill in the total number of pages in the line above the Signature section. Again, very carefully proofread your entire Living Trust. Be certain that there are no errors. If there are any errors, retype that particular page. Do not attempt to correct any errors with white-out type correcting fluid or tape or with erasures of any kind. Do not cross out or add anything to the typewritten words using a pen or pencil. Your Living Trust, when completed properly, should look similar to the sample Living Trust contained in the previous chapter, except that the signature and notary acknowledgement spaces should be blank.

④　When you have a perfect original of your Living Trust and Schedules, with no corrections and no additions, staple all of the pages together in the top left-hand corner.

⑤ Take the original of your Living Trust and Schedules before a Notary Public. Many banks, real estate offices, and government offices have notary services and most will be glad to assist you. In front of the Notary Public, you should sign your Living Trust and Schedules in the places indicated.

⑥ The final step is for the Notary Public to complete the Notary Acknowledgments, sign in the space indicated, and stamp with his or her Notary Seal. When this step is completed, your Living Trust is a valid legal document and you may be assured that your wishes will be carried out upon your death.

Once it has been properly executed following the steps above, you may make photocopies of your Living Trust. It is a good idea to label any of these as "COPIES."

Safeguarding Your Living Trust

Having completed your Living Trust according to the foregoing instructions, it is now time to place your Living Trust in a safe place. Many people keep their important papers in a safe deposit box at a local bank. Although this is an acceptable place for storing a Living Trust, be advised that there are certain drawbacks. Your Living Trust should be in a place which is readily accessible to your Successor Trustee at a moment's notice. Often there are certain unavoidable delays in gaining access to a safe deposit box in an emergency situation. If you are married and your safe deposit box is jointly held, many of these delays can be avoided. However, even in this situation, some states prevent immediate access to the safe deposit box of a deceased married person. If you decide to keep the original in your safe deposit box, it is a good idea to keep a clearly-marked copy of your Living Trust at home in a safe but easily-located place, with a note as to where the original may be found.

An acceptable alternative to a safe deposit box is a home file box or desk that is used for home storage of your important papers. If possible, this storage place should be fire-proof and under lock and key. Wherever you decide to store your Living Trust, you will need to inform your chosen Successor Trustee of its location. The Successor Trustee will need to obtain the original of your Living Trust shortly after your demise to determine if there are any necessary duties which must be looked after without delay, for example: funeral plans or organ donations.

It is also a good practice to store any life insurance policies and a copy of your birth certificate in the same location. Additionally, it is also prudent to store a copy of your Property Questionnaire, Beneficiary Questionnaire, and the Successor Trustee Information List with your Living Trust in order to provide your Successor Trustee with an inventory and location list of your assets and a list of information regarding your beneficiaries. Any title documents or deeds relating to property which is to be transferred under your Living Trust may also be stored with your Living Trust for the convenience of your Successor Trustee. A final precaution, if you desire, is to allow the Successor Trustee whom you have named to keep a copy of your Living Trust. Be careful, however, to be certain that you immediately inform him or her of any amendments to your Living Trust which you prepare or of any decision to revoke your Living Trust.

Transferring Property to Your Living Trust

After you have completed signing and having your Living Trust notarized, you will need to complete the transfers to the Trust of any property which has ownership documentation. It is very important that you make these transfers as soon as possible after completing your Living Trust. If you do not effectively transfer the property to your Trust, this property will not be considered part of your trust estate and your Successor Trustee will have no legal authority to distribute the property to your chosen beneficiaries. Such untransferred property would pass to the beneficiaries of any will you might have or, if you do not have a will, would be distributed to your heirs as determined by the state, or, in a worst case scenario, would actually be forfeited to the state if you have no living heirs.

To be certain that these events do not come to pass, you must complete the proper documents of title to pass ownership of the property from yourself to the Trust. The types of property and the necessary ownership documents that you will need to complete include the following:

- All real estate (transferred by deed, which must then be properly recorded in the county or parish clerk's office)
- Motor vehicles (transferred by title generally, which must then be filed with the state's motor vehicle department or Secretary of State)
- Boats (transferred by title generally, which must then be filed with the appropriate state department)
- Patents, copyrights, and trademarks (transferred generally, by an Assignment of Property to Living Trust form [provided in Chapter 7] which must then be filed with the appropriate federal agency)
- Bank accounts and safe deposit boxes (generally transferred by completing paperwork supplied by the particular financial institution)
- Stocks, bonds, and mutual funds (stocks and bonds are generally transferred by having a new stock certificate or bond issued. Mutual fund or brokerage accounts are transferred by completing paperwork supplied by the particular brokerage house or fund)
- Business interests (ownership of a sole proprietorship is transferred by listing it on your Schedule of Assets of Living Trust. Corporate ownership transfers require reissuing stock certificates in the name of the trust. Transfers of ownership for partnerships will generally require amending the partnership agreement to specify ownership by the trust)

When transferring property ownership to the Living Trust, you should specify ownership as follows:

"[your name], as Trustee of the [your name] Living Trust, dated [date of creation of the trust]."

So, for example, the name on a new deed which is used to transfer property to the trust would be "Andrea Ann Doria, as Trustee of the Andrea Ann Doria Living Trust, dated June 4, 2003."

If you add or delete property from your Schedule of Assets of Living Trust or if you entirely revoke your Living Trust as explained in the next chapter, you must be certain to officially transfer ownership of the property back to yourself using the appropriate ownership documentation.

CHAPTER 10:
Changing Your Living Trust

In this chapter, instructions will be given on when and how to change your Living Trust and how to revoke your Living Trust. It is most important to follow these instructions carefully should you desire to make any changes to your Living Trust. Failure to follow these instructions and an attempt to change your Living Trust by such methods as crossing out a name or penciling in an addition could have the disastrous effect of voiding portions of, or perhaps even your entire, Living Trust. Again, these instructions are not difficult to follow, but are very important to insure that your Living Trust remains legally valid.

Amending Your Living Trust

Regarding any potential changes which you may wish to make in your Living Trust at a later date, you should periodically review the provisions of your Living Trust, keeping in mind the following items as they relate to your present situation:

- Have there been any substantial changes in your personal wealth?
- Have there been any changes in your ownership of any property mentioned in your Living Trust or schedules?
- Have any of the beneficiaries named in your Living Trust died or fallen into your disfavor?
- Are any of the persons whom you named as successor or alternative successor trustee in your Living Trust no longer willing or able to serve?
- Have you changed the state of your residence?
- Have you been married since the date of your Living Trust?
- Have you been divorced since the date of your Living Trust?
- Have you had any children since the date of your Living Trust?
- Have you adopted any children since the date of your Living Trust?
- Do you simply wish to make any corrections, deletions, or additions to any provisions in your Living Trust or schedules?

If any of these matters apply, you will need to change your Living Trust accordingly. Although it is possible to completely rewrite your Living Trust to take account of any of these changes, an easier method is to prepare and sign a written Amendment to a Living Trust. Please bear in mind that all of the formalities surrounding the signing of your original Living Trust must again be followed for any such changes to your Living Trust to be valid.

Never attempt to change any portions of your Living Trust by any other method. For example, do not attempt to add provisions in the margin of your Living Trust, either by typing or writing them in. Do not attempt to cross out any portions of your Living Trust. These methods are not acceptable methods for the alteration of a Living Trust, and could subject your Living Trust to a court battle to determine its subsequent validity.

Following these instructions, you will find two separate Amendment of Living Trust forms: one for a single person or individual spouse and one for a married couple who have completed a Joint Living Trust. The Joint Living Trust forms provided in this book allow for the amendment of the trust or any schedules of the trust to be done only jointly by both spouses. Select the proper form and complete the information requested as shown on the instructions page.

When you have completed the form and retyped it, sign the form in the presence of a Notary Public and make certain that you store the original Amendment with the original of your Living Trust. You should also make certain that a copy of any amendment is provided to anyone who has a copy of your original Living Trust, such as your Successor Trustee.

If you delete property from your Schedule of Assets of Living Trust, you must be certain to officially transfer ownership of the property back to yourself using the appropriate ownership documentation as detailed in the previous chapter. And, of course, if you add property to your Schedule of Assets of Living Trusts, which requires additional ownership transfer documentation, you must complete these documents as soon as possible.

Amendment of Living Trust by Single Person or Individual Spouse

This form is for use by anyone who has created an individual Living Trust, whether or not he or she is married or has children. You may use this form for changes to the original Trust, Schedules of Assets, or Beneficiaries. For changes to the trust or schedules, you may use the following language in section 2 of the form:

- "The following wording is added to the Trust [here insert the added material]"
  OR
- "The following wording is deleted from the Trust [here insert the deleted material]"

To complete this form, you will need the following information:

①   Date of amendment,
     Full name of grantor,
     Name of Living Trust, and
     Date original Living Trust was created.
②   Additions or deletions to trust, asset, or beneficiary schedules.
③   No information needed.
④   Your signature and printed name (do not sign unless in front of a notary public).
⑤   The Notary Acknowledgment section (to be completed by notary public).

Amendment of Living Trust by Single Person or Individual Spouse

AMENDMENT OF LIVING TRUST

(1) This Amendment of Living Trust is made on _____ (date), by _____ , the grantor, to the _____ _____ Living Trust dated _____ .

(2) The grantor modifies the original Trust as follows:

(3) All other terms and conditions of the original Living Trust remain in effect without modification. This Amendment, including the original Living Trust, is the entire Living Trust as of this date. The grantor has signed this Amendment on the date specified at the beginning of this Amendment.

(4)

_____
Signature of Grantor

_____
Printed Name of Grantor

(5) **Notary Acknowledgment**

State of _____
County of _____

On _____ , _____ came before me personally and, under oath, stated that he or she is the person described in the above document and he or she signed the above document in my presence. I declare under penalty of perjury that the person whose name is subscribed to this instrument appears to be of sound mind and under no duress, fraud, or undue influence.

_____
Notary Public
My commission expires _____

Joint Amendment of Joint Living Trust by Married Couple

This form is for use by a married couple which has created a Joint Living Trust, whether or not they have children. Under the terms of the Joint Living Trusts in this book, both spouses must agree to any changes to the Joint Living Trust. They may use this form for changes to the original Trust, Schedules of Assets, or Beneficiaries. For changes to the trust or schedules, use the following language in section 2 of the form:

- "The following wording is added to the Trust [here insert the added material]"
  OR
- "The following wording is deleted from the Trust [here insert the deleted material]"

To complete this form, you will need the following information:

① Date of amendment,
Full names of grantors,
Name of Joint Living Trust, and
Date original Joint Living Trust was created.
② Additions or deletions to trust, asset, or beneficiary schedules.
③ No information needed.
④ Your signatures and printed names (do not sign unless in front of a notary public).
⑤ The Notary Acknowledgment section (to be completed by notary public).

Joint Amendment of Joint Living Trust by Married Couple

JOINT AMENDMENT OF JOINT LIVING TRUST

① This Joint Amendment of Joint Living Trust is made on _____ (date), by _____ and _____ , grantors, to the _____ and _____ _____ Joint Living Trust dated _____ .

② The grantors modify the original trust as follows:

③ All other terms and conditions of the original Joint Living Trust remain in effect without modification. This Joint Amendment, including the original Joint Living Trust, is the entire Joint Living Trust as of this date. The grantors have signed this Joint Amendment on the date specified at the beginning of this Joint Amendment.

④

_____ _____
Signature of Grantor   Signature of Grantor

_____ _____
Printed Name of Grantor   Printed Name of Grantor

⑤ **Notary Acknowledgment**

State of _____
County of _____

On _____ , _____ and _____ _____ came before me personally and, under oath, stated that they are the persons described in the above document and they signed the above document in my presence. I declare under penalty of perjury that the persons whose names are subscribed to this instrument appear to be of sound mind and under no duress, fraud, or undue influence.

_____
Notary Public
My commission expires _____

Revoking Your Living Trust

At some point in the future, you may desire to cancel or revoke your Living Trust entirely. Until you die, you have the right to revoke your Living Trust at any time.

Following these instructions, you will also find two separate Revocation of Living Trust forms: one for a single person or individual spouse and one for a married couple who have completed a Joint Living Trust. Select the proper form and complete the information requested. When you have completed the form and retyped it, sign the form in the presence of a Notary Public and make certain that you store the original where you had stored the original of your Living Trust. You should also make certain that a copy of any revocation is provided to anyone who has a copy of your original Living Trust, such as your Successor Trustee. You should also then destroy the original and all copies of your Living Trust or cross out each page of the forms and mark "REVOKED" across them in bold print.

If you entirely revoke your Living Trust, you must be certain to officially transfer ownership of any trust assets back to yourself using the appropriate ownership documentation as explained in the previous chapter.

Revocation of Living Trust by Single Person or Individual Spouse

This form should be used by a single person or individual or surviving spouse to revoke an individual or Joint Living Trust. Under the terms of the Joint Living Trusts in this book, either spouse may revoke a Joint Living Trust at any time and a surviving spouse may revoke a Joint Living Trust after the other spouse has died.

To complete this form, you will need the following information:

①   Date of revocation,
      Full name of grantor,
      Name of Living Trust, and
      Date original Living Trust was created.
②   Your signature and printed name (do not sign unless in front of a notary public).
③   The Notary Acknowledgment section (to be completed by notary public).

Revocation of Living Trust by Single Person or Individual Spouse

REVOCATION OF LIVING TRUST

① On this date _____ , I, _____ ,
the grantor, fully and completely revoke the _____
Living Trust dated _____ . All property that is held in trust
shall be returned to the grantor as my sole property.

②

_____
Signature of Grantor

_____
Printed Name of Grantor

③ **Notary Acknowledgment**

State of _____
County of _____

On _____ , _____ came before me per-
sonally and, under oath, stated that he or she is the person described in the above document
and he or she signed the above document in my presence. I declare under penalty of perjury
that the person whose name is subscribed to this instrument appears to be of sound mind and
under no duress, fraud, or undue influence.

_____
Notary Public
My commission expires _____

Joint Revocation of Joint Living Trust by Married Couple

This form should be used by both spouses to jointly revoke a Joint Living Trust. Under the terms of the Joint Living Trusts in this book, either spouse may revoke a Joint Living Trust at any time or the spouses may jointly revoke the Joint Living Trust.

To complete this form, you will need the following information:

① Date of revocation,
   Full names of grantors,
   Name of Joint Living Trust, and
   Date original Joint Living Trust was created.
② Your signatures and printed names (do not sign unless in front of a notary public).
③ The Notary Acknowledgment section (to be completed by notary public).

Joint Revocation of Joint Living Trust by Married Couple

JOINT REVOCATION OF JOINT LIVING TRUST

① On this date _____ , we, _____
and _____ , the grantors, fully and completely revoke the
_____ and _____
Joint Living Trust dated _____ . All property that is held in trust
shall be returned to the grantors as their sole or shared property, in the same ownership
that existed before the property was transferred to the trust.

②

_____   _____
Signature of Grantor   Signature of Grantor

_____   _____
Printed Name of Grantor   Printed Name of Grantor

③ **Notary Acknowledgment**

State of _____
County of _____

On _____ , _____ and _____
_____ came before me personally and, under oath, stated that they are the
persons described in the above document and they signed the above document in my presence. I declare under penalty of perjury that the persons whose names are subscribed to this
instrument appear to be of sound mind and under no duress, fraud, or undue influence.

_____
Notary Public
My commission expires _____

CHAPTER 11:
Supplemental Will

This chapter contains the instructions and form for preparing a basic simple will to supplement the use of your Living Trust. Even if you have used a Living Trust and other estate-planning tools such as joint tenancies, life insurance, or payable-on-death accounts, a will is still highly recommended. There may be assets that you have neglected, forgotten about, or that will not be uncovered until your death. If you have used a trust, joint-property agreements, and other estate-planning tools, these unknown or forgotten assets may wind up passing to your heirs as *intestate* property under your state's particular scheme for distributing property for persons who die without a will. Through the use of a simple will, you can avoid this possibility.

Since most of your property will be passed to your chosen beneficiaries using your Living Trust, it is also likely that any property that is distributed under your basic will may qualify for simplified probate proceedings in many states. A growing number of states have adopted laws which exempt estates which have a limited value from standard probate laws. These "estate value" limits typically range from $20,000.00 to $100,000.00. Since the "estate" which will be valued in order to determine the qualification for the simplified probate will consist only of the property which passes under the will itself, and not the Living Trust, it is likely that most basic wills used in conjunction with Living Trusts will qualify for simplified probate proceedings. Generally, this will significantly reduce both the expense and time delays normally associated with probate.

You have already used your Living Trust and other estate-planning tools to plan the distribution of the bulk of your assets to your chosen beneficiaries. You have completed your property and beneficiary questionnaires which allow you to understand the extent of your assets and your choices for beneficiaries. The use of a basic will under these circumstances is to assure that every single piece of property that you may have will pass to the beneficiaries of your choice.

Completing Your Supplemental Will

Carefully read through all of the clauses in the blank basic will to understand how the form is laid out. Make a photocopy of the basic will to use as a worksheet. If you wish, you may use this book itself as a worksheet (unless it is a library book!)

As you fill in the information for each section, keep in mind the following instructions:

① Identification Section

The identification section is mandatory—it must be filled in. In the first blank, include any other names by which you are known. Do this by adding the phrase: "also known as" after your principal full name. For example: "John James Smith, also known as Jimmy John Smith." In the spaces provided for your residence, use the location of your principal residence, that is, where you currently live permanently.

② Marital and Parental Status Section

Depending upon your current marital and parental status, you will choose one of the following clauses. If you have children, list the appropriate information for each child. This clause should be included in your basic will after the phrase "My marital status is that…:

- I am single and have no children."
- I am currently married to [name of spouse] and we have no children."
- I was previously married to [name of spouse] and that marriage ended on [date] by [death, divorce, or annulment] and we had no children."
- I am single and have [number] child[ren] currently living. Their names and dates of birth are: [fill in the necessary information]."
- I am currently married to [name of spouse] and we have [number] child[ren] currently living. Their names and dates of birth are: [fill in the necessary information]."
- I was previously married to [name of spouse] and that marriage ended on [date] by [death, divorce, or annulment] and we have [number] child[ren] currently living. Their names and dates of birth are: [fill in the necessary information]."

③ Specific Gifts Section

This section allows you to give certain specific gifts to the beneficiaries and alternate beneficiaries of your choice. If you have used your Living Trust to pass all of your important property and assets to your chosen beneficiaries, you may decide not to use any specific gift designations at all, but rather simply complete the Residuary Section below. If you do decide to use specific gift designations, complete the following for each item of property:

- Name of beneficiary
- Relationship of beneficiary
- Name of alternative beneficiary (if main beneficiary has died first)
- Relationship of alternative beneficiary
- Full description of property to be transferred

④ **Residuary Section**

Everyone who completes a basic will should complete this section. In fact, you may desire to complete this gift section only and leave no specific gifts, particularly if you believe that you have included all of your assets under your Living Trust. This section, however, is still important as it will direct that any property or other assets that have been overlooked or were unknown to you at your death will be left to your designated "residual" beneficiaries. To complete your residuary clause, complete the following:

- Name of residuary beneficiary
- Relationship of residuary beneficiary
- Name of alternative residuary beneficiary (if main beneficiary has died first)
- Relationship of alternative residuary beneficiary

⑤ **Survivorship Section**

This clause provides for two possibilities. First, it provides for a required period of survival for any beneficiary to receive a gift under your will. The practical effect of this is to be certain that your property passes under your will and not that of a beneficiary who dies shortly after receiving your gift. The second portion of this clause provides for a determination of how your property should pass in the eventuality that both you and a beneficiary (most likely your spouse) should die in a manner that makes it impossible to determine who died first.

Without this clause in your will it would be possible that property would momentarily pass to a beneficiary under your will. When that person dies (possibly immediately if a result of a common accident or disaster), your property could wind up being left to the person whom your beneficiary designated, rather than to your alternate beneficiary. If you and your spouse are both preparing individual wills, it is a good idea to be certain that each of your wills contains identical survivorship clauses. If you are each other's primary beneficiary, it is also wise to attempt to coordinate who your alternate beneficiaries may be in the event of a simultaneous death.

⑥ **Executor Section**

With this paragraph, you will make your choice of *executor* and alternative executor, the person who will administer and distribute your assets upon your death. The chosen alternate executor will assume the powers of the executor only if the executor that you have chosen is not surviving or is otherwise unable to serve. A spouse, sibling, or other trusted party is usually chosen to act as executor. You will most likely desire to select the same persons as executor and alternative executor to your basic will as you selected as successor trustee and alternative successor trustee to your Living Trust. The persons chosen should be residents of the state in which you currently reside. You also provide that they not be required to post a bond in order to be appointed to serve as executor and that they will not be compensated for their services as executor. Be sure to clearly identify the executor and alternate executor by his or her full name and address.

⑦ Powers of Executor Section

With this paragraph, you authorize your executor to perform any acts necessary for the management and distribution of your estate, including independent distribution of your estate if that alternative is allowed in your state.

⑧ Publication and Date Section

In this section, you declare that you are signing your will and you note how many pages it consists of. You also declare that you are of sound mind and legal age and that no one is forcing you to sign the will against your will. Fill in the date that you sign the will.

⑨ Signature Section

The signature lines of your basic will must be completed in front of three witnesses. Do not sign your will unless your witnesses are present. When you have assembled your three witnesses, do all the following in order:

- State to your witnesses that you are about to sign your will.
- Sign your will in the space indicated (as Testator).

⑩ Witness Section

After you have signed your will in the presence of your witnesses, do all the following in order:

- Pass the will signed by you to the first witness and ask that he or she sign as a witness. It is not required that he or she read the will or know the details of the will, only that he or she is aware that it is your will. Have each witness sign their full name, print their full name, and fill in their address.
- After the first witness signs, ask that the second and then the third witness sign the will.
- When all three witnesses have signed the will, place the original will with the original of your Living Trust and provide a copy to the persons whom you have named as executor and alternative executor (generally the same persons whom you have named as successor and alternative successor trustee).

If you wish to prepare a more complex will, please consult Nova Publishing's *Prepare Your Own Will: The National Will Kit.*

Supplemental Will

LAST WILL AND TESTAMENT

① Identification

I, _____ , residing at _____
_____ (address), declare that this is my Last Will and
Testament and I revoke all previous wills and codicils.

② Marital and Parental Status

My marital status is that _____
_____ .

③ Specific Gifts

I make the following specific gifts:

To _____ (name), who is my _____
(relationship), or if not surviving, to _____ (name), who is
my _____ (relationship), I give _____
_____
_____
_____
_____ .

To _____ (name), who is my _____
(relationship), or if not surviving, to _____ (name), who is
my _____ (relationship), I give _____
_____
_____
_____
_____ .

To _____ (name), who is my _____
(relationship), or if not surviving, to _____ (name), who is
my _____ (relationship), I give _____
_____
_____
_____
_____ .

To _____ (name), who is my _____
(relationship), or if not surviving, to _____ (name), who is
my _____ (relationship), I give _____
_____
_____
_____
_____ .

To _____ (name), who is my _____
(relationship), or if not surviving, to _____ (name), who is
my _____ (relationship), I give _____
_____
_____
_____
_____ .

To _____ (name), who is my _____
(relationship), or if not surviving, to _____ (name), who is
my _____ (relationship), I give _____
_____
_____
_____
_____ .

To _____ (name), who is my _____
(relationship), or if not surviving, to _____ (name), who is
my _____ (relationship), I give _____
_____
_____
_____
_____ .

④ Residuary

I give all the rest of my property, whether real or personal, wherever located, to
_____ (name), who is my _____
(relationship), or if not surviving, to _____ (name), who is
my _____ (relationship).

⑤ Survivorship

All beneficiaries named in this will must survive me by (30) thirty days to receive any gift under this will. If any beneficiary and I should die simultaneously, I shall be conclusively presumed to have survived that beneficiary for purposes of this will.

⑥ Executor

I appoint _____ (name), residing at _____
_____ (address), as Executor, to serve without bond or compensation. If not surviving or otherwise unable to serve, I appoint _____ (name), residing at _____
_____ (address), as Alternate Executor, also to serve without bond or compensation.

⑦ Powers of Executor

In addition to any powers, authority, and discretion granted by law, I grant such Executor or Alternate Executor any and all powers to perform any acts, in his or her sole discretion and without court approval, for the management and distribution of my estate, including independent administration of my estate.

⑧ Publication and Date

I publish and sign this Last Will and Testament, consisting of _____
pages, on the date of _____ , and declare that I do so freely, for the purposes expressed, under no constraint or undue influence, and that I am of sound mind and of legal age.

⑨ Signature

_____
Signature of Testator

_____
Printed Name of Testator

⑩ Witness Acknowledgment

On the date of _____ , in the presence of all of us, the above-named Testator published and signed this Last Will and Testament, and then at Testator's request, and in Testator's presence, and in each other's presence, we all signed below as witnesses, and we declare, under penalty of perjury, that, to the best of our knowledge, the Testator signed this instrument freely, under no constraint or undue influence, and is of sound mind and legal age.

_____   _____
Signature of Witness   Signature of Witness

_____   _____
Printed Name of Witness   Printed Name of Witness

_____   _____

_____   _____
Address of Witness   Address of Witness

_____
Signature of Witness

_____
Printed Name of Witness

_____

_____
Address of Witness

Appendix: State Laws Relating to Living Trusts

This book is part of Nova Publishing Company's *Law Made Simple Series*. This Appendix contains a summary of the laws relating to living trusts for all states and the District of Columbia (Washington D.C.). It has been compiled directly from the most recently-available statutes and has been abridged for clarity and succinctness. Every effort has been made to assure that the information contained in this guide is accurate and complete. However, laws are subject to constant change. Therefore, prior to reliance on any legal points, the current status of the specific law should be checked.

State Law Reference: This listing specifies the correct state statute book(s) and sections that contain wills or trust law.

State Website: This listing provides the internet website address of the location of the state's statutes relating to trust law. The addresses were current at the time of this book's publication; however, like most websites, the page addresses are subject to change. If an expired state webpage is not automatically redirected to a new site, laws can be searched at http://www.findlaw.com

Uniform Acts Adopted: This listing notes the various uniform acts relating to trusts that have been enacted and lists their citations (*i.e.*, Uniform Trustees' Powers Act, Uniform Gifts to Minors Act, etc.).

Trustee Residency Requirements: Here is noted if a trustee must be a resident of the state in which the trust is formed and any qualifications.

Minimum Age for Grantor or Trustee: This listing specifies the minimum age that a person must be to be either a grantor or trustee of a trust. There is no minimum age to be a beneficiary of a trust in any state.

Trust-Writing Requirements: Which trust provisions must be in writing are noted in this listing. All states require trusts relating to real estate to be in writing. Some states require that all trust provisions be in writing.

Trust Pour-Over to Will: The requirements for a trust that is used to add property to an existing will are noted in this section.

Spouse's Right to Property Regardless of Will: This listing notes the surviving spouse's right to a certain share of the deceased spouse's estate regardless of any provisions in the will. In most common-law states, a spouse's right extends to any property passed via a Living Trust as well.

Laws of Intestate Succession (Distribution If Decedent Leaves No Will): Under this listing are shown the complex state provisions regarding how property will be distributed in the event that a person dies without a valid will or trust.

Property Ownership: Whether the state follows the community property or common law system of ownership of property and details of joint ownership of property are noted in this section.

State Gift, Inheritance, or Estate Taxes: This listing shows the tax situation in each state as it relates to estates and wills.

Additional Requirements: Here are listed any additional state-specific requirements for trusts, such as registration of a trust, etc.

Alabama

State Law Reference: Code of Alabama Trust; Sections 35-4-250+. Code of Alabama, Title 43, Chapters 2-1 to 8-298.

State Website: http://www.legislature.state.al.us/CodeofAlabama/1975/coatoc.htm.

Uniform Acts Adopted:

Uniform Testamentary Additions to Trusts Act: (Section 43-8-140).

Uniform Trustee Powers Act: (Section 19-3-322)

Uniform Gift to Minors Act: (Sections 35-5A-1+).

Trustee Residency Requirements: No provision.

Minimum Age for Grantor or Trustee: Nineteen (19). (Section 26-1-1).

Trust-Writing Requirements: A trust holding real estate must be in writing. A trust holding personal or other property can be written or oral. (Section 8-9-2).

Trustee Bond Requirements: Trustee must provide bond of double the amount of the supposed value of the trust, unless waived by the trust itself. (Section 19-3-233).

Trustee Pour-Over to Will: The trust must be identified in the will. The terms of the trust must be in a document other than the will and signed before or at the same time as the will. (Section 43-8-140).

Spouse's Right to Property Regardless of Will: The surviving spouse is entitled to 1/3 of the "augmented" estate of the deceased spouse. In general, the "augmented" estate includes both the property that passes under the will and any other property that passes by other "non-will" transfers, such as under the terms of a living trust or a joint tenancy arrangement. (Section 43-8-70).

Laws of Intestate Succession (Distribution If Decedent Leaves No Will):

Spouse and children of spouse surviving: $50,000.00 and 1/2 of balance to spouse and 1/2 of balance to children.

Spouse and children not of spouse surviving: 1/2 to spouse and 1/2 to children.

Spouse, but no children or parent(s) surviving: All to spouse.

Spouse and parent(s), but no children surviving: $100,000.00 and 1/2 of balance to spouse and 1/2 of balance to parent(s).

Children, but no spouse surviving: All to children equally or to their children per stirpes.

Parent(s), but no spouse or children surviving: All to parents equally or to the surviving parent.

No spouse, children, or parent(s) surviving: All to brothers and sisters per stirpes; or if none, to grandparents or their children per stirpes; or if none, to deceased spouse's next of kin. (Sections 43-8-41 & 43-8-42).

Property Ownership: Common-law state. Tenancy-in-common is presumed if real estate is held jointly unless title creates joint tenancy with right of survivorship or similar words. No tenancy-in-entirety is recognized. Joint bank account deposits are payable to any survivor. (Section 35-4-7).

State Gift, Inheritance, or Estate Taxes: No gift tax; no inheritance tax; imposes state estate tax equal to federal credit for state death taxes. (Sections 40-15-1–40-15-19).

Alaska

State Law Reference: Alaska Statutes; Title 13, Chapters 36.005+ and Title 13.06+.

State Website: http://www.legis.state.ak.us/folhome.htm

Uniform Acts Adopted:

Uniform Probate Code: (Sections 13.06.005+).

Uniform Testamentary Additions to Trusts Act: (Section 13.12.511).

Uniform Transfer to Minors Act: (Sections 13.46.010+).

Uniform Powers of Trustees Act: (Section 13.36.109).

Trustee Residency Requirements: If out-of-state trustee is appointed, trust must be registered. (Section 13.36.025).

Minimum Age for Grantor or Trustee: Eighteen (18). (Section 25.20.010).

Trust-Writing Requirements: All trusts must be in writing. (Sections 9.25.010 & 34.40.070).

Trustee Bond Requirements: None, unless required by trust, requested by beneficiary, or ordered by court. (Section 13.36.085).

Trustee Pour-Over to Will: The trust must be identified in the will. The terms of the trust must be in a document other than the will and signed before or at the same time as the will. (Section 13.12.511).

Spouse's Right to Property Regardless of Will: The surviving spouse is entitled to 1/3 of the "augmented" estate of the deceased spouse. In general, the "augmented" estate includes both the property that passes under the will and any other property that passes by other "non-will" transfers, such as under the terms of a living trust or a joint tenancy arrangement. (Sections 13.12.202 & 13.12.203).

Laws of Intestate Succession (Distribution If Decedent Leaves No Will):

Spouse and children of spouse surviving: All to spouse.

Spouse and children not of spouse surviving: 1/2 to spouse and 1/2 to children or grandchildren per stirpes.

Spouse, but no children or parent(s) surviving: All to spouse.

Spouse and parent(s), but no children surviving: $200,000.00 and 3/4 of balance to spouse and 1/4 of balance to parent.

Children, but no spouse surviving: All to children equally or to their children per stirpes.

Parent(s), but no spouse or children surviving: All to parents equally or to the surviving parent.

No spouse, children, or parent(s) surviving: All to brothers and sisters per stirpes; or if none, 1/2 to paternal grandparents and their children per stirpes and 1/2 to maternal grandparents and their children per stirpes. (Sections 13.12.102 & 13.12.103).

Property Ownership: Common-law state. No joint tenancy in personal property. Persons with undivided interests in real estate are tenants-in-common. Spouses who acquire real estate hold it as tenants-by-entirety unless stated otherwise. Joint bank account deposits are payable to any survivor. (Sections 34.15.110 & 34.15.730).

State Gift, Inheritance, or Estate Taxes: No gift tax; no inheritance tax; imposes state estate tax equal to federal credit for state death taxes. (Sections 43.31.011–43.31.430).

Additional Requirements: Residents should register a "Registration of Living Trust" form with the local court in their county of residence. This requirement is mandatory, although there are no penalties or consequences for failure to register. Please see proper form in Chapter 7.

Arizona

State Law Reference: Arizona Revised Statutes Annotated; Sections 14-7201+ and Title 14, Chapters 1102+.

State Website: http://www.azleg.state.az.us/ars/ars.htm

Uniform Acts Adopted:

Uniform Probate Code: (Sections 14-1102+).

Uniform Trustees' Powers Act: (Sections 14-7232 & 14-7233).

Uniform Transfer to Minors Act: (Sections 14-7651+).

Uniform Testamentary Additions to Trusts Act: (Section 14-2511).

Trustee Residency Requirements: None.

Minimum Age for Grantor or Trustee: Eighteen (18). (Section 8-101).

Trust-Writing Requirements: A trust holding real estate must be in writing. A trust holding personal property can be written or oral. (Section 44-101).

Trustee Bond Requirements: None, unless required by trust, requested by beneficiary, or required by court order. (Section 14-7304).

Trustee Pour-Over to Will: The trust must be identified in the will. The terms of the trust must be in a document other than the will and signed before or at the same time as the will. (Section 14-2511).

Spouse's Right to Property Regardless of Will: Community property right to 1/2 of the deceased spouse's "community" property. In addition, the surviving spouse is entitled to an allowance of $18,000.00. (Section 14-2402).

Laws of Intestate Succession (Distribution If Decedent Leaves No Will):

Spouse and children of spouse surviving: All of decedent's separate property and 1/2 of decedent's community property to spouse and 1/2 of decedent's community property to children.

Spouse and children not of spouse surviving: 1/2 of decedent's separate property to spouse and 1/2 of decedent's separate property and all of decedent's community property to children.

Spouse, but no children or parent(s) surviving: All to spouse.

Spouse and parent(s), but no children surviving: All to spouse.

Children, but no spouse surviving: All to children equally or to their children per stirpes.

Parent(s), but no spouse or children surviving: All to parents equally or to the surviving parent.

No spouse, children, or parent(s) surviving: All to brothers and sisters per stirpes; or if none, to the next of kin. (Sections 14-2102 & 14-2103).

Property Ownership: Community property state. Property acquired during marriage outside state before moving into state is quasi-community property. Joint tenancy between spouses if stated. Tenancy-by-entirety is not recognized. Joint bank account deposits are payable to any survivor unless clear evidence exists that deposit is payable only to specified survivor. (Sections 25-211 and 33-431).

State Gift, Inheritance, or Estate Taxes: No gift tax; no inheritance tax; imposes state estate tax equal to federal credit for state death taxes. (Title 42, Sections 4051 & 4052).

Arkansas

State Law Reference: Arkansas Code of 1987 Annotated; Title 28, Chapters 28-24-101 to 28-72-507.

State Website: http://www.arkleg.state.ar.us/newwebcode

Uniform Acts Adopted:

Uniform Testamentary Additions to Trusts Act: (Sections 28-27-101+).

Uniform Trustees' Powers Act: (Sections 28-69-033 & 28-69-304).

Uniform Gifts to Minors Act: (Sections 9-26-201+).

Trustee Residency Requirements: Out-of-state trustee must qualify to do business in Arkansas. (Section 4-31-202).

Minimum Age for Grantor or Trustee: Eighteen (18). (Section 9-25-101).

Trust-Writing Requirements: A trust holding real estate must be in writing. (Section 4-59-103).

Trustee Bond Requirements: Yes, unless not required by trust. (Section 28-4-201).

Trustee Pour-Over to Will: The trust must be identified in the will. The terms of the trust must be in a document other than the will and signed before or at the same time as the will. (Section 28-27-101).

Spouse's Right to Property Regardless of Will: Intestate share: 1/3 of personal property and 1/3 of real estate for life. (Section 28-39-401).

Laws of Intestate Succession (Distribution If Decedent Leaves No Will):

Spouse and children of spouse surviving: Real estate: 1/3 life estate to spouse and 2/3 to children equally or their children per stirpes; personal property: 1/3 to spouse and 2/3 to children equally or their children per stirpes.

Spouse and children not of spouse surviving: Real estate: 1/3 life estate to spouse and 2/3 to children equally or their children per stirpes; personal property: 1/3 to spouse and 2/3 to children equally or their children per stirpes.

Spouse, but no children or parent(s) surviving: All to spouse if married over three (3) years. If married less than three (3) years, 1/2 to spouse and 1/2 to brothers and sisters equally or their children per stripes; or if none, all to ancestors (up to great-grandparents); or if none, all to spouse.

Spouse and parent(s), but no children surviving: All to spouse if married over three (3) years. If married less than three (3) years, 1/2 to spouse and 1/2 to parent(s).

Children, but no spouse surviving: All to children equally or to their children per capita.

Parent(s), but no spouse or children surviving: All to parents equally or to the surviving parent.

No spouse, children, or parent(s) surviving: All to brothers and sisters per stripes; or if none, to grandparents and their children per stirpes. (Sections 28-9-204, 28-9-205 & 28-9-206).

Property Ownership: Common-law state. Property acquired in a community property state is community property. Tenancy-in-common and joint tenancy are recognized. Tenancy-by-entirety is recognized when conveyance is to husband and wife. Joint bank account deposits are payable to any survivor. (Sections 18-12-106, 18-12-603, & 23-47-204).

State Gift, Inheritance, or Estate Taxes: No gift tax; no inheritance tax; imposes state estate tax equal to federal credit for state death taxes. (Title 26, Sections 59-101–59-122).

California

State Law Reference: Annotated California Code; Probate Code, Sections 1500+ and 6100+.

State Website: http://www.leginfo.ca.gov/index.html

Uniform Acts Adopted:

Uniform Testamentary Additions to Trusts Act: (Probate Code, Section 6300).

Uniform Trustees' Powers Act: (Sections 16200+).

Uniform Transfers to Minors Act: (Sections 3900+).

Trustee Residency Requirements: Out-of-state trustee's actions are severely restricted, please refer directly to the statute. (Probate Code, Sections 17003 & 17005).

Minimum Age for Grantor or Trustee: Eighteen (18). (Family Code, Section 6500-02).

Trust-Writing Requirements: A trust holding real estate must be in writing. Trusts holding personal property need clear and convincing evidence if not in writing. (Sections 15206 & 15207).

Trustee Bond Requirements: None, unless required by the trust or court order. (Section 15602).

Trustee Pour-Over to Will: The trust must be identified in the will. The terms of the trust must be in a document other than the will and signed before or at the same time as the will. (Section 6300).

Spouse's Right to Property Regardless of Will: Community property right to 1/2 of the deceased spouse's "community" property. (Section 100).

Laws of Intestate Succession (Distribution If Decedent Leaves No Will):

Spouse and children of spouse surviving: All of decedent's community property to spouse. If one (1) child, 1/2 of decedent's separate property to spouse and 1/2 to child per stirpes. If more than one (1) child, 1/3 of decedent's separate property to spouse and 2/3 to children per stirpes.

Spouse and children not of spouse surviving: Same as above "Spouse and children of spouse surviving."

Spouse, but no children or parent(s) surviving: All of decedent's community property to spouse. 1/2 of decedent's separate property to spouse and 1/2 of decedent's separate property to brothers and sisters equally or to their children per stirpes; or if none, all to spouse.

Spouse and parent(s), but no children surviving: All of decedent's community property to spouse. 1/2 of decedent's separate property to spouse and 1/2 of decedent's separate property to parent(s) or surviving parent.

Children, but no spouse surviving: All to children equally or to their children per stirpes.

Parent(s), but no spouse or children surviving: All to parents equally or to the surviving parent.

No spouse, children, or parent(s) surviving: All to brothers and sisters per stirpes; or if none, to the next of kin. (Sections 6401 & 6402).

Property Ownership: Community property state. Property in names of spouses as joint tenants is not community property unless stated. Joint tenancy must be stated. Tenancy-by-entirety is not recognized. Joint bank account deposits are payable to survivor if account had rights of survivorship stated. (Family Title, Sections 750, 760, & 770 and Civil Code Title, Section 683).

State Gift, Inheritance, or Estate Taxes: No gift tax; no inheritance tax; imposes state estate tax equal to federal credit for state death taxes. (Revenue and Taxation Title, Sections 13301 & 13302).

Additional Requirements: When a living trust becomes irrevocable in California (upon the death of the grantor or surviving grantor), the trustee must notify all beneficiaries of the trust in writing. There are specific requirements for the notice which are contained in California Probate Code, Section 16061.5+.

Colorado

State Law Reference: Colorado Revised Statutes Annotated; Sections 15-10-101+, 15-11-101+, and 15-12-101+.

State Website: http://64.78.178.125/stat01/index.html

Uniform Acts Adopted:

Uniform Probate Code: (Sections 15-10-101+ and 15-11-101+).

Uniform Testamentary Additions to Trusts Act: (Section 15-11-511).

Uniform Trustees' Powers Act: (Section 15-1-804).

Uniform Gifts to Minors Act: (Sections 11-50-101+).

Trustee Residency Requirements: Trust managed by out-of-state trustee must be registered. (Section 15-16-105).

Minimum Age for Grantor or Trustee: Eighteen (18). (Section 13-22-101).

Trust-Writing Requirements: A trust holding real estate must be in writing. (Section 38-10-118).

Trustee Bond Requirements: None unless required by trust or beneficiary. (Section 15-16-304).

Trustee Pour-Over to Will: The trust must be identified in the will. The terms of the trust must be in a document other than the will and signed before or at the same time as the will. (Section 15-15-101).

Spouse's Right to Property Regardless of Will: The surviving spouse is entitled to 1/2 of the "augmented" estate of the deceased spouse. However, the amount is also dependent on the length of the marriage in years. In general, the "augmented" estate includes both the property that passes under the will and any other property that passes by other "non-will" transfers, such as under the terms of a living trust or a joint tenancy arrangement. (Section 15-11-201).

Laws of Intestate Succession (Distribution If Decedent Leaves No Will):

Spouse and children of spouse surviving: Spouse receives entire estate. (Section 15-11-102(1)(b)).

Spouse and children not of spouse surviving: $150,000.00 and 1/2 to spouse and 1/2 to children and grandchildren per stirpes. (Section 15-11-102(3)).

Spouse, but no children or parent(s) surviving: $200,000.00 and 3/4 of remainder to spouse, 1/4 to parent(s). (Section 15-11-102(1)(A)).

Spouse and parent(s), but no children surviving: All to spouse. (Section 15-11-102(2)).

Children, but no spouse surviving: All to children equally or to their children per capita at each generation. (Section 15-11-103(1)).

Parent(s), but no spouse or children surviving: All to parents equally or to the surviving parent. (Section 15-11-103(2)).

No spouse, children, or parent(s) surviving: All to brothers and sisters per stirpes; or if none, to grandparents and their children per stirpes; or if none, to nearest lineal ancestors and their children. (Section 15-11-102).

Property Ownership: Common-law state. Tenancy-in-common is presumed unless otherwise stated. Joint tenancy is recognized. Tenancy-by-entirety is not recognized. Joint bank account deposits are payable to any survivor. (Sections 11-6-105 & 38-11-101).

State Gift, Inheritance, or Estate Taxes: No gift tax; no inheritance tax; imposes state estate tax equal to federal credit for state death taxes. (Sections 39-23.5+).

Additional Requirements: Residents should register a "Registration of Living Trust" form with the local court in their county of residence. This requirement is mandatory, although there are no penalties or consequences for failure to register. Please see proper form in Chapter 7.

Connecticut

State Law Reference: Connecticut General Statutes Annotated; Title 45a, Chapters 471+ and 802+.

State Website: http://www.cslib.org/psaindex.htm

Uniform Acts Adopted:

Uniform Testamentary Additions to Trusts Act: (Section 45a-260).

Uniform Gifts to Minors Act: (Sections 45a-557+).

Uniform Trustees' Powers Act: (Sections 45a-234+).

Trustee Residency Requirements: If out-of-state trustee is appointed, then a resident agent must also be appointed. (Section 45a-477).

Minimum Age for Grantor or Trustee: Eighteen (18). (Section 1-12).

Trust-Writing Requirements: A trust holding real estate must be in writing. (Section 52-550).

Trustee Bond Requirements: Yes, unless not required by trust. (Section 45a-473).

Trustee Pour-Over to Will: The trust must be identified in the will. The terms of the trust must be in a document other than the will and signed before or at the same time as the will. (Section 45a-260).

Spouse's Right to Property Regardless of Will: The surviving spouse is entitled to 1/3 of the deceased spouse's real estate and personal property for the rest of his or her life. (Section 45a-436).

Laws of Intestate Succession (Distribution If Decedent Leaves No Will):

Spouse and children of spouse surviving: $100,000.00 and 1/2 of balance to spouse and 1/2 of balance to children or grandchildren per stirpes. (Section 45a-437(3)).

Spouse and children not of spouse surviving: 1/2 to spouse and 1/2 to children or grandchildren per stirpes. (Sections 45a-437(4) & 45a-438).

Spouse, but no children or parent(s) surviving: All to spouse. (Section 45a-437(1)).

Spouse and parent(s), but no children surviving: $100,000.00 and 3/4 of balance to spouse and 1/4 of balance to parents or surviving parent. (Section 45a-437(2)).

Children, but no spouse surviving: All to children equally or to their children per stirpes. (Section 45a-438).

Parent(s), but no spouse or children surviving: All to parents equally or to the surviving parent. (Section 45a-439(a)(1)).

No spouse, children, or parent(s) surviving: All to brothers and sisters per stirpes; or if none, to next of kin. (Section 45a-439(2)-(3)).

Property Ownership: Common-law state. Tenancy-in-common is presumed unless words "joint tenants" follow names. Joint tenancy automatically includes right of survivorship. Tenancy-by-entirety is recognized. Joint bank account deposits are payable to any survivor. (Sections 39a-2720 and 47-14a).

State Gift, Inheritance, or Estate Taxes: No gift tax; no inheritance tax; imposes state estate tax equal to federal credit for state death taxes. (Section 12-391–399).

Delaware

State Law Reference: Delaware Code Annotated; Title 12, Chapters 101+ and 3501+.

State Website: http://www.legis.state.de.us

Uniform Acts Adopted:

Uniform Gifts to Minors Act: (Sections 12-4501+).

Trustee Residency Requirements: None.

Minimum Age for Grantor or Trustee: Eighteen (18). (Section 1-701).

Trust-Writing Requirements: A trust holding real estate must be in writing. (Section 6-2714).

Trustee Bond Requirements: No provision.

Trustee Pour-Over to Will: The trust must be identified in the will. The terms of the trust must be in a document other than the will and signed before or at the same time as the will. (Section 12-211).

Spouse's Right to Property Regardless of Will: The surviving spouse is entitled to 1/3 of the deceased spouse's estate or $20,000.00, whichever is less. (Section 12-901(a)).

Laws of Intestate Succession (Distribution If Decedent Leaves No Will):

Spouse and children of spouse surviving: Real estate: Life estate to spouse and all the rest to children or grandchildren per stirpes; personal property: $50,000.00 and 1/2 of balance to spouse and 1/2 of balance to children or grandchildren per stirpes. (Section 12-502(3)).

Spouse and children not of spouse surviving: Real estate: Life estate to spouse and all the rest to children or grandchildren per stirpes; personal property: 1/2 to spouse and 1/2 to children or grandchildren per stirpes. (Section 12-502(4)).

Spouse, but no children or parent(s) surviving: All to spouse. (Section 12-502(1)).

Spouse and parent(s), but no children surviving: Real estate: Life estate to spouse; all the rest to parents or surviving parent; personal property: $50,000.00 and 1/2 of balance to spouse and 1/2 of balance to parents or surviving parent. (Section 12-502).

Children, but no spouse surviving: All to children equally or to their children per stirpes. (Section 12-503(1)).

Parent(s), but no spouse or children surviving: All to parents equally or to the surviving parent. (Section 12-503(2)).

No spouse, children, or parent(s) surviving: All to brothers or sisters or their children per stirpes; or if none, to the next of kin per stirpes. (Section 12-503(3)(4)).

Property Ownership. Common-law state. Tenancy-in-common is presumed. If joint owners are married, tenancy-by-entirety is created. Joint tenancy created only if stated. Joint bank account deposits are payable to any survivor. (Sections 25-309, 25-311, & 25-701).

State Gift, Inheritance, or Estate Taxes: Imposes a state gift tax; imposes an inheritance tax of up to 16 percent; imposes state estate tax equal to federal credit for state death taxes less any amounts paid on state inheritance tax. Maximum total state inheritance and state estate tax is equal to the maximum allowable federal estate tax credit for state death taxes. (Sections 30-1501+).

District of Columbia (Washington D.C.)

State Law Reference: District of Columbia Code Annotated; Sections 16-101+, 18-101+, 20-101+, 21-1701+, and 45-101+.

State Website: http://dccouncil.washington.dc.us/

Uniform Acts Adopted:

Uniform Testamentary Additions to Trusts Act: (Section 18-306).

Uniform Transfers to Minors Act: (Sections 21-301+).

Uniform Fiduciaries Act: (Sections 21-1701+).

Trustee Residency Requirements: No provision.

Minimum Age for Grantor or Trustee: Eighteen (18). (Section 30-401).

Trust-Writing Requirements: A trust holding real estate must be in writing. (Section 28-3503).

Trustee Bond Requirements: Yes, if appointed by court or can be waived by the trust itself. (Section 16-601).

Trustee Pour-Over to Will: The trust must be identified in the will. The terms of the trust must be in a document other than the will and signed before or at the same time as the will. (Section 18-306).

Spouse's Right to Property Regardless of Will: The surviving spouse is entitled to 1/3 of the deceased spouse's real estate for the rest of his or her life. (Sections 19-114 & 19-303).

Laws of Intestate Succession (Distribution If Decedent Leaves No Will):

Spouse and children of spouse surviving: Real estate: 1/3 life estate to spouse and balance to children equally or their children per stirpes; personal property: 1/3 to spouse and 2/3 to children equally or their children per stirpes.

Spouse and children not of spouse surviving: Real estate: 1/3 life estate to spouse and balance to children equally or their children per stirpes; personal property: 1/3 to spouse and 2/3 to children equally or their children per stirpes.

Spouse, but no children or parent(s) surviving: Real estate: 1/3 life estate to spouse and balance to parent's children per stirpes; or if none, to collaterals; or if none, to grandparents; or if none, all to spouse; personal property: 1/2 to spouse and 1/2 to parent's children per stirpes; or if none, to collaterals; or if none, to grandparents; or if none, all to spouse.

Spouse and parent(s), but no children surviving: Real estate: 1/3 life estate to spouse and balance to parents or surviving parent; personal property: 1/2 to spouse and 1/2 to parents or surviving parent.

Children, but no spouse surviving: All to children equally or to their children per stirpes. (Section 19-306).

Parent(s), but no spouse or children surviving: All to parents equally or to the surviving parent.

No spouse, children, or parent(s) surviving: All to brothers and sisters or their children per stirpes; or if none, to collaterals; or if none, to grandparents. (Sections 19-301–19-312).

Property Ownership: Common-law state. Tenancy-in-common is presumed unless joint tenancy is stated. Joint ownership by husband and wife is presumed to be tenancy-by-entirety. Joint bank account deposits are payable to any survivor. (Section 45-216).

State Gift, Inheritance, or Estate Taxes: No gift tax; no inheritance tax; imposes state estate tax equal to federal credit for state death taxes. (Sections 47-3701–47-3723).

Florida

State Law Reference: Florida Statutes Annotated; Chapters 731.005+, 731.101+, 732.501+, and 733.101+.

State Website: http://www.leg.state.fl.us/statutes/index.cfm

Uniform Acts Adopted:

Uniform Trustees' Powers Act: (Sections 737.401+).

Uniform Testamentary Additions to Trusts Act: (Section 732.513).

Uniform Transfers to Minors Act: (Section 710).

Trustee Residency Requirements: If requested by beneficiary or directed by trust, an out-of-state trustee must register the trust. (Section 737.105).

Minimum Age for Grantor or Trustee: Eighteen (18). (Section 744.102).

Trust-Writing Requirements: A trust holding real estate must be in writing. (Section 689.05).

Trustee Bond Requirements: None, unless required by trust, requested by beneficiary, or ordered by court. (Section 737.304).

Trustee Pour-Over to Will: The trust must be identified in the will. The terms of the trust must be in a document other than the will and signed before or at the same time as the will. (Section 732.513).

Spouse's Right to Property Regardless of Will: The surviving spouse is entitled to 30 percent of the deceased spouse's estate. (Section 732.207).

Laws of Intestate Succession (Distribution If Decedent Leaves No Will):

Spouse and children of spouse surviving: $20,000.00 and 1/2 of balance to spouse and 1/2 of balance to children and grandchildren per stirpes. (Sections 732.102(1)(b) & 732.103).

Spouse and children not of spouse surviving: 1/2 to spouse and 1/2 to children and grandchildren per stirpes. (Section 732.102(1)(c)).

Spouse, but no children or parent(s) surviving: All to spouse. (Section 732.102 (1)(a)).

Spouse and parent(s), but no children surviving: All to spouse. (Section 732.102).

Children, but no spouse surviving: All to children equally or to their children per stirpes. (Section 732.103(1)).

Parent(s), but no spouse or children surviving: All to parents equally or to the surviving parent. (Section 732.103(2)).

No spouse, children, or parent(s) surviving: All to brothers and sisters or their children per stirpes; or if none, 1/2 to maternal next of kin and 1/2 to paternal next of kin beginning with grandparents. (Section 732.103(4)).

Property Ownership: Common-law state. Personal property or real estate owned by husband and wife is presumed to be a tenancy-by-entirety with survivorship. Joint tenancy includes survivorship only if stated. Joint bank account deposits are payable to any survivor. (Sections 689.11 & 689.15).

State Gift, Inheritance, or Estate Taxes: No gift tax; no inheritance tax; imposes state estate tax equal to federal credit for state death taxes. (Sections 198.01–198.44).

Additional Requirements: Upon the Grantor's death, the Successor Trustee must notify all beneficiaries of the existence of the trust. Additionally, residents should register a "Registration of Living Trust" form with the local court in their county of residence. This requirement is mandatory, although there are no penalties or consequences for failure to register. Please see proper form in Chapter 7.

Georgia

State Law Reference: Code of Georgia Annotated; Title 53-2-1+.

State Website: http://www.state.ga.us/services/ocode/ocgsearch.htm

Uniform Acts Adopted:

Uniform Testamentary Additions to Trusts Act: (Section 53-12-71).

Uniform Trustees' Powers Act: (Section 53-12-55).

Uniform Gifts to Minors Act: (Sections 44-5-110+).

Georgia Transfer to Minors Act. (Sections 45-5-110+).

Trustee Residency Requirements: None. (Section 53-12-24).

Minimum Age for Grantor or Trustee: Eighteen (18). (Section 53-12-22).

Trust-Writing Requirements: A trust holding real estate must be in writing. (Section 13-5-30).

Trustee Bond Requirements: Court may require a successor trustee to post bond; otherwise, no bond unless required by trust or requested by beneficiary. (Section 53-12-174).

Trustee Pour-Over to Will: The trust must be identified in the will. The terms of the trust must be in a document other than the will and signed before or at the same time as the will. (Section 53-12-71).

Spouse's Right to Property Regardless of Will: The surviving spouse is entitled to one (1) year's support from the deceased spouse's estate. (Section 53-3-1).

Laws of Intestate Succession (Distribution If Decedent Leaves No Will):

Spouse and children of spouse surviving: Children or grandchildren and spouse all take equal shares with at least 1/4 to spouse. (Section 53-4-2(2)).

Spouse and children not of spouse surviving: Children or grandchildren and spouse all take equal shares with at least 1/4 to spouse. (Section 53-4-2(2)).

Spouse, but no children or parent(s) surviving: All to spouse. (Section 53-4-2(1)).

Spouse and parent(s), but no children surviving: All to spouse. (Section 53-4-2(1)).

Children, but no spouse surviving: All to children equally or to their children per stirpes. (Section 53-4-2(4)).

Parent(s), but no spouse or children surviving: All to parents, brothers, and sisters equally or to their children per stirpes. (Section 53-4-2).

No spouse, children, or parent(s) surviving: All to brothers and sisters or their children per stirpes; or if none, to paternal and maternal next of kin. (Section 53-4-2).

Property Ownership: Common-law state. Tenancy-in-common is presumed unless "joint tenants" or similar language is stated specifically. Tenancy-by-entirety is not recognized. Joint bank account deposits are payable to any survivor unless clear evidence exists that deposit is payable only to specified survivor. (Section 44-6-120).

State Gift, Inheritance, or Estate Taxes: No gift tax; no inheritance tax; imposes state estate tax equal to federal credit for state death taxes. (Sections 48-12-1–48-12-6).

Hawaii

State Law Reference: Hawaii Revised Statutes; Title 560, Sections 2+ and 7-201+.

State Website: http://www.capitol.hawaii.gov

Uniform Acts Adopted:

Uniform Probate Code: (Sections 5601:1-201+).

Uniform Trustees' Powers Act: (Sections 554A-3 & 560:7-401).

Uniform Testamentary Additions to Trusts Act: (Section 560:2-511).

Uniform Gifts to Minors Act: (Sections 553A-1+).

Trustee Residency Requirements: If out-of-state trustee is appointed to a living trust, trust must be registered. (Section 560:7-101).

Minimum Age for Grantor or Trustee: Eighteen (18). (Section 577-1).

Trust-Writing Requirements: A trust holding real estate must be in writing. (Section 656-1).

Trustee Bond Requirements: None, unless required by trust, requested by beneficiary, or ordered by court. (Section 560:7-304).

Trustee Pour-Over to Will: The trust must be identified in the will. The terms of the trust must be in a document other than the will and signed before or at the same time as the will. (Section 560:2-511).

Spouse's Right to Property Regardless of Will: The surviving spouse right to property regardless of provisions in the will depends on the length of the marriage. Please refer to the statute for details. (Section 560:2-202).

Laws of Intestate Succession (Distribution If Decedent Leaves No Will):

Spouse and children of spouse surviving: 1/2 to spouse and 1/2 to children equally or to the grandchildren. (Section 560:2-102(1)(A)).

Spouse and children not of spouse surviving: 1/2 to spouse and 1/2 to children equally or to the grandchildren. (Section 560:2-102(3)).

Spouse, but no children or parent(s) surviving: All to spouse. (Section 560:2-102(1)(A)).

Spouse and parent(s), but no children surviving: 1/2 to spouse and 1/2 to parents or surviving parent.

Children, but no spouse surviving: All to children equally or to their children per stirpes. (Section 560:2-103(1)).

Parent(s), but no spouse or children surviving: All to parents equally or to the surviving parent. (Section 560:2-103(a)).

No spouse, children, or parent(s) surviving: All to brothers and sisters or their children per stirpes; or if none, to grandparents; or if none, to uncles and aunts equally. (Section 560:2-103(3)(4)).

Property Ownership: Community property state. Tenancy-in-common is presumed unless joint tenancy or tenancy-by-entirety is stated. Joint bank account deposits are payable to any survivor unless clear evidence exists that deposit is payable only to a specified survivor. (Sections 509-1, 509-2, & 510-22+).

State Gift, Inheritance, or Estate Taxes: No gift tax; no inheritance tax; imposes state estate tax equal to federal credit for state death taxes. (Section 236D-3).

Additional Requirements: Residents should register a "Registration of Living Trust" form with the local court in their county of residence. This requirement is mandatory, although there are no penalties or consequences for failure to register. Please see proper form in Chapter 7.

Idaho

State Law Reference: Idaho Code; Title 15, Chapter 7-101+ and Idaho Code; Title 15, Chapter 1+.

State Website: http://www.state.id.us/idstat/TOC/idstTOC.html

Uniform Acts Adopted:

Uniform Probate Code: (Sections 15-1-101+).

Uniform Trustees' Power Act. (Sections 15-7-401 & 15-7-402).

Uniform Testamentary Additions to Trusts Act: (Section 15-2-511).

Uniform Gifts to Minors Act: (Sections 68-801+).

Trustee Residency Requirements: Out-of-state trustee must qualify to do business in Idaho. A trustee, whether a resident or not, must register the trust. (Section 5-7-105).

Minimum Age for Grantor or Trustee: Eighteen (18). (Section 32-101).

Trust-Writing Requirements: A trust holding real estate must be in writing. (Section 9-503).

Trustee Bond Requirements: None, unless required by trust, requested by beneficiary, or ordered by court. (Section 15-7-304).

Trustee Pour-Over to Will: The trust must be identified in the will. The terms of the trust must be in a document other than the will and signed before or at the same time as the will. (Section 15-2-511).

Spouse's Right to Property Regardless of Will: Community property right to 1/2 of the deceased spouse's "community" property. (Section 15-2-301).

Laws of Intestate Succession (Distribution If Decedent Leaves No Will):

Spouse and children of spouse surviving: All of decedent's community property to spouse; $50,000.00 and 1/2 of balance of decedent's separate property to spouse and 1/2 of balance to children or grandchildren per stirpes. (Sections 15-2-102(1)(3) & 15-2-103(a)).

Spouse and children not of spouse surviving: All of decedent's community property to spouse; 1/2 of decedent's separate property to spouse and 1/2 to children or grandchildren per stirpes. (Section 15-2-102(a)(4)).

Spouse, but no children or parent(s) surviving: All to spouse. (Section 15-2-102(a)(1)).

Spouse and parent(s), but no children surviving: All of decedent's community property to spouse; $50,000.00 and 1/2 of balance of decedent's separate property to spouse and 1/2 of balance to parents or surviving parent. (Section 15-2-102(a)(2)).

Children, but no spouse surviving: All to children or to their children per stirpes. (Section 15-2-103(a)).

Parent(s), but no spouse or children surviving: All to parents equally or to the surviving parent. (Section 15-2-103(b)).

No spouse, children, or parent(s) surviving: All to brothers and sisters or their children, if surviving. If not, then 1/2 to living maternal grandparents or their children and 1/2 to paternal grandparents or their children. (Section 15-2-103(d)).

Property Ownership: Community property state. Tenancy-in-common is presumed unless joint tenancy is stated or property is acquired as partnership or as community property. Tenancy-by-entirety is not recognized. Joint bank account deposits are payable to any survivor unless clear evidence exists that deposit is payable only to specified survivor. (Sections 32-903, 32-906, & 55-508).

State Gift, Inheritance, or Estate Taxes: No gift tax; imposes an inheritance tax of up to 30 percent; imposes state estate tax equal to federal credit for state death taxes less any amounts paid on state inheritance tax. Maximum total state inheritance and state estate tax is equal to the maximum allowable federal estate tax credit for state death taxes. (Sections 14-401–14-430).

Additional Requirements: Residents should register a "Registration of Living Trust" form with the local court in their county of residence. This requirement is mandatory, although there are no penalties or consequences for failure to register. Please see proper form in Chapter 7.

Illinois

State Law Reference: Illinois Compiled Statutes; Chapter 755, Paragraphs 5/1+ and Chapter 760, Paragraphs 5/1+.

State Website: http://www.legis.state.il.us/ilcs/chapterlist.html

Uniform Acts Adopted:

Uniform Testamentary Additions to Trusts Act: (Paragraph 5/4-4).

Uniform Gifts to Minors Act: (Paragraphs 20/1+).

Uniform Trustees' Powers Act: (Paragraphs 5/4.01+).

Trustee Residency Requirements: None.

Minimum Age for Grantor or Trustee: Eighteen (18). (Section 760 ILCS 5/11-1).

Trust-Writing Requirements: A trust holding real estate must be in writing. (Section 740 ILCS 80/9).

Trustee Bond Requirements: None, unless required by trust.

Trustee Pour-Over to Will: The trust must be identified in the will. The terms of the trust must be in a document other than the will and signed before or at the same time as the will. (Section 5/4-4).

Spouse's Right to Property Regardless of Will: Generally, the surviving spouse is entitled to 1/2 of the deceased spouse's estate if there are no children and only 1/3 if there are children. However, please refer directly to the statute as the provisions are detailed. (Paragraph 5/2-8).

Laws of Intestate Succession (Distribution If Decedent Leaves No Will):

Spouse and children of spouse surviving: 1/2 to spouse and 1/2 to children equally or to the grandchildren per stirpes.

Spouse and children not of spouse surviving: 1/2 to spouse and 1/2 to children equally or to the grandchildren per stirpes.

Spouse, but no children or parent(s) surviving: All to spouse.

Spouse and parent(s), but no children surviving: All to spouse.

Children, but no spouse surviving: All to children equally or to their children per stirpes.

Parent(s), but no spouse or children surviving: All to parents, brothers, sisters, or children of brother and sisters per stirpes. If only one surviving parent, he or she takes a double share.

No spouse, children, or parent(s) surviving: 1/2 to maternal and 1/2 to paternal grandparents equally or to surviving grandparent; or if none, to their children per stirpes; or if none, 1/2 to maternal and 1/2 to paternal great-grandparents equally or to surviving great-grandparent; or if none, to their children per stipes; or if none of the above, all to the next of kin. (Paragraph 5/2-1).

Property Ownership: Common-law state. Tenancy-in-common is presumed. Joint tenancy with right of survivorship created only by statement that property is held in joint tenancy and not tenancy-in-common. Tenancy-by-entirety is recognized. Joint bank account deposits are payable to any survivor. (Chapter 205, Paragraph 105/4-8 and Chapter 765, Paragraphs 1005/1–1005/4a).

State Gift, Inheritance, or Estate Taxes: No gift tax; no inheritance tax; imposes state estate tax equal to federal credit for state death taxes. (Chapter 35, Paragraphs 405/1–405/18).

Indiana

State Law Reference: Indiana Code Annotated; Title 29, Sections 1-1+ and Title 30, Sections 4-1-1+.

State Website: http://www.state.in.us/legislative/ic/code

Uniform Acts Adopted:

Uniform Testamentary Additions to Trusts Act: (Section 29-1-6-1).

Uniform Gifts to Minors Act: (Sections 30-2-8.5-1+).

Uniform Trustees' Powers Act: (Section 30-4-3-3).

Trustee Residency Requirements: None.

Minimum Age for Grantor or Trustee: Eighteen (18). (Sections 30-4-2-10 & 30-4-2-11).

Trust-Writing Requirements: Yes. (Section 32-2-1-3).

Trustee Bond Requirements: None, unless required by trust. (Section 30-4-6-8).

Trustee Pour-Over to Will: The trust must be identified in the will. The terms of the trust must be in a document other than the will and signed before or at the same time as the will. (Section 29-1-6-1).

Spouse's Right to Property Regardless of Will: The surviving spouse is entitled to 1/2 of the deceased spouse's estate. If there are surviving children of a prior spouse, a second or subsequent spouse is entitled to 1/3 of the deceased's personal property and 1/3 of the deceased's real estate for the rest of her or his life. (Section 29-1-3-1).

Laws of Intestate Succession (Distribution If Decedent Leaves No Will):

Spouse and children of spouse surviving: 1/2 to spouse and 1/2 to children.

Spouse and children not of spouse surviving: Real estate: life estate of 1/3 of real estate to spouse and balance to children; personal property: 1/2 to spouse and 1/2 to children.

Spouse, but no children or parent(s) surviving: All to spouse.

Spouse and parent(s), but no children surviving: 3/4 to spouse and 1/4 to parents or surviving parent.

Children, but no spouse surviving: All to children equally or to their children per stirpes.

Parent(s), brothers, sisters, and children of brothers and sisters, but no spouse or children surviving: Surviving parents, brothers, sisters all share equally, but parents are entitled to at least 1/4 of estate.

No spouse, children, parent(s), or brothers or sisters surviving: All to brothers' and sisters' children per stirpes; or if none, to grandparents; or if none, to aunts and uncles per stirpes. (Section 29-1-2-1).

Property Ownership: Common-law state. Joint tenancy, tenancy-in-common, and tenancy-by-entirety are recognized. Tenancy-in-common is presumed unless joint tenancy stated. Joint ownership by husband and wife is presumed to be a tenancy-by-entirety. Joint bank account deposits are payable to any survivor. (Sections 6-4.1-8-4, 32-4-1.5-15, & 32-4-2-1).

State Gift, Inheritance, or Estate Taxes: No gift tax; imposes an inheritance tax of up to 20 percent; imposes state estate tax equal to federal credit for state death taxes less any amounts paid on state inheritance tax. Maximum total state inheritance and state estate tax is equal to the maximum allowable federal estate tax credit for state death taxes. (Sections 6-4.1-5-1 & 6-4.1-11-2).

Iowa

State Law Reference: Iowa Code Annotated; Sections 633.1+, 633.63+, and 633.699+.

State Website: http://www.legis.state.ia.us/Code.html

Uniform Acts Adopted:

Uniform Testamentary Additions to Trusts Act: (Sections 633-275+).

Uniform Gifts to Minors Act: (Sections 565B.1+).

Uniform Trustees' Powers Act: (Section 633.699).

Trustee Residency Requirements: None. (Section 633.64).

Minimum Age for Grantor or Trustee: Eighteen (18). (Section 599.1).

Trust-Writing Requirements: A trust holding real estate must be in writing. (Section 557.10).

Trustee Bond Requirements: Yes, unless not required by trust. (Section 633.169).

Trustee Pour-Over to Will: The trust must be identified in the will. The terms of the trust must be in a document other than the will and signed before or at the same time as the will. (Section 633.275).

Spouse's Right to Property Regardless of Will: The surviving spouse is entitled to 1/3 of the deceased spouse's estate. (Section 633.238).

Laws of Intestate Succession (Distribution If Decedent Leaves No Will):

Spouse and children of spouse surviving: All to spouse.

Spouse and children not of spouse surviving: $50,000.00 and 1/2 of balance to spouse and 1/2 of balance to children.

Spouse, but no children or parent(s) surviving: All to spouse.

Spouse and parent(s), but no children surviving: All to spouse.

Children, but no spouse surviving: All to children equally or to their children per stirpes.

Parent(s), but no spouse or children surviving: All to parents equally or to the surviving parent.

No spouse, children, or parent(s) surviving: All to brothers and sisters or their children per stirpes; or if none, to ancestors and their children per stirpes; or if none, to spouse or heirs of spouse. (Sections 633.211, 633.212, & 633.219).

Property Ownership: Common-law state. Tenancy-in-common is presumed unless joint tenancy stated. Tenancy-by-entirety not recognized. Joint bank account deposits are payable to any survivor. (Sections 534.302 & 557.15).

State Gift, Inheritance, or Estate Taxes: No gift tax; imposes an inheritance tax of up to 15 percent; imposes state estate tax equal to federal credit for state death taxes less any amounts paid on state inheritance tax. Maximum total state inheritance and state estate tax is equal to the maximum allowable federal estate tax credit for state death taxes. (Sections 451.2 & 450.10).

Kansas

State Law Reference: Kansas Statutes Annotated; Chapter 58, Sections 1001+ and Chapter 59, Sections 59-101+ & 59-601+.

State Website: http://www.accesskansas.org/legislative/statutes/index.cgi

Uniform Acts Adopted:

Uniform Trustees' Powers Act: (Sections 58-1202 & 58-1203).

Uniform Testamentary Additions to Trusts Act: (Sections 58-1201+).

Uniform Gifts to Minors Act: (Sections 38-1701+).

Trustee Residency Requirements: None, but if out-of-state trustee is appointed, a resident agent must also be appointed. (Section 59-1706).

Minimum Age for Grantor or Trustee: Eighteen (18). (Section 38-101).

Trust-Writing Requirements: A trust holding real estate must be in writing. (Section 33-106).

Trustee Bond Requirements: Yes, unless not required by trust. (Section 59-1101).

Trustee Pour-Over to Will: The trust must be identified in the will. The terms of the trust must be in a document other than the will and signed before or at the same time as the will. (Section 59-3101).

Spouse's Right to Property Regardless of Will: The amount is dependent on length of marriage. Please refer directly to the statute as the provisions are detailed. (Section 59-6a202).

Laws of Intestate Succession (Distribution If Decedent Leaves No Will):

Spouse and children of spouse surviving: 1/2 to spouse and 1/2 to children or grandchildren per stirpes.

Spouse and children not of spouse surviving: 1/2 to spouse and 1/2 to children or grandchildren per stirpes.

Spouse, but no children or parent(s) surviving: All to spouse.

Spouse and parent(s), but no children surviving: All to spouse.

Children, but no spouse surviving: All to children equally or to their children per stirpes.

Parent(s), but no spouse or children surviving: All to parents equally or to the surviving parent.

No spouse, children, or parent(s) surviving: All to brothers and sisters per stirpes. (Sections 59-504–59-508).

Property Ownership: Common-law state. Tenancy-in-common is presumed unless joint tenancy is stated. Tenancy-by-entirety not recognized. Joint bank account deposits are payable to any survivor. (Sections 17-2213, 58-501, & 59-2286).

State Gift, Inheritance, or Estate Taxes: No gift tax; imposes an inheritance tax of up to 15 percent; imposes state estate tax equal to federal credit for state death taxes less any amounts paid on state inheritance tax. Maximum total state inheritance and state estate tax is equal to the maximum allowable federal estate tax credit for state death taxes. (Sections 79-15, 79-102, & 79-1537).

Kentucky

State Law Reference: Kentucky Revised Statutes, Chapters 386.010+, 394.000+, and 395.000+.

State Website: http://www.lrc.state.ky.us/statrev/frontpg.htm

Uniform Acts Adopted:

Uniform Trustees' Powers Act: (Sections 386.800+).

Uniform Testamentary Additions to Trusts Act: (Section 394.075).

Uniform Gifts to Minors Act: (Sections 385.012+).

Trustee Residency Requirements: No provision.

Minimum Age for Grantor or Trustee: Eighteen (18). (Section 2.015).

Trust-Writing Requirements: A trust holding real estate must be in writing. (Section 371.010).

Trustee Bond Requirements: None, unless required by trust, requested by beneficiary, or ordered by court. (Section 386.720).

Trustee Pour-Over to Will: The trust must be identified in the will. The terms of the trust must be in a document other than the will and signed before or at the same time as the will. (Section 394.076).

Spouse's Right to Property Regardless of Will: The surviving spouse is entitled to 1/3 of the deceased spouse's real estate for the rest of his or her life. (Section 394.020).

Laws of Intestate Succession (Distribution If Decedent Leaves No Will):

Spouse and children of spouse surviving: Real estate: life estate of 1/3 of fee simple property acquired during marriage and 1/2 of other real estate to spouse; balance to children or grandchildren per stirpes. Personal property: 1/2 to spouse and 1/2 to children equally or to grandchildren per stirpes.

Spouse and children not of spouse surviving: Same as above for "Spouse and children of spouse surviving."

Spouse, but no children or parent(s) surviving: 1/2 to parents' children; or if none, all to spouse.

Spouse and parent(s), but no children surviving: 1/2 to spouse and 1/2 to parents or surviving parent.

Children, but no spouse surviving: All to children equally or to their children per stirpes.

Parent(s), but no spouse or children surviving: All to parents equally or to the surviving parent.

No spouse, children, or parent(s) surviving: All to brothers and sisters or their children per stirpes; or if none, 1/2 to maternal next of kin and 1/2 to paternal next of kin and their children per stirpes. (Sections 391.010 & 391.030).

Property Ownership: Common-law state. Tenancy-in-common is presumed between husband and wife unless joint tenancy stated. Tenancy-by-entirety is recognized. Joint bank account deposits are payable to any survivor. (Sections 381.130, 381.720, & 391.315).

State Gift, Inheritance, or Estate Taxes: No gift tax; imposes an inheritance tax of up to 16 percent; imposes state estate tax equal to federal credit for state death taxes less any amounts paid on state inheritance tax. Maximum total state inheritance and state estate tax is equal to the maximum allowable federal estate tax credit for state death taxes. (Sections 140.070 & 140.130).

Louisiana

State Law Reference: Louisiana Revised Statutes; Sections 9:172+ and Louisiana Revised Statutes and Louisiana Civil Code Annotated, Sections 1570+.

State Website: http://www.legis.state.la.us/tsrs/search.htm

Uniform Acts Adopted:

Uniform Gifts to Minors Act: (Revised Statutes, Sections 9:751+).

Trustee Residency Requirements: None.

Minimum Age for Grantor or Trustee: Eighteen (18). (Civil Code, Section 29).

Trust-Writing Requirements: A trust holding real estate must be in writing. (Civil Code, Section 2440).

Trustee Bond Requirements: Yes, unless not required by trust. (Revised Statutes, Section 9:2157).

Trustee Pour-Over to Will: The trust must be identified in the will. The terms of the trust must be in a document other than the will and signed before or at the same time as the will and with the same formalities as required for a will in Louisiana. (Revised Statutes, Sections 9:1733 & 9:1751).

Spouse's Right to Property Regardless of Will: The Louisiana Civil Code provisions regarding this matter are detailed and should be consulted directly.

Laws of Intestate Succession (Distribution If Decedent Leaves No Will):

Spouse and children of spouse surviving: All community property to descendants per stirpes. However, the spouse has the right to use the property until remarried. All separate property to children equally or to grandchildren per stirpes.

Spouse and children not of spouse surviving: Same as above for "Spouse and children of spouse surviving."

Spouse, but no children or parent(s) surviving: All community property to spouse. All separate property to brothers and sisters or to their children per stirpes; or if none, to parents; or if none, all to spouse.

Spouse and parent(s), but no children surviving: All community property to spouse. All separate property to brothers and sisters or their children per stirpes; or if none, to parents; or if none, all to spouse.

Children, but no spouse surviving: All to children equally or to their children per stirpes.

Parent(s), but no spouse or children surviving: All to parents equally or to the surviving parent.

No spouse, children, or parent(s) surviving: To brothers and sisters equally or their children per stirpes; or if none, to next of kin. (Civil Code, Sections 880–991).

Property Ownership. Community property state. Joint ownership is presumed if two or more persons are listed as owners. No tenancy-by-entirety or tenancy-in-common. Joint bank account deposits are payable to any survivor. (Revised Statutes, Sections 6:1255; Civil Code, Sections 2334 & 2345).

State Gift, Inheritance, or Estate Taxes: Imposes a state gift tax; imposes an inheritance tax of up to 10 percent; imposes a state estate tax equal to federal credit for state death taxes less any amounts paid on state inheritance tax. Maximum total state inheritance and state estate tax is equal to the maximum allowable federal estate tax credit for state death taxes. (Revised Statutes, Sections 47:2403 & 47:2432).

Maine

State Law Reference: Maine Revised Statutes Annotated, Title 18A, Sections 1-101+, 2-501+, and 3-101+.

State Website: http://janus.state.me.us/legis/statutes/

Uniform Acts Adopted:

Uniform Probate Code: (Sections 18A, 1-101+).

Uniform Testamentary Additions to Trusts Act: (Section 18A, 2-511).

Uniform Gifts to Minors Act: (Sections 33, 1651+).

Uniform Trustees' Powers Act: (Sections 18A, 7-401+).

Trustee Residency Requirements: Out-of-state trustee must qualify to do business in Maine. (Section 18A, 7-105).

Minimum Age for Grantor or Trustee: Eighteen (18). (Section 1, 1-72).

Trust-Writing Requirements: A trust holding real estate must be in writing. (Section 33, 851).

Trustee Bond Requirements: None, unless required by trust, requested by beneficiary, or ordered by court. (Section 18A, 7-304).

Trustee Pour-Over to Will: The trust must be identified in the will. The terms of the trust must be in a document other than the will and signed before or at the same time as the will. (Section 18A, 2-511).

Spouse's Right to Property Regardless of Will: The surviving spouse is entitled to 1/3 of the entire estate of the deceased spouse. (Section 18A, 2-201).

Laws of Intestate Succession (Distribution If Decedent Leaves No Will):

Spouse and children of spouse surviving: $50,000.00 and 1/2 of balance to spouse and 1/2 of balance to children or grandchildren per capita at each generation.

Spouse and children not of spouse surviving: 1/2 to spouse and 1/2 to children or grandchildren per capita at each generation.

Spouse, but no children or parent(s) surviving: All to spouse.

Spouse and parent(s), but no children surviving: $50,000.00 and 1/2 of balance to spouse and 1/2 of balance to parents or surviving parent.

Children, but no spouse surviving: All to children equally or to their children per capita at each generation.

Parent(s), but no spouse or children surviving: All to parents equally or to the surviving parent.

No spouse, children, or parent(s) surviving: All to children of parents per capita; or if none, then 1/2 to paternal grandparents or their children per capita and 1/2 to maternal grandparents or their children per capita. (Sections 18A, 2-102 & 18A, 2-103).

Property Ownership: Common-law state. Ownership by two (2) or more is presumed to be a tenancy-in-common unless joint tenancy is stated. Tenancy-by-entirety not recognized. Joint bank account deposits are payable to any survivor. (Sections 33-159 & 33-160).

State Gift, Inheritance, or Estate Taxes: No gift tax; no inheritance tax; imposes state estate tax equal to federal credit for state death taxes. (Section 18A, 3-916).

Additional Requirements: Residents should register a "Registration of Living Trust" form with the local court in their county of residence. This requirement is mandatory, although there are no penalties or consequences for failure to register. Please see proper form in Chapter 7.

Maryland

State Law Reference: Maryland Code; Estates and Trusts, Sections 14-101+ and Title 3, Sections 3-101+.

State Website: http://mgasearch.state.md.us/verity.asp

Uniform Acts Adopted:

Uniform Gifts to Minors Act: (Estates and Trusts, Sections 13-301+).

Uniform Trustees' Powers Act: (Estates and Trusts, Sections 15-101 & 15-102).

Trustee Residency Requirements: No provision.

Minimum Age for Grantor or Trustee: Eighteen (18). (Contracts, Section 1-103).

Trust-Writing Requirements: A trust holding real estate must be in writing. (Real Property, Section 5-105).

Trustee Bond Requirements: None.

Trustee Pour-Over to Will: The trust must be identified in the will. The terms of the trust must be in a document other than the will and signed before or at the same time as the will. (Estates and Trusts, Sections 4-411 & 4-412).

Spouse's Right to Property Regardless of Will: Generally, the surviving spouse is entitled to 1/2 of the deceased spouse's estate if there are no children, and only 1/3 if there are children. However, please refer directly to the statute for details. (Estates and Trusts, Section 3-203).

Laws of Intestate Succession (Distribution If Decedent Leaves No Will):

Spouse and children of spouse surviving: If any surviving children are minors, 1/2 to spouse and 1/2 to children equally or grandchildren per stirpes; if no surviving children are minors, $15,000.00 and 1/2 of balance to spouse and 1/2 of balance to children equally or grandchildren per stirpes.

Spouse and children not of spouse surviving: Same as above for "Spouse and children of spouse surviving."

Spouse, but no children or parent(s) surviving: All to spouse.

Spouse and parent(s), but no children surviving: First $15,000.00 to spouses and then 1/2 to spouse and 1/2 to parents or surviving parent.

Children, but no spouse surviving: All to children or to their children per stirpes.

Parent(s), but no spouse or children surviving: All to parents equally or to the surviving parent.

No spouse, children, or parent(s) surviving: All to brothers and sisters equally or to their children per stirpes; or if none, 1/2 to paternal grandparents and 1/2 to maternal grandparents and their next of kin. (Estates and Trusts, Sections 3-102–3-104).

Property Ownership: Common-law state. Tenancy-in-common is recognized. Joint tenancy must be stated. Joint ownership by spouses is presumed to be a tenancy-by-entirety unless stated otherwise. Joint bank accounts are payable to any survivor. (Financial Institutions 1-204; Real Property 2-117 & 4-108).

State Gift, Inheritance, or Estate Taxes: No gift tax; imposes an inheritance tax of up to 10 percent; imposes state estate tax equal to federal credit for state death taxes less any amounts paid on state inheritance tax. Maximum total state inheritance and state estate tax is equal to the maximum allowable federal estate tax credit for state death taxes. (Tax, Sections 7-204 & 7-304).

Massachusetts

State Law Reference: Massachusetts General Laws; Chapter 191, Sections 1+ and Chapter 203, Sections 1+.

State Website: http://www.lawlib.state.ma.us/cmr.html

Uniform Acts Adopted:

Uniform Testamentary Additions to Trusts Act: (Chapter 203, Section 3B).

Uniform Gifts to Minors Act: (Chapter 201A, Sections 1+).

Uniform Trustees' Powers Act: (Chapter 184B, Section 2).

Trustee Residency Requirements: If out-of-state trustee is appointed and trust holds Massachusetts land, trust must be registered. (Chapter 203, Section 10).

Minimum Age for Grantor or Trustee: Eighteen (18). (Chapter 231, Section 850).

Trust-Writing Requirements: A trust holding real estate must be in writing. (Chapter 203, Section 1).

Trustee Bond Requirements: None, unless required by trust. (Chapter 205, Section 5).

Trustee Pour-Over to Will: The trust must be identified in the will. The terms of the trust must be in a document other than the will and signed be fore or at the same time as the will. (Chapter 203, Section 3B).

Spouse's Right to Property Regardless of Will: Generally, the surviving spouse is entitled to $25,000.00 and 1/2 of the deceased spouse's remaining estate if there are no children, and only 1/3 if there are children. However, please refer directly to the statute as the provisions are detailed. (Chapter 191, Section 15).

Laws of Intestate Succession (Distribution If Decedent Leaves No Will):

Spouse and children of spouse surviving: 1/2 to spouse and 1/2 to children equally or grand-children per stirpes.

Spouse and children not of spouse surviving: 1/2 to spouse and 1/2 to children equally or grandchildren per stirpes.

Spouse, but no children or parent(s) surviving: $200,000.00 and 1/2 of balance to spouse and 1/2 of balance to brothers and sisters equally or their children per stirpes; or if none, to next of kin; or if none, all to spouse.

Spouse and parent(s), but no children surviving: $200,000.00 and 1/2 of balance to spouse and 1/2 of balance to parents equally or the surviving parent.

Children, but no spouse surviving: All to children equally or to their children per stirpes.

Parent(s), but no spouse or children surviving: All to parents equally or to the surviving parent.

No spouse, children, or parent(s) surviving: All to brothers and sisters equally or their children per stirpes; or if none, to the next of kin. (Chapter 190, Section 1).

Property Ownership: Common-law state. Tenancy-in-common, joint tenancy, and tenancy-by-entirety are recognized. Joint ownership by husband and wife creates a tenancy-in-common, unless otherwise stated. Joint bank account deposits are payable to any survivor. (Chapter 184, Section 7; Chapter 201E, Section 301).

State Gift, Inheritance, or Estate Taxes: No gift tax; no inheritance tax; imposes state estate tax of up to 16 percent (not tied to federal estate tax credit).

Michigan

State Law Reference: Michigan Compiled Laws Annotated; Sections 600.801+ and 700.1101+.

State Website: http://MichiganLegislature.org

Uniform Acts Adopted:

Uniform Probate Code: (Sections 720-1-101+).

Trustee Residency Requirements: Out-of-state trustee must qualify to do business in Michigan. (Section 700.7105).

Minimum Age for Grantor or Trustee: Eighteen (18). (Section 722.522).

Trust-Writing Requirements: Yes. (Section 566.106).

Trustee Bond Requirements: None, unless required by trust, requested by beneficiary, or re-quired by court. (Section 700.7304).

Trustee Pour-Over to Will: The trust must be identified in the will. The terms of the trust must be in a document other than the will and signed before or at the same time as the will. (Sections 555.461–555.464).

Spouse's Right to Property Regardless of Will: Generally, the surviving spouse is entitled to 1/2 of the deceased spouse's estate if there are no children, and only 1/3 if there are children. However, please refer directly to the statute as the provisions are detailed. (Sections 700.2102–700.2103, & 700.2201).

Laws of Intestate Succession (Distribution If Decedent Leaves No Will):

Spouse and children of spouse surviving: $60,000.00 and 1/2 of balance to spouse and 1/2 of balance to children per stirpes.

Spouse and children not of spouse surviving: 1/2 to spouse and 1/2 to children per stirpes.

Spouse, but no children or parent(s) surviving: All to spouse.

Spouse and parent(s), but no children surviving: $60,000.00 and 1/2 of balance to spouse and 1/2 of balance to parents or surviving parent.

Children, but no spouse surviving: All to children or to their children per stirpes.

Parent(s), but no spouse or children surviving: All to parents equally or to the surviving parent.

No spouse, children, or parent(s) surviving: All to brothers and sisters equally or to their children per stirpes; or if none, 1/2 to maternal grandparents or their children per stirpes and 1/2 to paternal grandparents or their children per stirpes. (Section 700.2101).

Property Ownership: Common-law state. Tenancy-in-common, joint tenancy, and tenancy-by-entirety are recognized. Joint tenancy created only if stated. Joint tenancy by spouses and joint ownership of real estate by spouses is presumed to be a tenancy-by-entirety unless otherwise stated. Joint tenancy with right of survivorship must be in writing. Joint bank account deposits are payable to any survivor. (Sections 554.44, 554.45, & 557.101).

State Gift, Inheritance, or Estate Taxes: No gift tax; imposes an inheritance tax of up to 17 percent; imposes state estate tax equal to federal credit for state death taxes less any amounts paid on state inheritance tax. Maximum total state inheritance and state estate tax is equal to the maximum allowable federal estate tax credit for state death taxes. (Sections 720.11–720.21).

Additional Requirements: Residents should register a "Registration of Living Trust" form with the local court in their county of residence. This requirement is mandatory, although there are no penalties or consequences for failure to register. Please see proper form in Chapter 7. (Section 700.7101).

Minnesota

State Law Reference: Minnesota Statutes Annotated; Chapters 501B.09+ and 524.1-101+.

State Website: http://www.leg.state.mn.us/leg/statutes.htm

Uniform Acts Adopted:

Uniform Probate Code: (Sections 524.1-101+).

Uniform Trustees' Powers Act: (Section 501B.81).

Uniform Testamentary Additions to Trusts Act: (Section 525.223).

Uniform Gifts to Minors Act: (Sections 527.21+).

Trustee Residency Requirements: No, unless in trust. (Section 524.3-913).

Minimum Age for Grantor or Trustee: Eighteen (18). (Section 645.451).

Trust-Writing Requirements: Yes. (Section 513.03).

Trustee Bond Requirements: No provision.

Trustee Pour-Over to Will: The trust must be identified in the will. The terms of the trust must be in a document other than the will and signed before or at the same time as the will. (Section 524.2-511).

Spouse's Right to Property Regardless of Will: The elective share amount is dependent on length of marriage. (Sections 524.2-201 & 524.2-202).

Laws of Intestate Succession (Distribution If Decedent Leaves No Will):

Spouse and children of spouse surviving: $70,000.00 and 1/2 of balance to spouse and 1/2 of balance to children or grandchildren per stirpes.

Spouse and children not of spouse surviving: 1/2 to spouse and 1/2 to children or grandchildren per stirpes.

Spouse, but no children surviving: All to spouse.

Spouse and parent(s), but no children surviving: 1/2 to spouse and 1/2 to parents.

Children, but no spouse surviving: All to children equally or to their children per stirpes.

Parent(s), but no spouse or children surviving: All to parents equally or to the surviving parent.

No spouse, children, or parent(s) surviving: All to brothers and sisters equally or their children per stirpes; or if none, to the next of kin. (Sections 524.2-102 & 524.2-103).

Property Ownership: Common-law state. Tenancy-in-common is presumed unless joint tenancy in writing. Tenancy-by-entirety not recognized. Joint bank account deposits are payable to any survivor unless clear evidence exists that deposit is payable only to specified survivor. (Sections 500.19 & 524.6-203).

State Gift, Inheritance, or Estate Taxes: No gift tax; no inheritance tax; imposes state estate tax equal to federal credit for state death taxes. (Section 291.03).

Mississippi

State Law Reference: Mississippi Code Annotated; Title 91, Chapters 1-1+.

State Website: http://www.mscode.com/

Uniform Acts Adopted:

Uniform Trustees' Powers Act: (Sections 91-9-101+).

Uniform Testamentary Additions to Trusts Act: (Section 91-5-11).

Uniform Gifts to Minors Act: (Sections 91-20-1+).

Trustee Residency Requirements: Out-of-state trustee must qualify to do business in Mississippi.

Minimum Age for Grantor or Trustee: Eighteen (18). (Section 645.451).

Trust-Writing Requirements: Yes. (Section 91-9-1).

Trustee Bond Requirements: None, unless required by trust.

Trustee Pour-Over to Will: The trust must be identified in the will. The terms of the trust must be in a document other than the will and signed before or at the same time as the will. (Section 91-5-11).

Spouse's Right to Property Regardless of Will: Generally, the surviving spouse is entitled to 1/2 of the deceased spouse's estate if there are no children, and only 1/3 if there are children. However, please refer directly to the statute as the provisions are detailed. (Sections 91-5-25 & 91-5-27).

Laws of Intestate Succession (Distribution If Decedent Leaves No Will):

Spouse and children of spouse surviving: Spouse and any surviving children or grandchildren each take equal shares.

Spouse and children not of spouse surviving: Spouse and any surviving children or grandchildren each take equal shares.

Spouse, but no children or parent(s) surviving: All to spouse.

Spouse and parent(s), but no children surviving: All to spouse.

Children, but no spouse surviving: All to children equally or to their children per stirpes.

Parent(s), but no spouse or children surviving: All to parents, brothers, and sisters equally, or to children of brothers and sisters per stirpes. If no brothers or sisters or children of brothers or sisters, all to parents equally or the surviving parent.

No spouse, children, or parent(s) surviving: All to brothers and sisters equally, or to their children per stirpes; or if none, to grandparents, uncles, and aunts equally, or to their children per stirpes; or if none, to the next of kin. (Sections 91-1-3, 91-1-7, & 91-1-11).

Property Ownership: Common-law state. Tenancy-in-common, joint tenancy and tenancy-by-entirety are recognized. Ownership by two (2) or more persons is presumed to be tenancy-in-common unless joint tenancy is stated. Joint bank account deposits are payable to any survivor. (Section 89-1-7).

State Gift, Inheritance, or Estate Taxes: No gift tax; no inheritance tax; imposes state estate tax of up to 16 percent. State estate tax not tied to federal credit for state death taxes. (Section 27-9-5).

Missouri

State Law Reference: Missouri Annotated Statutes; Sections 456.010+, 472.005+, and 474.010+.
State Website: http://www.moga.state.mo.us/homestat.htm
Uniform Acts Adopted:
>   Uniform Trustees' Powers Act: (Section 456.520).
>   Uniform Gifts to Minors Act: (Sections 404.005+).

Trustee Residency Requirements: Out-of-state trustee must qualify to do business in Missouri.
Minimum Age for Grantor or Trustee: Eighteen (18). (Section 431.055).
Trust-Writing Requirements: A trust holding real estate must be in writing. (Section 456.010).
Trustee Bond Requirements: Yes, unless not required by trust, or court. (Section 456.130).
Trustee Pour-Over to Will: The trust must be identified in the will. The terms of the trust must be in a document other than the will and signed before or at the same time as the will. (Section 456.232).
Spouse's Right to Property Regardless of Will: Generally, the surviving spouse is entitled to 1/2 of the deceased spouse's estate if there are no children, and only 1/3 if there are children. However, please refer directly to the statute as the provisions are detailed. (Section 474.160).
Laws of Intestate Succession (Distribution If Decedent Leaves No Will):
>   *Spouse and children of spouse surviving*: $20,000.00 and 1/2 of balance to spouse and 1/2 of balance to children or grandchildren per stirpes.
>   *Spouse and children not of spouse surviving*: 1/2 to spouse and 1/2 to children or grandchildren per stirpes.
>   *Spouse, but no children or parent(s) surviving*: All to spouse.
>   *Spouse and parent(s), but no children surviving*: All to spouse.
>   *Children, but no spouse surviving*: All to children equally or to their children per stirpes.
>   *Parent(s), but no spouse or children surviving*: All to parents, brothers, and sisters equally, or to their children per stirpes; or if none, all to parents or to the surviving parent.
>   *No spouse, children, or parent(s) surviving*: All to brothers and sisters equally or to their children per stirpes; or if none, to grandparents, uncles, and aunts and their children per stirpes; or if none, to the nearest lineal ancestor and their children. (Section 474.010).

Property Ownership: Common-law state. Tenancy common, joint tenancy and tenancy-by-entirety are recognized. Ownership by two (2) or more persons is presumed to be a tenancy-in-common unless joint tenancy is stated. Joint bank account deposits are payable to any survivor. (Sections 442.025, 442.030, & 442.035).
State Gift, Inheritance, or Estate Taxes: No gift tax; no inheritance tax; imposes state estate tax equal to federal credit for state death taxes. (Section 145.011).
Additional Requirements: Residents should register a "Registration of Living Trust" form with the local court in their county of residence. This requirement is mandatory, although there are no penalties or consequences for failure to register. Please see proper form in Chapter 7.

Montana

State Law Reference: Montana Code Annotated; Section 72, Titles 1-101+.
State Website: http://leg.state.mt.us/services/legal/laws.htm
Uniform Acts Adopted:
>   Uniform Probate Code: (Sections 72-1-101+).
>   Uniform Trustees' Powers Act: (Sections 72-34-301+).
>   Uniform Testamentary Additions to Trusts Act: (Sections 72-2-531+).
>   Uniform Gifts to Minors Act: (Sections 72-26-501+).

Trustee Residency Requirements: Out-of-state trustee must qualify to do business in Montana.
Minimum Age for Grantor or Trustee: Eighteen (18). (Section 431.055).

Trust-Writing Requirements: Yes. (Section 72-33-208).

Trustee Bond Requirements: None, unless required by trust or court. (Section 72-33-603).

Trustee Pour-Over to Will: The trust must be identified in the will. The terms of the trust must be in a document other than the will and signed before or at the same time as the will. (Section 72-2-531).

Spouse's Right to Property Regardless of Will: The surviving spouse is entitled to 1/3 of the "augmented" estate of the deceased spouse. In general, the "augmented" estate includes both the property that passes under the will and any other property that passes by other "non-will" transfers, such as under the terms of a living trust or a joint tenancy arrangement. (Section 72-2-221).

Laws of Intestate Succession (Distribution If Decedent Leaves No Will):

Spouse and children of spouse surviving: All to spouse.

Spouse and children not of spouse surviving: If one (1) child surviving, 1/2 to spouse and 1/2 to child; if more than one (1) child surviving, 1/3 to spouse and 2/3 to children equally.

Spouse, but no children or parent(s) surviving: All to spouse.

Spouse and parent(s), but no children surviving: All to spouse.

Children, but no spouse surviving: All to children equally or to their children per stirpes.

Parent(s), but no spouse or children surviving: All to parents equally or to the surviving parent.

No spouse, children, or parent(s) surviving: All to brothers and sisters equally or their children per stirpes; or if none, 1/2 to paternal and 1/2 to maternal grandparents or their children per stirpes. (Sections 72-2-112 & 72-2-113).

Property Ownership: Common-law state. Tenancy-in-common and joint tenancy (called interests in common and joint interests) are recognized. No tenancy-by-entirety is recognized in personal property. Tenancy-in-common is presumed unless joint tenancy stated. Joint bank account deposits are payable to any survivor. (Sections 40-2-105 & 70-1-310).

State Gift, Inheritance, or Estate Taxes: No gift tax; imposes an inheritance tax of up to 16 percent; imposes state estate tax equal to federal credit for state death taxes less any amounts paid on state inheritance tax. Maximum total state inheritance and state estate tax is equal to the maximum allowable federal estate tax credit for state death taxes. (Section 72-16-904).

Nebraska

State Law Reference: Revised Statutes of Nebraska; Chapter 30, Sections 2201+ and 2326+.

State Website: http://www.unicam.state.ne.us/laws

Uniform Acts Adopted:

Uniform Probate Code: (Section 30-2201).

Uniform Testamentary Additions to Trusts Act: (Sections 30-2336+).

Uniform Trustees' Powers Act: (Sections 30-2819+).

Uniform Gifts to Minors Act: (Sections 43-2701+).

Trustee Residency Requirements: Out-of-state trustee must qualify to do business in Nebraska. (Section 30-2805).

Minimum Age for Grantor or Trustee: Eighteen (18). (Section 19-43-2101).

Trust-Writing Requirements: A trust holding real estate must be in writing. (Section 36-103).

Trustee Bond Requirements: None, unless required by trust, requested by beneficiary, or court order. (Section 30-2815).

Trustee Pour-Over to Will: The trust must be identified in the will. The terms of the trust must be in a document other than the will and signed before or at the same time as the will. (Section 30-2336).

Spouse's Right to Property Regardless of Will: The surviving spouse is entitled to 1/2 of the "augmented" estate of the deceased spouse. In general, the "augmented" estate includes both the property that passes under the will and any other property that passes by other "non-will" transfers, such as under the terms of a living trust or a joint tenancy arrangement. (Section 30-2313).

Laws of Intestate Succession (Distribution If Decedent Leaves No Will):

Spouse and children of spouse surviving: $50,000.00 and 1/2 of balance to spouse and 1/2 of balance to children.

Spouse and children not of spouse surviving: 1/2 to spouse and 1/2 to children.

Spouse, but no children or parent(s) surviving: All to spouse.

Spouse and parent(s), but no children surviving: $50,000.00 and 1/2 of balance to spouse and 1/2 of balance to parents or surviving parent.

Children, but no spouse surviving: All to children equally or to their children per stirpes.

Parent(s), but no spouse or children surviving: All to parents equally or to the surviving parent.

No spouse, children, or parent(s) surviving: All to brothers and sisters equally, or their children per stirpes; or if none, 1/2 to paternal and 1/2 to maternal grandparents or their children per stirpes. (Sections 30-2302 & 30-2303).

Property Ownership: Common-law state. Tenancy-in-common and joint tenancy are recognized. Tenancy-by-entirety is not recognized. Joint bank account deposits are payable to any survivor unless clear evidence exists that deposit is payable only to specified survivor. (Section 76-118).

State Gift, Inheritance, or Estate Taxes: No gift tax; imposes an inheritance tax of up to 18 percent; imposes state estate tax equal to federal credit for state death taxes less any amounts paid on state inheritance tax. Maximum total state inheritance and state estate tax is equal to the maximum allowable federal estate tax credit for state death taxes. (Sections 77-2001–77-2006 & 77-2101.01).

Additional Requirements: Residents should register a "Registration of Living Trust" form with the local court in their county of residence. This requirement is mandatory, although there are no penalties or consequences for failure to register. Please see proper form in Chapter 7.

Nevada

State Law Reference: Nevada Revised Statutes Annotated; Chapters 133.000–150.999, 163.010, & 164.010.

State Website: http://www.leg.state.nv.us/law1.cfm

Uniform Acts Adopted:

Uniform Testamentary Additions to Trusts Act: (Sections 136-220+).

Uniform Trustees' Powers Act: (Sections 163.260+).

Uniform Gifts to Minors Act: (Sections 167.010+).

Trustee Residency Requirements: No provision.

Minimum Age for Grantor or Trustee: Eighteen (18). (Section 129.010).

Trust-Writing Requirements: A trust holding real estate must be in writing. (Section 111.235).

Trustee Bond Requirements: None, unless required by trust or ordered by court. (Section 153.120).

Trustee Pour-Over to Will: Trust must be identified in the will. Terms of the trust must be in a document other than the will and signed before or at the same time as the will. (Sections 163.220–163.250).

Spouse's Right to Property Regardless of Will: Community property right to 1/2 of the deceased spouse's "community" property. (Section 123.250).

Laws of Intestate Succession (Distribution If Decedent Leaves No Will):

Spouse and children of spouse surviving: All of decedent's community property to spouse. If only one (1) child is surviving, 1/2 of decedent's separate property to spouse and 1/2 to child or grandchildren per stirpes; if more than one (1) child is surviving, 1/3 of separate property to spouse and 2/3 to the children or grandchildren per stirpes.

Spouse and children not of spouse surviving: Same as above for "Spouse and children of spouse surviving."

Spouse, but no children or parent(s) surviving: All of decedent's community property to spouse. 1/2 of decedent's separate property to spouse and 1/2 to brothers and sisters equally or their children per stirpes; or if none, all to spouse.

Spouse and parent(s), but no children surviving: All of decedent's community property to spouse. 1/2 of decedent's separate property to spouse and 1/2 to parents or surviving parent.

Children, but no spouse surviving: All to children or to their children per stirpes.

Parent(s), but no spouse or children surviving: All to parents equally or to the surviving parent.

No spouse, children, or parent(s) surviving: All to brothers and sisters equally, or their children per stirpes; or if none, to the next of kin. (Sections 134.040 & 134.050).

Property Ownership: Community property state. Tenancy-in-common, joint tenancy, and community property are recognized. Tenancy-by-entirety is not recognized. Joint bank account deposits are payable to any survivor. (Sections 111.060 & 111.065).

State Gift, Inheritance, or Estate Taxes: No gift tax; no inheritance tax; no state estate tax.

New Hampshire

State Law Reference: New Hampshire Revised Statutes; Chapters 547:1+, 551:1+, and 564.

State Website: http://sudoc.nhsl.lib.nh.us/rsa/

Uniform Acts Adopted:

Uniform Trustees' Powers Act: (Sections 564-A:1+).

Uniform Testamentary Additions to Trusts Act: (Sections 563-A:1+).

Uniform Gifts to Minors Act: (Sections 463-A:1+).

Trustee Residency Requirements: If out-of-state trustee is appointed, a resident agent must also be appointed.

Minimum Age for Grantor or Trustee: Eighteen (18). (Section 21-B:1).

Trust-Writing Requirements: A trust holding real estate must be in writing. (Section 477:17).

Trustee Bond Requirements: None, unless required by trust or ordered by court. (Section 553:15).

Trustee Pour-Over to Will: The trust must be identified in the will. The terms of the trust must be in a document other than the will and signed before or at the same time as the will. (Sections 563-A:1 & 563-A:4).

Spouse's Right to Property Regardless of Will: Generally, the surviving spouse is entitled to 1/2 of the deceased spouse's estate if there are no children, and only 1/3 if there are children. However, please refer directly to the statute as the provisions are detailed. (Section 560:10).

Laws of Intestate Succession (Distribution If Decedent Leaves No Will):

Spouse and children of spouse surviving: $50,000.00 and 1/2 of balance to spouse and 1/2 of balance to children or grandchildren per stirpes.

Spouse and children not of spouse surviving: 1/2 to spouse and 1/2 to children or grandchildren per stirpes.

Spouse, but no children or parent(s) surviving: All to spouse.

Spouse and parent(s), but no children surviving: $50,000.00 and 1/2 of balance to spouse and 1/2 of balance to parents or surviving parent.

Children, but no spouse surviving: All to children or to their children per stirpes.

Parent(s), but no spouse or children surviving: All to parents equally or to the surviving parent.

No spouse, children, or parent(s) surviving: All to brothers and sisters equally, or their children per stirpes; or if none, 1/2 to maternal and 1/2 to paternal grandparents or their children per stirpes. (Section 561:1).

Property Ownership: Common-law state. Tenancy-in-common is presumed unless joint tenancy stated. Ownership by spouses creates joint tenancy. Tenancy-by-entirety is not recognized. Joint bank account deposits are payable to any survivor. (Sections 477:18 & 477:19).

State Gift, Inheritance, or Estate Taxes: No gift tax; imposes an inheritance tax of up to 15 percent; imposes state estate tax equal to federal credit for state death taxes less any amounts paid on state inheritance tax. Maximum total state inheritance and state estate tax is equal to the maximum allowable federal estate tax credit for state death taxes. (Sections 86:01–89).

New Jersey

State Law Reference: New Jersey Revised Statutes; Title 3B: Chapters 3-1+ and 11-1.
State Website: http://www.njleg.state.nj.us/
Uniform Acts Adopted:
    Uniform Probate Code: (Sections 3B:3-1+).
    Uniform Testamentary Additions to Trusts Act: (Sections 3B:4-1+).
    Uniform Trustees' Powers Act: (Section 3B:14-23).
    Uniform Gifts to Minors Act: (Sections 46:38A-1+).
Trustee Residency Requirements: None.
Minimum Age for Grantor or Trustee: Eighteen (18). (Section 9:17B-4).
Trust-Writing Requirements: A trust holding real estate must be in writing. (Section 25:1-11).
Trustee Bond Requirements: Yes, if the trustee is not the appointed trustee, the trust requires it, or court orders it. (Section 3B:15-1).
Trustee Pour-Over to Will: The trust must be identified in the will. The terms of the trust must be in a document other than the will and signed before or at the same time as the will. (Sections 3B: 4-1–3B:4-6).
Spouse's Right to Property Regardless of Will: The surviving spouse is entitled to 1/3 of the "augmented" estate of the deceased spouse. In general, the "augmented" estate includes both the property that passes under the will and any other property that passes by other "non-will" transfers, such as under the terms of a living trust or a joint tenancy arrangement. (Section 3B:8-1).
Laws of Intestate Succession (Distribution If Decedent Leaves No Will):
Spouse and children of spouse surviving: $50,000.00 and 1/2 of balance to spouse and 1/2 of balance to children or grandchildren per stirpes.
Spouse and children not of spouse surviving: 1/2 to spouse and 1/2 to children or grandchildren per stirpes.
Spouse, but no children or parent(s) surviving: All to spouse.
Spouse and parent(s), but no children surviving: $50,000.00 and 1/2 of balance to spouse and 1/2 of balance to parents or surviving parent.
Children, but no spouse surviving: All to children or to their children per stirpes.
Parent(s), but no spouse or children surviving: All to parents equally or to the surviving parent.
No spouse, children, or parent(s) surviving: All to brothers and sisters equally, or their children per stirpes; or if none, 1/2 to maternal and 1/2 to paternal grandparents or their children per stirpes. (Sections 3B:5-3 & 3B:5-4).
Property Ownership: Common-law state. Tenancy-in-common, joint tenancy, and tenancy-by-entirety are recognized. Ownership by spouses is presumed to be a tenancy-by-entirety unless stated otherwise. Tenancy-in-common is presumed unless joint tenancy stated. Joint bank account deposits are payable to any survivor. (Sections 46:3-17, 46:3-17.1, & 46:3-17.2).
State Gift, Inheritance, or Estate Taxes: No gift tax; imposes an inheritance tax of up to 16 percent; imposes state estate tax equal to federal credit for state death taxes less any amounts paid on state inheritance tax. Maximum total state inheritance and state estate tax is equal to the maximum allowable federal estate tax credit for state death taxes. (Sections 54:34-2 & 54:38-1).

New Mexico

State Law Reference: New Mexico Statutes Annotated; Sections 45-2-101+ and 46-2-1+.
State Website: http://legis.state.nm.us
Uniform Acts Adopted:
    Uniform Probate Code: (Sections 45-1-101+).
    Uniform Trustees' Powers Act: (Section 45-7-401).
    Uniform Testamentary Additions to Trusts Act: (Sections 45-2-511+)
    Uniform Gifts to Minors Act: (Sections 46-7-11+).
Trustee Residency Requirements: None.
Minimum Age for Grantor or Trustee: Eighteen (18). (Section 28-6-1).
Trust-Writing Requirements: A trust holding real estate must be in writing, requested by beneficiaries, or court order. (Section 45-7-304).
Trustee Bond Requirements: None, unless required by trust.
Trustee Pour-Over to Will: The trust must be identified in the will. The terms of the trust must be in a document other than the will and signed before or at the same time as the will. (Section 46-5-2).
Spouse's Right to Property Regardless of Will: Community property right to 1/2 of the deceased spouse's "community" property. (Section 45-2-805).
Laws of Intestate Succession (Distribution If Decedent Leaves No Will):
Spouse and children of spouse surviving: All of decedent's community property to spouse. 1/4 of decedent's separate property to spouse and 3/4 to children or grandchildren per stirpes.
Spouse and children not of spouse surviving: All of decedent's community property to spouse. 1/4 of decedent's separate property to spouse and 3/4 to children or grandchildren per stirpes.
Spouse, but no children or parent(s) surviving: All to spouse.
Spouse and parent(s), but no children surviving: All to spouse.
Children, but no spouse surviving: All to children equally or to their children per stirpes.
Parent(s), but no spouse or children surviving: All to parents equally or to the surviving parent.
No spouse, children, or parent(s) surviving: All to brothers and sisters equally, or their children per stirpes; or if none, 1/2 to maternal and 1/2 to paternal grandparents or their children per stirpes. (Sections 45-2-102 & 45-2-103).
Property Ownership: Community property state. Tenancy-in-common, joint tenancy, and community property are recognized. Spouses may hold real estate as joint tenants. Tenancy-by-entirety is not recognized. Joint bank account deposits are payable to any survivor unless clear evidence exists that deposit is payable only to specified survivor. (Section 47-1-15).
State Gift, Inheritance, or Estate Taxes: No gift tax; no inheritance tax; imposes state estate tax equal to federal credit for state death taxes. (Sections 7-7-3 & 7-7-4).

New York

State Law Reference: New York Consolidated Laws; Estates, Powers, and Trusts. Article 11, Sections 1.1+ and 3-1.1+.
State Website: http://assembly.state.ny.us/leg/?ul=0
Uniform Acts Adopted:
    Uniform Testamentary Additions to Trusts Act: (Sections 3.1-7+).
    Uniform Trustees' Powers Act: (Section 11-1.1).
    Uniform Gifts to Minors Act: (Sections 7-6.1+).
Trustee Residency Requirements: None.
Minimum Age for Grantor or Trustee: Eighteen (18). (Section 2.10).
Trust-Writing Requirements: Yes. (Section 13-2.1).

Trustee Bond Requirements: None, unless required by trust.

Trustee Pour-Over to Will: The trust must be identified in the will. The terms of the trust must be in a document other than the will and signed before or at the same time as the will. (Section 3-3.7).

Spouse's Right to Property Regardless of Will: Generally, the surviving spouse is entitled to $50,000.00 or 1/3 of the deceased spouse's estate. However, please refer directly to the statute as the provisions are detailed. (Section 5-1.1-A).

Laws of Intestate Succession (Distribution If Decedent Leaves No Will):

Spouse and children of spouse surviving: $50,000.00 and 1/2 of balance to spouse and 1/2 of balance to children or grandchildren per stirpes.

Spouse and children not of spouse surviving: Same as above for "Spouse and children of spouse surviving."

Spouse, but no children or parent(s) surviving: All to spouse.

Spouse and parent(s), but no children surviving: All to spouse.

Children, but no spouse surviving: All to children equally or to their children per stirpes.

Parent(s), but no spouse or children surviving: All to parents equally or to the surviving parent.

No spouse, children, or parent(s) surviving: All to brothers and sisters equally, or their children per stirpes; or if none, to grandparents equally or their children per capita; or if none, to the next of kin. (Section 4-1.1).

Property Ownership: Common-law state. Tenancy-in-common, joint tenancy, and tenancy-by-entirety are recognized, however, tenancy-by-entirety in personal property is not recognized. Joint ownership by spouses is presumed to be a tenancy-by-entirety unless specified otherwise. Tenancy-in-common is presumed unless joint tenancy is stated. Joint bank account deposits are payable to any survivor. (Real Property, Section 240b).

State Gift, Inheritance, or Estate Taxes: Imposes gift tax; no inheritance tax; state estate tax of up to 21 percent or not less than any federal credit for state death taxes. (Tax, Sections 249-a, 1001, & 1002).

Additional Requirements: Residents of New York will need to prepare a "Notice of Assignment Property to Living Trust." Please see proper form in Chapter 7.

North Carolina

State Law Reference: North Carolina General Statutes; Chapters 28A-1+, 31-1+, 32, 36a, and 47-1+.

State Website: http://www.ncga.state.nc.us/

Uniform Acts Adopted:

Uniform Testamentary Additions to Trusts Act: (Section 31-47).

Uniform Trustees' Powers Act: (Sections 32-25+).

Uniform Gifts to Minors Act: (Sections 31A-1+).

Trustee Residency Requirements: If out-of-state trustee is appointed, a resident agent must also be appointed.

Minimum Age for Grantor or Trustee: Eighteen (18). (Section 48A-2).

Trust-Writing Requirements: A trust holding real estate must be in writing. (Section 22-2).

Trustee Bond Requirements: Yes, if the trustee is not the appointed trustee. Otherwise, not unless required by trust or ordered by court.

Trustee Pour-Over to Will: The trust must be identified in the will. The terms of the trust must be in a document other than the will and signed before or at the same time as the will. (Section 31-47).

Spouse's Right to Property Regardless of Will: Generally, the surviving spouse is entitled to 1/2 of the deceased spouse's estate if there are no children, and only 1/3 if there are children. Please refer directly to the statute for details. (Section 29-30).

Laws of Intestate Succession (Distribution If Decedent Leaves No Will):

Spouse and children of spouse surviving: If only one (1) child surviving, $15,000.00 (from any personal property, if any) and 1/2 of balance to spouse and 1/2 of balance to children or grandchildren per stirpes. If more than one (1) child, $15,000.00 (from any personal property, if any) and 1/3 of balance to spouse and 2/3 of balance to children or grandchildren per stirpes.

Spouse and children not of spouse surviving: Same as for "Spouse and children of spouse surviving."

Spouse, but no children or parent(s) surviving: All to spouse.

Spouse and parent(s), but no children surviving: $25,000.00 (from any personal property, if any) and 1/2 of balance to spouse and 1/2 of balance to parents or surviving parent.

Children, but no spouse surviving: All to children equally or to their children per stirpes.

Parent(s), but no spouse or children surviving: All to parents equally or to the surviving parent.

No spouse, children, or parent(s) surviving: All to brothers and sisters equally, or their children per stirpes; or if none, 1/2 to maternal and 1/2 to paternal grandparents or their children per stirpes. (Sections 29-14 & 29-15).

Property Ownership: Common-law state. Tenancy-in-common, joint tenancy, and tenancy-by-entirety are recognized. However, a tenancy-by-entirety in personal property not recognized. Joint bank account deposits are payable to any survivor. (Sections 37-7+).

State Gift, Inheritance, or Estate Taxes: Imposes a gift tax; imposes an inheritance tax of up to 17 percent; imposes a state estate tax equal to federal credit for state death taxes less any amounts paid on state inheritance tax. Maximum total state inheritance and state estate tax is equal to the maximum allowable federal estate tax credit for state death taxes. (Section 105-32.2).

North Dakota

State Law Reference: North Dakota Century Code; Chapters 30.1-01+ and Sections 59-01-01+.

State Website: http://www.state.nd.us/lr/statutes/centurycode.html

Uniform Acts Adopted:

Uniform Probate Code: (Sections 30.1-01-01+).

Uniform Testamentary Additions to Trusts Act: (Sections 30.1-08-11+).

Uniform Trustees' Powers Act: (Sections 59-05-01+).

Uniform Gifts to Minors Act: (Sections 47-24.1-01+).

Trustee Residency Requirements: No provision.

Minimum Age for Grantor or Trustee: Eighteen (18). (Sections 9-02-01 & 9-02-02).

Trust-Writing Requirements: A trust holding real estate must be in writing. (Section 59-03-03).

Trustee Bond Requirements: Yes, unless trust expressly states otherwise. (Section 30.1-34-04).

Trustee Pour-Over to Will: The trust must be identified in the will. The terms of the trust must be in a document other than the will and signed before or at the same time as the will. (Section 30.1-08-11).

Spouse's Right to Property Regardless of Will: The surviving spouse is entitled to 1/3 of the "augmented" estate of the deceased spouse. In general, the "augmented" estate includes both the property that passes under the will and any other property that passes by other "non-will" transfers, such as under the terms of a living trust or a joint tenancy arrangement. (Section 30.1-05-01).

Laws of Intestate Succession (Distribution If Decedent Leaves No Will):

Spouse and children of spouse surviving: $50,000.00 and 1/2 of balance to spouse and 1/2 of balance to children or grandchildren per stirpes.

Spouse and children not of spouse surviving: 1/2 to spouse and 1/2 to children or grandchildren per stirpes.

Spouse, but no children or parent(s) surviving: All to spouse.

Spouse and parent(s), but no children surviving: $50,000.00 and 1/2 of balance to spouse and 1/2 of balance to parents or surviving parent.

Children, but no spouse surviving: All to children equally or to their children per stirpes.
Parent(s), but no spouse or children surviving: All to parents equally or to the surviving parent.
No spouse, children, or parent(s) surviving: All to brothers and sisters equally, or their children per stirpes; or if none, 1/2 to maternal and 1/2 to paternal next of kin. (Sections 30.1-04-02 & 30.1-04-03).

Property Ownership: Common-law state. Tenancy-in-common and joint tenancy are recognized. Tenancy-by-entirety is not recognized. Joint bank account deposits are payable to any survivor. (Sections 30.1-04-02 & 30.1-04-03).

State Gift, Inheritance, or Estate Taxes: No gift tax; no inheritance tax; imposes state estate tax equal to federal credit for state death taxes. (Section 57-37.1-03).

Additional Requirements: Residents should register a "Registration of Living Trust" form with the local court in their county of residence. This requirement is mandatory, although there are no penalties or consequences for failure to register. Please see proper form in Chapter 7.

Ohio

State Law Reference: Ohio Revised Code Annotated; Sections 2101.01+, 2105.01+, 2107.01+, and 2109+.

State Website: http://onlinedocs.andersonpublishing.com/revisedcode/

Uniform Acts Adopted:
   Uniform Testamentary Additions to Trusts Act: (Section 2107.63).
   Uniform Trustees' Powers Act: (Sections 2109.39+).
   Uniform Gifts to Minors Act: (Sections 1339.31+).

Trustee Residency Requirements: None. (Section 2109.21).

Minimum Age for Grantor or Trustee: Eighteen (18). (Section 3109.01).

Trust-Writing Requirements: A trust holding real estate must be in writing. (Section 1335.04).

Trustee Bond Requirements: Yes, unless not required by trust. (Section 2109.05).

Trustee Pour-Over to Will: The trust must be identified in the will. The terms of the trust must be in a document other than the will and signed before or at the same time as the will. (Section 2107.63).

Spouse's Right to Property Regardless of Will: Generally, the surviving spouse is entitled to 1/2 of the deceased spouse's estate if there are no children, and only 1/3 if there are children. However, please refer directly to the statute as the provisions are detailed. (Section 2106.01).

Laws of Intestate Succession (Distribution If Decedent Leaves No Will):
   Spouse and children of spouse surviving: If only one (1) child surviving, $60,000.00 and 1/2 of balance to spouse and 1/2 of balance to children or grandchildren per stirpes. If more than one (1) child surviving, $60,000.00 and 1/3 of balance to spouse and 2/3 of balance to children or grandchildren per stirpes.
   Spouse and children not of spouse surviving: If only one (1) child surviving, $20,000.00 and 1/2 of balance to spouse and 1/2 of balance to children or grandchildren per stirpes. If more than one (1) child surviving, $20,000.00 and 1/3 of balance to spouse and 2/3 of balance to children or grandchildren per stirpes.
   Spouse, but no children or parent(s) surviving: All to spouse.
   Spouse and parent(s), but no children surviving: All to spouse.
   Children, but no spouse surviving: All to children or to their children per stirpes.
   Parent(s), but no spouse or children surviving: All to parents equally or to the surviving parent.
   No spouse, children, or parent(s) surviving: All to brothers and sisters equally or their children per stirpes; or if none, 1/2 to maternal and 1/2 to paternal grandparents or their children per stirpes; or if none, to the next of kin. (Section 2105.06).

Property Ownership: Common-law state. Tenancy-in-common, joint tenancy, and tenancy-by-entirety are recognized Joint tenancy must be stated. Joint bank account deposits are payable to any survivor. (Sections 5302.19 & 5302.20).

State Gift, Inheritance, or Estate Taxes: No gift tax; no inheritance tax; imposes a state estate tax of up to seven (7) percent or not less than any federal credit for state death taxes. (Section 5731.02).

Additional Requirements: Upon the grantor's death, the Successor Trustee must record an affidavit regarding any real estate held by the trust. The affidavit must contain all names and address of trustees and all legal descriptions of property.

Oklahoma

State Law Reference: Oklahoma Statutes Annotated; Title 58, Sections 1+, Title 60, Sections 175.1+, and Title 84, Sections 1+ and 101+.

State Website: http://oklegal.onenet.net/statutes.basic.html

Uniform Acts Adopted:

Uniform Testamentary Additions to Trusts Act: (Sections 301+).

Uniform Trustees' Powers Act: (Title 60, Section 171).

Uniform Gifts to Minors Act: (Title 58, Sections 1201+).

Trustee Residency Requirements: If out-of-state trustee is appointed a resident agent must also be appointed.

Minimum Age for Grantor or Trustee: Eighteen (18). (Title 15, Section 13).

Trust-Writing Requirements: Yes. (Title 60, Section 136).

Trustee Bond Requirements: Yes, unless not required by trust.

Trustee Pour-Over to Will: Trust must be identified in the will. Terms of the trust must be in a document other than the will and signed before or at the same time as the will. (Title 84, Sections 301.59–304).

Spouse's Right to Property Regardless of Will: Generally, the surviving spouse is entitled to 1/2 of the deceased spouse's estate if there are no children, and only 1/3 if there are children. However, please refer to the statute for details. (Title 84, Section 44).

Laws of Intestate Succession (Distribution If Decedent Leaves No Will):

Spouse and children of spouse surviving: If one (1) child, then 1/2 to spouse and 1/2 to child or grandchildren. If deceased had more than one (1) child, then 1/3 to spouse and 2/3 to children or grandchildren per stirpes.

Spouse and children not of spouse surviving: All of property acquired during the marriage by joint effort to spouse, and balance to children and spouse in equal shares.

Spouse, but no children or parent(s) surviving: 1/2 of other property to spouse and 1/3 to maternal and 1/3 to paternal grandparents or their children per stirpes; or if none, to the next of kin.

Spouse and parent(s), but no children surviving: 1/2 of to spouse and 1/2 to parents or surviving parent per stirpes.

Children, but no spouse surviving: All to children equally or grandchildren per stirpes.

Parent(s), but no spouse or children surviving: All to parents equally or to the surviving parent.

No spouse, children, or parent(s) surviving: All to brothers and sisters equally, or their children per stirpes; or if none, 1/2 to maternal and 1/2 to paternal grandparents or their children per stirpes; or if none, to the next of kin. (Title 84, Section 213).

Property Ownership: Common-law state. Tenancy-in-common, joint tenancy, and tenancy-by-entirety are recognized. Rights of survivorship must be stated. Joint bank account deposits are payable to any survivor. (Title 60, Section 74).

State Gift, Inheritance, or Estate Taxes: No gift tax; no inheritance tax; imposes a state estate tax of up to 15 percent but not less that the federal credit for state death taxes. (Title 68, Section 803).

Oregon

State Law Reference: Oregon Revised Statutes; Chapter 12, Sections 112.015+, 115.000+, & 117.000+, and Chapter 13, Sections 128.001+.

State Website: http://www.leg.state.or.us/ors/

Uniform Acts Adopted:

Uniform Trustees' Powers Act: (Sections 128.003+).

Uniform Testamentary Additions to Trusts Act: (Section 112.265).

Uniform Gifts to Minors Act: (Sections 126.805+).

Trustee Residency Requirements: No provision.

Minimum Age for Grantor or Trustee: Eighteen (18). (Section 109.510).

Trust-Writing Requirements: A trust holding real estate must be in writing. (Section 93.020).

Trustee Bond Requirements: No provision.

Trustee Pour-Over to Will: The trust must be identified in the will. The terms of the trust must be in a document other than the will and signed before or at the same time as the will. (Section 112.265).

Spouse's Right to Property Regardless of Will: The surviving spouse is entitled to up to 1/4 of the deceased spouse's estate, including any property which was received under the deceased's will. (Section 114.105).

Laws of Intestate Succession (Distribution If Decedent Leaves No Will):

Spouse and children of spouse surviving: All to spouse.

Spouse and children not of spouse surviving: 1/2 to spouse and 1/2 to children or grandchildren per stirpes.

Spouse, but no children or parent(s) surviving: All to spouse.

Spouse and parent(s), but no children surviving: All to spouse.

Children, but no spouse surviving: All to children equally or to their children per stirpes.

Parent(s), but no spouse or children surviving: All to parents equally or to the surviving parent.

No spouse, children, or parent(s) surviving: All to brothers and sisters equally, or their children per stirpes; or if none, to the next of kin. (Sections 112.025–112.045).

Property Ownership: Common-law state. Tenancy-in-common and tenancy-by-entirety are recognized. Right of survivorship must be stated. Joint bank account deposits are payable to any survivor unless clear evidence exists that deposit is payable only to specified survivor. (Section 93.180).

State Gift, Inheritance, or Estate Taxes: No gift tax; no inheritance tax; imposes state estate tax equal to federal credit for state death taxes. (Section 118.010).

Pennsylvania

State Law Reference: Pennsylvania Consolidated Statutes; Title 20, Sections 1001+.

State Website: http://members.aol.com/StatutesPA/Index.html

Uniform Acts Adopted:

Uniform Testamentary Additions to Trusts Act: (Sections 2515+).

Uniform Trustees' Powers Act: (Sections 7131+).

Uniform Gifts to Minors Act: (Sections 5301+).

Trustee Residency Requirements: None.

Minimum Age for Grantor or Trustee: Eighteen (18). (Title 23, Section 5101).

Trust-Writing Requirements: Yes. (Title 33, Section 2).

Trustee Bond Requirements: None, unless required by trust or ordered by court. (Title 20, Section 7111).

Trustee Pour-Over to Will: The trust must be identified in the will. The terms of the trust must be in a document other than the will and signed before or at the same time as the will. (Title 20, Section 2515).

Spouse's Right to Property Regardless of Will: The surviving spouse is entitled to 1/3 of the deceased spouse's estate. (Title 20, Section 2203).

Laws of Intestate Succession (Distribution If Decedent Leaves No Will):

Spouse and children of spouse surviving: $30,000.00 and 1/2 of balance to spouse and 1/2 of balance to children or grandchildren per stirpes.

Spouse and children not of spouse surviving: 1/2 to spouse and 1/2 to children or grandchildren per stirpes.

Spouse, but no children or parent(s) surviving: All to spouse.

Spouse and parent(s), but no children surviving: $30,000.00 and 1/2 of balance to spouse and 1/2 of balance to parents or surviving parent.

Children, but no spouse surviving: All to children equally or to their children per stirpes.

Parent(s), but no spouse or children surviving: All to parents equally or to the surviving parent.

No spouse, children, or parent(s) surviving: All to brothers and sisters equally, or their children per stirpes; or if none, 1/2 to maternal and 1/2 to paternal grandparents; or if none, all to aunts and uncles or their children per stirpes. (Title 20, Sections 2102 & 2103).

Property Ownership: Common-law state. Tenancy-in-common and tenancy-by-entirety are recognized. Joint tenancy with right of survivorship only if stated. Real estate jointly owned by spouses is presumed to be a tenancy-by-entirety unless stated otherwise. Joint bank account deposits are payable to any survivor. (Title 61, Section 1401.31).

State Gift, Inheritance, or Estate Taxes: No gift tax; imposes an inheritance tax of up to 15 percent; imposes state estate tax equal to federal credit for state death taxes less any amounts paid on state inheritance tax. Maximum total state inheritance and state estate tax is equal to the maximum allowable federal estate tax credit for state death taxes. (Title 72, Sections 9117 & 9116).

Rhode Island

State Law Reference: Rhode Island General Laws; Title 18, Sections 1-1+ and Title 33, Sections 33-5-1+.

State Website: http://www.rilin.state.ri.us/Statutes/Statutes.html

Uniform Acts Adopted:

Uniform Trustees' Powers Act: (Sections 18-4-1+).

Uniform Gifts to Minors Act: (Sections 18-7-1+).

Trustee Residency Requirements: No provision.

Minimum Age for Grantor or Trustee: Eighteen (18). (Section 15-12-1).

Trust-Writing Requirements: A trust holding real estate must be in writing. (Section 9-1-4).

Trustee Bond Requirements: None, unless trust requires court order. (Section 18-13-14).

Trustee Pour-Over to Will: Trust must be identified in the will. Terms of the trust must be in a document other than the will and signed before or at the same time as the will. (Sections 18-14-1–6).

Spouse's Right to Property Regardless of Will: The surviving spouse is entitled to all of the deceased spouse's real estate for the rest of his or her life. (Section 33-25-2).

Laws of Intestate Succession (Distribution If Decedent Leaves No Will):

Spouse and children of spouse surviving: Real estate: life estate to spouse and balance to children equally or grandchildren per stirpes; personal property: 1/2 to spouse and 1/2 to children or grandchildren per stirpes.

Spouse and children not of spouse surviving: Same as above for "Spouse and children of spouse surviving."

Spouse, but no children or parent(s) surviving: Real estate: life estate and $75,000.00 to spouse (if court approves), balance to brothers and sisters equally; or if none, 1/2 to maternal and 1/2 to paternal grandparents; or if none, to aunts and uncles equally or their children per stirpes; or if none, to the next of kin; or if none, to the spouse. Personal property: $50,000.00 and 1/2 of balance to spouse and 1/2 of balance same as for real estate.

Spouse and parent(s), but no children surviving: Real estate: life estate and $75,000.00 to spouse (if court approves), balance to parents or surviving parent; personal property: $50,000.00 and 1/2 of balance to spouse and 1/2 of balance to parents or surviving parent.

Children, but no spouse surviving: All to children or grandchildren per stirpes.

Parent(s), but no spouse or children surviving: All to parents equally or to parent.

No spouse, children, or parent(s) surviving: All to brothers and sisters equally, or their children per stirpes; or if none, 1/2 to maternal and 1/2 to paternal grandparents; or if none, to the next of kin. (Sections 33-1-5–6 & 33-1-10).

Property Ownership: Common-law state. Tenancy-in-common is presumed unless stated otherwise. Tenancy-in-common, joint tenancy, and tenancy-by-entirety are recognized. Joint bank account deposits are payable to any survivor. (Sections 33-1-5, 33-1-6, & 33-1-10).

State Gift, Inheritance, or Estate Taxes: No gift tax; no inheritance tax; imposes state estate tax equal to federal credit for state death taxes. (Section 44-22-1.1).

South Carolina

State Law Reference: Code of Laws of South Carolina Annotated; Title 62, Sections 62-1-100+.

State Website: http://www.lpitr.state.sc.us/

Uniform Acts Adopted:

Uniform Probate Code: (Sections 62-1-100+).

Uniform Trustees' Powers Act: (Sections 62-7-701+).

Uniform Testamentary Additions to Trusts Act: (Sections 62-2-510+).

Uniform Gifts to Minors Act: (Sections 20-7-140+).

Trustee Residency Requirements: Out-of-state trustees must qualify to do business in South Carolina and if a corporate trustee, must have capital of at least $250,000.00.

Minimum Age for Grantor or Trustee. Eighteen (18). (Sections 20-7 and 25+).

Trust-Writing Requirements: Yes. (Section 62-7-101).

Trustee Bond Requirements: None, unless required by trust.

Trustee Pour-Over to Will: The trust must be identified in the will. The terms of the trust must be in a document other than the will and signed before or at the same time as the will. (Section 62-2-510).

Spouse's Right to Property Regardless of Will: The surviving spouse is entitled to 1/3 of the deceased spouse's real estate for the rest of his or her life. (Section 62-2-201).

Laws of Intestate Succession (Distribution If Decedent Leaves No Will):

Spouse and children of spouse surviving: 1/2 to spouse and 1/2 to children or grandchildren.

Spouse and children not of spouse surviving: 1/2 to spouse and 1/2 to children or grandchildren.

Spouse, but no children or parent(s) surviving: All to spouse.

Spouse and parent(s), but no children surviving: 1/2 to spouse and 1/2 to parents, brothers, and sisters or their children per stirpes.

Children, but no spouse surviving: All to children equally or to their children per stirpes.

Parent(s), but no spouse or children surviving: All to parents equally or to the surviving parent if no brothers and sisters.

No spouse, children, or parent(s) surviving: All to brothers and sisters equally or their children per stirpes; or if none, to lineal ancestors equally or to survivor; or if none, to aunts and uncles equally or their children per stirpes; or if none, to the next of kin. (Sections 62-2-102 & 62-2-103).

Property Ownership: Common-law state. Tenancy-in-common and joint tenancy are recognized. Right of survivorship only if stated. Tenancy-by-entirety is not recognized. Joint bank account deposits are payable to any survivor. (Title 27, Sections 1+).

State Gift, Inheritance, or Estate Taxes: Imposes a gift tax; no inheritance tax; imposes a state estate tax of up to eight (8) percent but not less than the federal credit for state death taxes. (Section 12-16-510).

South Dakota

State Law Reference: South Dakota Codified Laws Annotated; Title 29A, Chapters 29-2-1 to 29-6-25.

State Website: http://legis.state.sd.us/statutes/index.cfm

Uniform Acts Adopted:

Uniform Testamentary Additions to Trusts Act: (Sections 29A-2-511+).

Uniform Trustees' Powers Act: (Sections 55-1A-1+).

Uniform Gifts to Minors Act: (Sections 55-10A-1+).

Uniform Probate Code: (Sections 29A-1-101+).

Trustee Residency Requirements: No provision.

Minimum Age for Grantor or Trustee: Eighteen (18). (Section 26-1-1).

Trust-Writing Requirements: A trust holding real estate must be in writing. A trust holding personal or other property may be written or oral. (Section 43-25-1).

Trustee Bond Requirements: Yes, unless not required by trust. (Section 21-22-10).

Trustee Pour-Over to Will: The trust must be identified in the will. The terms of the trust must be in a document other than the will and signed before or at the same time as the will. (Section 29A-2-511).

Spouse's Right to Property Regardless of Will: Dependent on length of marriage. (Section 29A-2-202).

Laws of Intestate Succession (Distribution If Decedent Leaves No Will):

Spouse and children of spouse surviving: If one (1) child surviving, 1/2 to spouse and 1/2 to child or grandchildren; if more than one (1) child surviving, 1/3 to spouse and 2/3 to child or grandchildren per stirpes.

Spouse and children not of spouse surviving: Same as above for "Spouse and children of spouse surviving."

Spouse, but no children or parent(s) surviving: $100,000.00 and 1/2 of balance to spouse, 1/2 of balance to brothers and sisters equally or their children per stirpes; or if none, to the spouse.

Spouse and parent(s), but no children surviving: $100,000.00 and 1/2 of balance to spouse, 1/2 of balance to parents or the surviving parent.

Children, but no spouse surviving: All to children or to their children per stirpes.

Parent(s), but no spouse or children surviving: All to parents equally or to the surviving parent.

No spouse, children, or parent(s) surviving: All to brothers and sisters equally, or their children per stirpes; or if none, to the next of kin. (Sections 29-A-2-101+).

Property Ownership: Common-law state. Tenancy-in-common and joint tenancy are recognized. Tenancy-by-entirety is not recognized. Joint bank account deposits are payable to any survivor. (Sections 43-2-11–43-2-15).

State Gift, Inheritance, or Estate Taxes: No gift tax; imposes an inheritance tax of up to 30 percent; imposes state estate tax equal to federal credit for state death taxes less any amounts paid on state inheritance tax. Maximum total state inheritance and state estate tax is equal to the maximum allowable federal estate tax credit for state death taxes. (Sections 10-40A-3 & 10-40-21).

Tennessee

State Law Reference: Tennessee Code Annotated; Title 32, Sections 32-1-101+ and Title 35, Sections 35-1-101+.

State Website: http://www.michie.com/

Uniform Acts Adopted:

Uniform Testamentary Additions to Trusts Act: (Sections 32-3-106+).

Uniform Trustees' Powers Act: (Section 35-50-110).

Uniform Gifts to Minors Act: (Sections 35-7-201+).

Trustee Residency Requirements: Out-of-state trustee must qualify to do business in Tennessee. (Section 66-24-123).

Minimum Age for Grantor or Trustee: Eighteen (18). (Section 1-3-105).

Trust-Writing Requirements: A trust may be oral or written. (Section 29-2-100).

Trustee Bond Requirements: None, unless required by trust or required by court. (Section 35-1-103).

Trustee Pour-Over to Will: The trust must be identified in the will. The terms of the trust must be in a document other than the will and signed before or at the same time as the will. (Section 32-3-106).

Spouse's Right to Property Regardless of Will: Dependent on length of marriage. (Section 31-4-101).

Laws of Intestate Succession (Distribution If Decedent Leaves No Will):

Spouse and children of spouse surviving: Family homestead and one (1) year's support allowance and one (1) child's share of estate (at least 1/3) to spouse, balance to children equally or grandchildren per stirpes.

Spouse and children not of spouse surviving: Family homestead and one (1) year's support allowance and one (1) child's share of estate (at least 1/3) to spouse, balance to children equally or grandchildren per stirpes.

Spouse, but no children or parent(s) surviving: All to spouse.

Spouse and parent(s), but no children surviving: All to spouse.

Children, but no spouse surviving: All to children equally or to their children per stirpes.

Parent(s), but no spouse or children surviving: All to parents equally or to the surviving parent.

No spouse, children, or parent(s) surviving: All to brothers and sisters equally, or their children per stirpes; or if none, 1/2 to maternal and 1/2 to paternal grandparents or surviving grandparent; or if none to the children of grandparents per stirpes. (Section 31-2-104).

Property Ownership: Common-law state. Tenancy-in-common and tenancy-by-entirety are recognized. Joint bank account deposits are payable to any survivor. (Sections 45-2-703 & 66-1-1074).

State Gift, Inheritance, or Estate Taxes: Imposes a gift tax; imposes an inheritance tax of up to 16 percent; imposes state estate tax equal to federal credit for state death taxes less any amounts paid on state inheritance tax. Maximum total state inheritance and state estate tax is equal to the maximum allowable federal estate tax credit for state death taxes. (Sections 67-8-102, 67-8-204, & 67-8-314).

Texas

State Law Reference: Texas Statutes and Code Annotated; Trusts, Title 9, Sections 101+ and Texas Statutes and Code Annotated; Probate Title, Chapters 1+.

State Website: http://www.capitol.state.tx.us/statutes/statutes.html

Uniform Acts Adopted:

Uniform Testamentary Additions to Trusts Act: (Section 58A).

Uniform Trustees' Powers Act: (Sections 113.001+).

Uniform Gifts to Minors Act: (Property, Sections 141.001+).

Trustee Residency Requirements: No provision.

Minimum Age for Grantor or Trustee: Eighteen (18). (Civil Practice and Remedies, Section 129.001)

Trust-Writing Requirements: Yes. (Section 112.004).

Trustee Bond Requirements: Yes, if corporate trustee. Otherwise, yes unless not required by trust. (Section 113.058).

Trustee Pour-Over to Will: The trust must be identified in the will. The terms of the trust must be in a document other than the will and signed before or at the same time as the will. (Section 58a).

Spouse's Right to Property Regardless of Will: Community property right to 1/2 of the deceased spouse's "community" property. (Section 270).

Laws of Intestate Succession (Distribution If Decedent Leaves No Will):

Spouse and children of spouse surviving: 1/2 of community property, 1/3 life estate in separate real property, and 1/3 separate personal property to spouse; balance to children or grandchildren per stirpes.

Spouse and children not of spouse surviving: Same as above for "Spouse and children of spouse surviving."

Spouse, but no children or parent(s) surviving: All community property, separate personal property and 1/2 separate real property to spouse; balance to brothers and sisters equally or their children per stirpes; or if none, to grandparents or their descendants; or if none, to spouse.

Spouse and parent(s), but no children surviving: All community property, separate personal property and 1/2 separate real property to spouse; balance to parents (if both surviving); if only one (1) surviving, 1/4 balance to parent and 1/4 to brothers and sisters equally or their children per stirpes; or if none, entire 1/2 to parent.

Children, but no spouse surviving: All to children or to their children per stirpes.

Parent(s), but no spouse or children surviving: If both parents are surviving, all to parents equally; if only one (1) surviving, 1/2 to parent and 1/2 to brothers and sisters equally or their children per stirpes; or if none, all to parent.

No spouse, children, or parent(s) surviving: All to brothers and sisters equally, or their children per stirpes; or if none, 1/2 to maternal and 1/2 to paternal grandparents or their children per stirpes. (Section 38).

Property Ownership: Community property state. Tenancy-in-common is recognized. Tenancy-by-entirety is not recognized. Joint bank account deposits are payable to any survivor. (Chapter 11, Section 436).

State Gift, Inheritance, or Estate Taxes: No gift tax; no inheritance tax; imposes state estate tax equal to federal credit for state death taxes. (Sections 211:051–211:056).

Utah

State Law Reference: Utah Code Annotated; Sections 75-1-101+ and 75-2-101+.

State Website: http://www.le.state.ut.us/Documents/code_const.htm

Uniform Acts Adopted:

Uniform Probate Code: (Sections 75-1-101+).

Uniform Trustees' Powers Act: (Sections 75-7-401+).

Uniform Testamentary Additions to Trusts Act: (Section 75-2-511).

Uniform Gifts to Minors Act: (Sections 75-5a-101+).

Trustee Residency Requirements: Out-of-state trustee must qualify to do business in Utah.

Minimum Age for Grantor or Trustee: Eighteen (18). (Section 15-2-1).

Trust-Writing Requirements: A trust holding real estate must be in writing. (Section 25-5-1).

Trustee Bond Requirements: None, unless required by trust, requested by beneficiaries, or ordered by the court. (Section 75-7-304).

Trustee Pour-Over to Will: The trust must be identified in the will. The terms of the trust must be in a document other than the will and signed before or at the same time as the will. (Section 72-5-511).

Spouse's Right to Property Regardless of Will: The surviving spouse is entitled to 1/3 of the deceased spouse's augmented estate. (Section 75-2-202).

Laws of Intestate Succession (Distribution If Decedent Leaves No Will):

Spouse and children of spouse surviving: 1/2 to spouse and 1/2 to children or grandchildren per stirpes.

Spouse and children not of spouse surviving: 1/2 to spouse and 1/2 to children or grandchildren per stirpes.

Spouse, but no children or parent(s) surviving: All to spouse.

Spouse and parent(s), but no children surviving: $100,000.00 and 1/2 of balance to spouse and 1/2 to parents or surviving parent.

Children, but no spouse surviving: All to children equally or to their children per stirpes.

Parent(s), but no spouse or children surviving: All to parents equally or to the surviving parent.

No spouse, children, or parent(s) surviving: All to brothers and sisters equally, or their children per stirpes; 1/2 to maternal and 1/2 to paternal grandparents or their descendants per stirpes; or if none, to the next of kin. (Sections 75-2-102 & 75-2-103).

Property Ownership: Common-law state. Tenancy-in-common, joint tenancy and tenancy-by-entirety are recognized. Real estate is presumed to be in tenancy-in-common, unless joint tenancy is stated. Joint bank account deposits are payable to any survivor. (Section 57-1-5).

State Gift, Inheritance, or Estate Taxes: No gift tax; no inheritance tax; imposes state estate tax equal to federal credit for state death taxes. (Sections 59-11-103 & 59-11-104).

Vermont

State Law Reference: Vermont Statutes Annotated; Title 14, Sections 1+ and 1001+.

State Website: http://www.leg.state.vt.us/

Uniform Acts Adopted:

Uniform Testamentary Additions to Trusts Act: (Section 2329).

Uniform Gifts to Minors Act: (Title 14, Sections 3201+).

Trustee Residency Requirements: If out-of-state trustee is appointed, a resident agent must also be appointed.

Minimum Age for Grantor or Trustee: Eighteen (18). (Section 1-173).

Trust-Writing Requirements: A trust holding real estate must be in writing; otherwise may be written or oral. (Title 27, Section 303).

Trustee Bond Requirements: Yes, unless not required by trust. (Title 14, Section 2301).

Trustee Pour-Over to Will: The trust must be identified in the will. The terms of the trust must be in a document other than the will and signed before or at the same time as the will. (Title 14, Section 2329).

Spouse's Right to Property Regardless of Will: If there are none or more than one (1) child of the surviving spouse and the deceased, the surviving spouse is entitled to 1/3 of the deceased spouse's real estate. If there is only one (1) child of the surviving spouse and the deceased, the surviving spouse is entitled to 1/2 of the deceased spouse's real estate. Please refer, however, directly to the statute for instances when this may be barred. (Title 14, Section 461).

Laws of Intestate Succession (Distribution If Decedent Leaves No Will):

Spouse and children of spouse surviving: If one (1) child surviving: 1/2 of deceased's estate; balance to child or grandchildren per stirpes. If more than one (1) child surviving: 1/3 to spouse and 2/3 to child or grandchildren per stirpes.

Spouse and children not of spouse surviving: If one (1) child surviving: 1/3 of deceased's estate; balance to child or grandchildren per stirpes.

Spouse, but no children or parent(s) surviving: If spouse waives the statutory share and any will provisions, then $25,000.00 and 1/2 of balance to spouse and 1/2 of balance as if surviving spouse had not survived.

Spouse and parent(s), but no children surviving: $25,000.00 and 1/2 of balance to spouse and 1/2 of balance as if surviving spouse had not survived.

Children, but no spouse surviving: All to children equally or to their children per stirpes.

Parent(s), but no spouse or children surviving: All to parents equally or to the surviving parent.

No spouse, children, or parent(s) surviving: All to brothers and sisters equally, or their children per stirpes; or if none, to the next of kin. (Title 14, Section 551).

Property Ownership: Common-law state. Tenancy-in-common, tenancy-by-entirety, and joint tenancy are recognized. Real estate is presumed to be held by tenancy-in-common unless joint tenancy is stated. Joint bank account deposits are payable to any survivor. (Title 27, Section 2).

State Gift, Inheritance, or Estate Taxes: No gift tax; no inheritance tax; imposes state estate tax equal to federal credit for state death taxes. (Title 32, Section 7442a).

Virginia

State Law Reference: Virginia Code Annotated; Title 26, Section 1+.

State Website: http://leg1.state.va.us/

Uniform Acts Adopted:

Uniform Gifts to Minors Act: (Sections 31-37+).

Trustee Residency Requirements: If out-of-state trustee is appointed, a resident agent must also be appointed unless trustee is a corporation authorized to do business in Virginia or is a parent, sister, or brother of decedent and has qualified to do business in Virginia. (Section 2-9-59).

Minimum Age for Grantor or Trustee: Eighteen (18). (Section 1-13-42).

Trust-Writing Requirements: A trust may be written or oral. (Section 11-2).

Trustee Bond Requirements: No provision.

Trustee Pour-Over to Will: The trust must be identified in the will. The terms of the trust must be in a document other than the will and signed before or at the same time as the will. (Section 64.1-73.1).

Spouse's Right to Property Regardless of Will: The surviving spouse is entitled to 1/3 of the deceased spouse's real estate for the rest of his or her life. (Section 64.1-16).

Laws of Intestate Succession (Distribution If Decedent Leaves No Will):

Spouse and children of spouse surviving: All to spouse.

Spouse and children not of spouse surviving: 1/3 to spouse and 2/3 to children or grandchildren per stirpes.

Spouse, but no children or parent(s) surviving: All to spouse.

Spouse and parent(s), but no children surviving: All to spouse.

Children, but no spouse surviving: All to children equally or to their children per stirpes.

Parent(s), but no spouse or children surviving: All to parents equally or to the surviving parent.

No spouse, children, or parent(s) surviving: All to brothers and sisters equally, or their children per stirpes; or if none, 1/2 to maternal grandparents or maternal next of kin (or if none, to paternal side) and 1/2 to paternal grandparents, or their children, or paternal next of kin (or if none to maternal side). (Section 64.1-1).

Property Ownership: Common-law state. Joint tenancy is recognized only if right of survivorship is stated. Tenancy-in-common and tenancy-by-entirety are recognized. Joint bank account deposits are payable to any survivor unless clear evidence exists that deposit is payable only to specified survivor. (Section 55-20-1).

State Gift, Inheritance, or Estate Taxes: No gift tax; no inheritance tax; imposes state estate tax equal to federal credit for state death taxes. (Sections 58.1-361–58.1-363).

Washington

State Law Reference: Washington Revised Code Annotated; Title 11.

State Website: http://www.leg.wa.gov/

Uniform Acts Adopted:

Uniform Testamentary Additions to Trusts Act: (Section 11.12.250).

Uniform Trustees' Powers Act: (Section 11.98.070).

Uniform Gifts to Minors Act: (Sections 11.114.010+).

Trustee Residency Requirements: No provision.

Minimum Age for Grantor or Trustee. Eighteen (18). (Section 26.28.010).

Trust-Writing Requirements: A trust holding real estate must be in writing. A trust holding personal property can be either oral or in writing. (Section 19.36.010).

Trustee Bond Requirements: No provision.

Trustee Pour-Over to Will: The trust must be identified in the will. The terms of the trust must be in a document other than the will and signed before or at the same time as the will. (Section 11.12.250).

Spouse's Right to Property Regardless of Will: Community property right to 1/2 of the deceased spouse's "community" property.

Laws of Intestate Succession (Distribution If Decedent Leaves No Will):

Spouse and children of spouse surviving: All of decedent's community property and 1/2 of decedent's separate property to spouse; 1/2 of decedent's separate property to children or grandchildren per stirpes.

Spouse and children not of spouse surviving: All of decedent's community property and 1/2 of decedent's separate property to spouse; 1/2 of decedent's separate property to children or grandchildren per stirpes.

Spouse, but no children or parent(s) surviving: All to spouse.

Spouse and parent(s), but no children surviving: All decedent's community property and 3/4 decedent's separate property to spouse; 1/4 decedent's separate property to parents or surviving parent or their children.

Children, but no spouse surviving: All to children equally or to their children per stirpes.

Parent(s), but no spouse or children surviving: All to parents equally or to the surviving parent.

No spouse, children, or parent(s) surviving: All to brothers and sisters equally, or their children per stirpes; or if none, to grandparents or their children. (Section 11.04.015).

Property Ownership: Community property state. Tenancy-in-common and joint tenancy are recognized. Joint tenancy with right of survivorship is created if specifically stated. No survivorship rights in tenancy-by-entirety. Joint bank account deposits are payable to any survivor unless evidence exists that deposit is payable only to specified survivor, and is subject to community property rights. (Section 64-28).

State Gift, Inheritance, or Estate Taxes: No gift tax; no inheritance tax; imposes state estate tax equal to federal credit for state death taxes. (Sections 83.110.030–83.100.040).

West Virginia

State Law Reference: West Virginia Code Annotated; Sections 41, 42, and 44-1-1.

State Website: http://www.legis.state.wv.us/

Uniform Acts Adopted:

Uniform Testamentary Additions to Trusts Act: (Section 41-3-8).

Uniform Gifts to Minors Act: (Sections 36-7-1+).

Trustee Residency Requirements: None.

Minimum Age for Grantor or Trustee: Eighteen (18). (Section 49-5-1).

Trust-Writing Requirements: Yes. (Section 36-1-4).

Trustee Bond Requirements: No provision.

Trustee Pour-Over to Will: The trust must be identified in the will. The terms of the trust must be in a document other than the will and signed before or at the same time as the will. (Sections 41-3-8–41-3-11).

Spouse's Right to Property Regardless of Will: Dependent on length of marriage. (Section 42-3-1).

Laws of Intestate Succession (Distribution If Decedent Leaves No Will):

Spouse and children of spouse surviving: All to spouse.

Spouse and children not of spouse surviving: 3/5 to spouse if all of deceased's children are also children of surviving spouse and surviving spouse also has children who are not deceased's children; balance to deceased's children or grandchildren per stirpes.

Spouse, but no children or parent(s) surviving: All to spouse.

Spouse and parent(s), but no children surviving: All to spouse.

Children, but no spouse surviving: All to children equally or to their children per stirpes.

Parent(s), but no spouse or children surviving: All to parents equally or to the surviving parent.

No spouse, children, or parent(s) surviving: All to brothers and sisters equally, or their children per stirpes; or if none, 1/2 to maternal grandparents or their children or maternal uncles and aunts or their children, or maternal next of kin (or if none, to paternal side) and 1/2 to paternal grandparents, or their children, or paternal uncles and aunts or their children, or paternal next of kin (or if none to maternal side). (Sections 42-1-3 & 42-1-3a).

Property Ownership: Common-law state. Tenancy-in-common, joint tenancy, and tenancy-by-entirety are recognized. Right of survivorship is created if stated. Joint bank account deposits are payable to any survivor. (Section 36-1-19).

State Gift, Inheritance, or Estate Taxes: No gift tax; no inheritance tax; imposes state estate tax equal to federal credit for state death taxes. (Section 11-11-3).

Wisconsin

State Law Reference: Wisconsin Statutes Annotated; Sections 701+, 851.001+, 852.01+, and 853.01+.

State Website: http://www.legis.state.wi.us/

Uniform Acts Adopted:

Uniform Trustees' Powers Act: (Section 701.09).

Uniform Gifts to Minors Act: (Sections 880.61+).

Trustee Residency Requirements: Out-of-state trustee must qualify to do business in Wisconsin.

Minimum Age for Grantor or Trustee: Eighteen (18). (Section 48.02).

Trust-Writing Requirements: Yes. (Section 234.01).

Trustee Bond Requirements: Yes, unless not required by trust or ordered by court. (Section 701.16).

Trustee Pour-Over to Will: The trust must be identified in the will. The terms of the trust must be in a document other than the will and signed before or at the same time as the will. (Section 701.09).

Spouse's Right to Property Regardless of Will: Modified community property right to 1/2 of the deceased spouse's "community" property. (Section 861.02).

Laws of Intestate Succession (Distribution If Decedent Leaves No Will):

Spouse and children of spouse surviving: All to spouse.

Spouse and children not of spouse surviving: 1/2 to spouse and 1/2 to children or grandchildren per stirpes.

Spouse, but no children or parent(s) surviving: All to spouse.

Spouse and parent(s), but no children surviving: All to spouse.

Children, but no spouse surviving: All to children or to their children per stirpes.

Parent(s), but no spouse or children surviving: All to parents equally or to the surviving parent.

No spouse, children, or parent(s) surviving: All to brothers and sisters equally, or their children per stirpes; or if none, to grandparents or surviving grandparent; or if none, to the next of kin. (Section 852.01).

Property Ownership: Community property state. The Wisconsin statute, however, uses unique terminology to describe this treatment of property. Tenancy-in-common and joint tenancy are recognized. Ownership by spouses is presumed to be joint tenancy unless stated otherwise. Tenancy-by-entirety is not recognized. Joint bank account deposits are payable to any survivor. (Sections 700.17, 700.19, & 700.20).

State Gift, Inheritance, or Estate Taxes: Imposes a gift tax; imposes an inheritance tax of up to 20 percent; imposes state estate tax equal to federal credit for state death taxes less any amounts paid on state inheritance tax. Maximum total state inheritance and state estate tax is equal to the maximum allowable federal estate tax credit for state death taxes. (Sections 72.02, 72.18, & 72.77–72.75).

Wyoming

State Law Reference: Wyoming Statutes; Titles 2, 4, & 34.

State Website: http://legisweb.state.wy.us/

Uniform Acts Adopted:

Uniform Trustees Powers Act: (Sections 4-8-101+).

Uniform Testamentary Additions to Trusts Act: (Section 2-6-102).

Uniform Gifts to Minors Act: (Section 34-13-114).

Trustee Residency Requirements: None.

Minimum Age for Grantor or Trustee: Eighteen (18). (Section 14-1-101).

Trust-Writing Requirements: A trust holding real estate must be in writing. (Section 1-23-105).

Trustee Bond Requirements: No provision.

Trustee Pour-Over to Will: The trust must be identified in the will. The terms of the trust must be in a document other than the will and signed before or at the same time as the will. (Section 2-6-103).

Spouse's Right to Property Regardless of Will: Generally, the surviving spouse is entitled to 1/2 of the deceased spouse's estate if there are no children or if surviving spouse is parent of deceased's children; and only 1/4 if the surviving spouse is not the parent of any surviving children of the deceased. However, please refer directly to the statute as the provisions are detailed. (Section 2-5-101).

Laws of Intestate Succession (Distribution If Decedent Leaves No Will):

Spouse and children of spouse surviving: 1/2 to spouse and 1/2 to children or grandchildren per stirpes.

Spouse and children not of spouse surviving: 1/2 to spouse and 1/2 to children or grandchildren per stirpes.

Spouse, but no children or parent(s) surviving: All to spouse.

Spouse and parent(s), but no children surviving: All to spouse.

Children, but no spouse surviving: All to children equally or to their children per stirpes.

Parent(s), but no spouse or children surviving: All to parents, brothers, and sisters equally, or to children of brothers and sisters per stirpes.

No spouse, children, or parent(s) surviving: All to grandparents, uncles, or aunts or their children per stirpes. (Section 2-4-101).

Property Ownership: Common-law state. Tenancy-in-common, joint tenancy, and tenancy-by-entirety are recognized. Right of survivorship created if stated. Joint bank account deposits are payable to any survivor. (Chapter 34).

State Gift, Inheritance, or Estate Taxes: No gift tax; no inheritance tax; imposes state estate tax equal to federal credit for state death taxes. (Section 39-6-812).

Glossary of Legal Terms

Abatement: A reduction or complete extinguishment of a gift in a will where the estate does not have sufficient assets to make full payment.

Accounts Payable: Money owed to another and due to be paid.

Accounts Receivable: Money owed from another and due to be paid.

Acknowledgment: Formal declaration before a Notary Public.

Ademption: The withdrawal of a gift in a will by an act of the *testator*'s which shows an intent to revoke it. For example; by giving the willed property away as a gift during his or her life.

Administrator/Administratrix: One who is appointed to administer the estate of a deceased person who has died without a will or who has died with a will but has not named an *executor*. The distinction between the two titles (male and female) has largely been removed and *administrator* is proper usage for either male or female.

Advancement: A lifetime gift made to a child by a parent, with the intent that the gift be all or a portion of what the child will be entitled to on the parent's death.

Affidavit: A person's signed and notarized statement.

Alternate Beneficiary: A person chosen to receive a gift under a will or trust should the originally chosen beneficiary not be available or surviving.

Amend: To change or alter.

Ancestor: One from whom a person is descended.

Annuity contract: A form of investment in which the purchaser is guaranteed a certain periodic payment for life or a certain term.

Appraisal: Valuation of a piece of property, generally by a person certified to conduct such a valuation.

Assets: Any property that you own. Your assets may consist of *real estate* or *personal property*. Your personal property may consist of cash, securities, or actual tangible property.

Attestation: To sign one's name as a witness to a will.

Augmented: An augmented estate is your estate left under a will plus the value of property transferred by other means, such as joint tenancies and living trusts. The augmented estate is used to calculate the value of a *spousal share* of an estate in those states that use this concept.

Bank Trust Account: A type of *payable-on-death account* under which the main account holder retain full and unilateral control of the account until death. Same as a *Totten Trust*.

Basic Will: A simple standardized type of will.

Beneficiary: One who is named in a will to receive property; one who receives a benefit or gift, as under the terms of a trust.

Bequest: Traditionally, a gift of personal property in a will. Synonymous with legacy. Now, *gift* is the appropriate usage for either a gift of real estate or personal property.

Blood Relative: A person who is directly related to another through birth descent.

Bond: A document by which a bonding company guarantees to pay an amount of money if the bonded person does not carry out his or her legal duties.

Bonds: A form of investment through which a company is indebted to the holder and, generally, pays interest to the holder.

Business Interest: Ownership of any form of business, such as a sole proprietorship, partnership, corporation, or limited liability company.

Buy-Out Provisions: Contractual terms contained in a business ownership agreement (such as a partnership agreement) which specify the terms under which other owners may be required to or have the option to purchase (buy-out) another owner's interest in the business, often upon the death of an owner.

Certificate of Deposit: A form of investment under which a bank issues a certificate indicating that it holds a deposit and will pay a certain rate of interest for a certain term.

Charitable Organization: A group which holds a Federal 501(c)3 "charitable organization" tax exemption status, and is able to receive tax-exempt donations.

Children's Trust: A form of trust under which gifts to children may be held in trust beyond the child's attainment of the legal age of majority.

Close Corporation: A corporation operated by a small number of individuals, often family members. Often is exempt from certain state laws and may operate more informally. Also referred to as a "closely-held corporation."

Codicil: A formally-signed supplement to a will.

Common Law: System of law which originated in England based on general legal principles rather than legislative acts.

Common-Law Property: Property held by a spouse in a common-law state. Generally, can be jointly-held property or solely-owned property. The name(s) on the title document is the determining factor. See Appendix for those states in which this system of marital property applies.

Community Property: The property acquired by either spouse during marriage, other than by gift or inheritance. Each spouse owns a half-interest in the community property. See Appendix for those states in which this system of marital property applies.

Conservator: Temporary court-appointed custodian of property.

Contest: Challenging the validity of a will.

Curtesy: In ancient common law, a husband's right to all of his wife's real estate for life upon her death. Now generally abolished in most jurisdictions and replaced with a right to a certain *statutory share* of a spouse's property.

Death Benefits: Money, generally from either insurance policies or pension plans, which are payable to the *beneficiaries* of a *decedent*.

Decedent: One who has died.

Descendant: One who is descended from another.

Descent: Inheritance by operation of law rather than by will.

Devise: Traditionally, a gift of real estate under a will. Now, *gift* is the appropriate usage for either a gift of real estate or personal property.

Domicile: A person's principal and permanent home.

Dower: In ancient common law, a wife's right to one-third of her husband's real estate for her life upon his death. Now generally abolished in most jurisdictions and replaced with a right to a certain *statutory share* of a spouse's property.

Employee Benefits: Money or other benefits which are payable to an employee, such as health-care insurance, travel-expense compensation, etc.

Escheat: The reversion of property to the state, if there is no family member found to inherit it.

Estate: All property owned by a person.

Estate Tax: A tax imposed on property that passes to another upon death.

Execution: The formal signing of a will.

Executor/Executrix: The person appointed in a will to carry out the *testator*'s wishes and to administer the property.

Federal Estate Tax: A percentage tax which is imposed on the estate of a deceased person for the benefit of being able to pass estate to others upon death. In 2002, the first $1 million dollars of a person's estate value are fully exempt from this tax, as are all estate property which passes from one spouse to another. The dollar value of the exemption is scheduled to rise to $3.5 million by 2009.

Fiduciary: A person with a duty of care to another. For example, a trustee has a duty of care to any *beneficiary* of a trust, and thus, is a *fiduciary*.

Gift: A voluntary transfer of property to another without any compensation.

Grantor: The person who creates a trust. Also may be referred to as a *settlor*.

Guardian: A person with the legal power and duty to care for another person and/or a person's property.

Heirlooms: Treasured pieces of property that have been passed down from ancestors.

Heirs: Those persons who inherit from a person by operation of law if there is no will present.

Holographic: A will that is entirely handwritten by the *testator* and unwitnessed. No longer valid in most states.

Homestead Allowance: A monetary allowance given in some states to spouses and children to insure that they are not abruptly cut off from their support by any terms of a Living Trust.

Incapacitated: Being unable to care for one's self or handle one's own financial or other affairs.

Income Property: Real estate which is held for a commercial purpose; the generation of income.

Inheritance: The receipt of property from someone who has died.

Inheritance Tax: A tax on property received that is paid by the person who has actually inherited the property.

Intestate: To die without leaving a valid will.

Intestate Distribution: A state scheme which is used to determine the distribution of the property of any person who dies without leaving a valid will or other determination of how their property is to be distributed upon their death.

IRA: Individual Retirement Accounts under IRS regulations.

Joint Tenancy: Joint ownership of property under which the surviving owner automatically owns the deceased owner's share. This is called the *right of survivorship*. May be abbreviated as JTWROS or *joint tenancy with right of survivorship*.

JTWROS: Joint tenancy with right of survivorship.

KEOGH: A form of retirement account.

Legacy: A gift of personal property in a will. Now, *gift* is the appropriate usage for either a gift of real estate or personal property. Synonymous with *bequest*.

Letters of Administration: The court order which officially appoints a person to administer the estate of another.

Letters Testamentary: The court order which officially appoints an *executor* named in a will as the person to administer the estate of the *testator*.

Liabilities: Something for which a person is liable, such as a debt.

Living Trust: A form of *revocable trust* which becomes irrevocable upon the death of the grantor.

Living Will: A document that can be used to state your desire that extraordinary life support means not be used to artificially prolong your life in the event that you are stricken with a terminal illness or injury.

Loans Payable: Loans for which a person owes money to another.

Minor Child: A child who is under the legal age of majority (generally 18 or 21 years old).

Mortgage: A written statement of a debt owned for the purchase of real estate, under which the property is used as collateral.

Net Worth: A person's net value, determined by subtracting *liabilities* from *assets*.

Notarize: To have a notary public acknowledge the signing of a document.

Notes Payable: Money owed to another based on a promissory note and which is due to be paid.

Notes Receivable: Money owed from another based on a promissory note and which is due to be paid.

Nuncupative: An oral will, usually during a person's last illness and later reduced to writing by another. No longer valid in most states.

Obituary: A written statement regarding a person's death, usually in a newspaper.

Payable-on-Death Account: An account, generally a bank account, for which a *beneficiary* is chosen who will receive the proceeds of the account upon the death of the primary account holder.

Pension Plan: Any plan under which an employee will receive any benefits after the end of his or her employment.

Per Capita: Equally; share and share alike. For example: if a gift is made to ones' descendants, per capita, and one has two children and two grandchildren and one of the children dies, then the gift is divided equally among the surviving child and the two grandchildren. This amounts to one-third to the child and one-third to each grandchild.

Per Stirpes: To share by representation. For example: if a gift is made to two children, per stirpes, and one should die but leave two grandchildren, the deceased child's share is given to the two grandchildren in equal shares. This amounts then to one-half to the surviving child and one-fourth to each of the grandchildren.

Personal Property: Movable property, as opposed to *real estate*.

Personal Representative: A person who is appointed to administer a deceased's estate. Modern usage which replaces *Executor* and/or *Administrator*.

Posthumous Child: A child born after the father's death.

Pretermitted Child: A child who is left nothing in a parent's will and where there is no intent shown to disinherit.

Probate: The court proceeding to determine the validity of a will and, in general, the administration of the property which passes under the will.

Proprietorship: See *Sole Proprietorship*.

Proved: Determined whether or not the document presented is actually the deceased's will.

Pour-Over Will: A will under which a trust is the main *beneficiary*.

Publication: For a will, the statement by the testator that the document that is being signed is his or her will.

Real Estate/Real Property: Land and that which is attached permanently to it, as opposed to *personal property*.

Relative: A person who is related by blood or marriage to another.

Residuary: The remainder of an estate after all debts, taxes, and gifts have been distributed.

Residuary Clause: A clause in a will or trust which designates a *beneficiary* of the *residuary* of an estate.

Revocable Trust: Another name for *Living Trust*. Upon death, a Living Trust becomes irrevocable and can no longer be changed or altered in any way. In general, however, any type of trust that can be revoked by the grantor.

Revocation: The annulment of a will, which renders it invalid. Accomplished either by complete destruction of the original will or by executing a later will which revokes the earlier one.

Right of Survivorship: The right of a joint owner of property to automatically obtain ownership over another deceased owner's share of the property. Generally true in a *joint tenancy* or a *tenancy-by-the-entireties*.

Self-Proving Affidavit: A document which may be completed by witnesses to the signing of a will by which they affirm that they did indeed witness the signing. This affidavit may then be used later in a probate proceeding to prove the signing without the necessity of calling the witnesses to testify in person at the probate court.

Separate Property: The property of a spouse in a *community property* or *common-law* state which is considered the solely owned property of that spouse, generally property which is solely-owned prior to the marriage and any property which is obtained by gift or *inheritance* during the marriage.

Settlor: See *Grantor*.

Shared Property: The property of a spouse in a *community property* or common-law state which is considered property of both spouses jointly. In community property states, this would be all property which is not *separate property*. In common-law property states, this would be all property which is not *separate property* and which is actually held in some form of joint ownership, such as t*enants-in-common* or as a *joint tenancy*.

Sibling: A brother or sister.

Sole Proprietorship: A business which is owned by one owner and which is not a corporation or limited liability company.

Sound Mind: A legal term which refers to the *testator*'s ability to understand what gifts you are making and who your chosen beneficiaries are.

Spouse's Share: See *Statutory Share*.

Statutory Share: In *common law* states, that portion of a person's property that a spouse is entitled to by law, regardless of any provisions in a will. In *community property* states, a surviving spouse receives half of all of the community property, regardless of any provisions in a will.

Successor Trustee: The person who is chosen to manage and distribute trust assets upon either the incapacitation or death of the original trustee of the trust.

Supplemental Will: A will which is used to supplement a living trust. Not a *pour-over will*.

Survivorship Clause: A clause in a trust or will which provides that a beneficiary must outlive the decedent by a certain period of time in order to be considered a rightful beneficiary.

Tenancy-by-the-Entireties: A form of Joint Tenancy that is only allowed for husbands and wives in certain states.

Tenancy-in-Common: A form of joint ownership under which each owner own a certain specific share of the property (perhaps one-half or another fraction). Upon the death of a co-owner, that co-owner's share is passed to the heirs or beneficiaries of the deceased co-owner, not to the other co-owner(s). Compare to *Joint Tenancy*.

Testamentary: The expression of intent to dispose of property by will.

Testator/Testratrix: A male or female who makes a will.

Totten Trust: A type of payable-on-death account at a financial institution that allows a person to name a beneficiary. Similar to a joint account, but where the joint co-owner has no rights until the death of the creator of the account.

Transfer Documents: Any documents that may be necessary to formalize the change in ownership of property, such as a deed in the case of real estate, or a title in the case of a motor vehicle.

Trust: In general, an arrangement created by one party, the *grantor*, under which property is held by another party, the *trustee*, for the benefit of yet another party, the *beneficiary*. Under a Living Trust, one person may initially be all three of these parties.

Trust Estate: The assets which have been transferred into a trust by a grantor.

Trustee: A person appointed to administer a trust. In a Living Trust, the trustee and the *grantor* may be the same person.

Vacant Land: Real estate on which there are no buildings present.

Vacation House: Real estate which is owned for the purpose of being used for the owner's vacations.

Will: A formally signed and witnessed document by which a person makes a disposition of his or her property to take effect upon death.

Witness: A person who is present and sees another person sign a document.

Index

Accounts receivable, 38
Accounts payable, 45
Administrator, 61
Adopted, 152
Affidavit of Assumption of Duties by Successor
     Trustee, 63, 139
Age requirements, 22
Alternate beneficiary, 50
Amend, 20
Amending a Living Trust, 152
Amendment of Living Trust by Single Person or
     Individual Spouse, 155
Amendments and Revocations, 81
Annuity contracts, 38
Appraisal, 67
Artwork, 44
Assets, 22, 37, 43, 45
Assignment to Living Trust by Single Person or
     Individual Spouse, 111

Bank accounts, 24, 150
Banks, 21
Bank trust account, 24
Basic Will, 162
Beneficiary, 10, 14, 16, 21, 31, 48
Beneficiary Questionnaire, 26, 29, 48–59, 149
Blood relative, 16
Boat, 43, 150
Bond, 19, 40
Bonds, 150
Brother, 17
Business interests, 150
Buy-out provisions, 31

Car, 43
Cash, 37
Cemetery, 65
Certificate of deposit, 37
Charitable organizations, 48
Checking account, 37
Children, 17, 53, 152
Children's trust, 19, 51, 79
Churches, 48

Close corporation, 42
Contest, 61
Common law property, 33
Community property, 31, 32
Copyrights, 43, 150
Corporate ownership, 150
Corporations, 42
Credit cards, 46
Creditors, 67
Cremation arrangements, 69

Death benefits, 65
Death certificate, 66
Deed, 21
Dependent, 57
Divorce, 152
Durable Power of Attorney for Health Care, 25

Employee benefits, 44
Escheat, 16, 18
Estate Planning Tools, 23
Estate, 10, 23
Estate tax, 34
Execute, 22
Execution, 26
Executor, 15, 164

Federal estate tax, 9, 34
Finance companies, 21
Friends, 58
Friends to Contact, 72
Funeral arrangements, 69
Funeral expenses, 67
Funeral home, 65
Fur, 44

Gift, 32
Governing law, 81
Grandchildren, 17, 54
Grantor, 14, 22
Grantor's rights, 78

Health insurance, 65

Heirs, 16
Homestead exemptions, 78
Household furnishings, 43

Identification and Date clause, 77
Immediate Successor Trustee duties, 65
Incapacitated, 25, 79
Income property, 43
Individual proprietorship,
Inheritance, 32
Inheritance tax, 34
Intestate distribution, 16
Intestate property, 162
Inventory, 67
IRA, 31, 66

Jewelry, 44
Joint Amendment of Joint Living Trust by
    Married Couple, 157
Joint Assignment to Joint Living Trust by
    Married Couple, 113
Jointly-held property, 31
Joint tenancy, 23, 37, 42
Joint property, 23, 31–34
Joint Schedule of Beneficiaries of Joint Living
    Trust of Married Couple, 129
Joint Living Trust
    -of Married Couple without a Children's
        Trust, 105
    -of Married Couple with Children's Trust
        Included, 99
Joint Tenancy with Right of Survivorship, 23
Joint Revocation of Joint Living Trust by
    Married Couple, 161

KEOGH, 31, 66

Land, 49
Letters of Administration, 61
Letters Testamentary, 60
Liabilities, 45
Life insurance, 24, 31, 38, 65
Living will, 24
Living Trust Preparation Checklist, 29
Living Trust
    -for Single Person or Individual Spouse
        without a Children's Trust, 95
    -for Single Person or Individual Spouse with
        Children's Trust Included, 89
    -Joint, of Married Couple without a Children's
        Trust, 105

-Joint, of Married Couple with Children's
    Trust Included, 99
Living Trusts, 86–139
Loans payable, 45
Location of records, 69

Marital property, 31–34
Marital/Parental status clause, 77
Marital status, 163
Married, 152
Married couples, 82
Medicare, 65
Minor Child, 19
Mortgages, 46
Mortuary, 65
Motor vehicles, 150
Mutual funds, 39, 150

Name of trust clause, 77
Net worth, 47
New York Notice of Assignment of Property to
    Living Trust, 135
Notary Public, 81, 149
Notes receivable, 38
Notes payable, 45

Obituary, 65, 73
Organizations, 58

Patents, 43, 150
Parental status, 163
Parent, 17, 56
Partnership, 42, 150
Payable-on-death account, 24, 31, 37
Pension plan, 31, 44, 65
Personal property, 43
Persons to Contact, 70
Powers of executor, 165
Probate, 14, 15, 23, 60, 162
Profit-sharing plan, 44
Property Questionnaire, 26, 29, 30–47, 149
Property transfer, 78
Proprietorship, 41
Publication, 165

Qualifications, 22

Real estate/real property, 20, 42, 150
Registration of Living Trust, 137
Relative, 58
Relatives to Contact, 71

Residence, 20, 152
Residuary clause, 50, 84, 164
Retirement plan, 31
Revocable trust, 14
Revocation of Living Trust by Single Person or
    Individual Spouse, 159
Revocation of living trust, 158
Revoke, 20

Safe deposit box, 149, 150
Safeguarding of living trust, 149
Sample living trust, 140
Savings accounts, 37
Schedules
    -Joint Schedule of Beneficiaries of Joint
        Living Trust of Married Couple, 129
    -of Assets of Joint Living Trust for Husband,
        117
    -of Assets of Joint Living Trust for Wife, 121
    -of Assets of Living Trust for Single Person
        or Individual Spouse, 115
    -of Assets of Living Trust instructions, 81
    -of Beneficiaries of Living Trust for Single
        Person or Individual Spouse, 125
    -of Beneficiaries of Living Trust instructions,
        82
Separate property, 32
Shared gifts, 49
Siblings, 56
Signature, 81, 165
Sister, 17
Social security, 66
Sole proprietorship, 42, 150
Sound mind, 22
Specific gifts, 83, 163
Spouse, 17, 53
Spouse's share, 34

State inheritance/estate taxes, 34
State laws, 171
Statutory share, 34
Stocks, 39, 150
Successor Trustee, 10, 14, 18, 20, 60–73, 78
    -Duties checklist, 63
    -Duties within first month, 65
    -Information list, 26, 68, 149
    -Financial duties, 67
Supplemental Will, 162–170
Survivorship, 51, 80, 164

Taxation of estates, 24
Taxes, 23, 67
Tenants-by-the-entirety, 23, 33, 42
Tenants-in-common, 23, 33, 42, 43
Termination of trust, 80
Title, 21
Title clause, 77
Totten trust, 24
Trademarks, 43, 150
Transfer documents, 21
Transfer taxes, 21
Transferring property, 150
Trust bank account, 31
Trustee, 14, 18
Trustee clause, 77
Trustee's powers, 79
Trust estate, 10, 19, 49

U.S. Savings Bonds, 31
Vacant land, 43
Vacation house, 43

Will, 21, 162–170
Witness, 165

★ Nova Publishing Company ★
Small Business and Consumer Legal Books and Software

Law Made Simple Series
Liwing Trusts Simplified

ISBN 0-935755-53-5	Book only	$22.95
ISBN 0-935755-51-9	Book w/Forms-on-CD	$28.95

Living Wills Simplified

ISBN 0-935755-52-7	Book only	$22.95
ISBN 0-935755-50-0	Book w/Forms-on-CD	$28.95

Small Business Library Series
Simplified Small Business Accounting (3rd Edition)

ISBN 0-935755-91-8	Book only	$19.95

The Complete Book of Small Business Legal Forms (3rd Edition)

ISBN 0-935755-84-5	Book w/Forms-on-CD	$24.95

Incorporate Your Business: The National Corporation Kit (3rd Edition)

ISBN 0-935755-88-8	Book w/Forms-on-CD	$24.95

The Complete Book of Small Business Management Forms

ISBN 0-935755-56-X	Book w/Forms-on-CD	$24.95

Small Business Start-up Series
C-Corporations: Small Business Start-up Kit

ISBN 0-935755-78-0	Book w/Forms-on-CD	$24.95

S-Corporations: Small Business Start-up Kit

ISBN 0-935755-77-2	Book w/Forms-on-CD	$24.95

Partnerships: Small Business Start-up Kit

ISBN 0-935755-75-6	Book w/Forms-on-CD	$24.95

Limited Liability Company: Small Business Start-up Kit

ISBN 0-935755-76-4	Book w/Forms-on-CD	$24.95

Sole Proprietorship: Small Business Start-up Kit

ISBN 0-935755-79-9	Book w/Forms-on-CD	$24.95

Quick Reference Law Series
Bankruptcy Exemptions: Laws of the United States

ISBN 0-935755-71-3	Book only	$16.95

Corporations: Laws of the United States

ISBN 0-935755-67-5	Book only	$16.95

Divorce: Laws of the United States

ISBN 0-935755-68-3	Book only	$16.95

Limited Liability Companies: Laws of the United States

ISBN 0-935755-80-2	Book only	$16.95

Partnerships: Laws of the United States

ISBN 0-935755-69-1	Book only	$16.95

Wills and Trusts: Laws of the United State

ISBN 0-935755-70-5	Book only	$16.95

Legal Self-Help Series
Debt Free: The National Bankruptcy Kit (2nd Edition)

ISBN 0-935755-62-4	Book only	$19.95

The Complete Book of Personal Legal Forms (3rd Edition)

ISBN 0-935755-92-6	Book w/Forms-on-CD	$24.95

Divorce Yourself: The National No-Fault Divorce Kit (5th Edition)

ISBN 0-935755-93-4	Book only	$24.95
ISBN 0-935755-94-2	Book w/Forms-on-CD	$34.95

Prepare Your Own Will: The National Will Kit (5th Edition)

ISBN 0-935755-72-1	Book only	$17.95
ISBN 0-935755-73-X	Book w/Forms-on-CD	$27.95

★ Ordering Information ★

Distributed by:
National Book Network
4720 Boston Way
Lanham MD 20706

Shipping/handling: $4.50 for first book or disk and $.75 for each additional
Phone orders with Visa/MC: (800) 462-6420
Fax orders with Visa/MC: (800) 338-4550
Internet: www.novapublishing.com